VOLUME 565

SEPTEMBER 1999

THE ANNALS

of The American Academy *of* Political *and* Social Science

ALAN W. HESTON, *Editor*
NEIL A. WEINER, *Assistant Editor*

CIVIL SOCIETY AND DEMOCRATIZATION

Special Editors of this Volume
ISIDRO MORALES
GUILLERMO DE LOS REYES
PAUL RICH
Universidad de las Américas–Puebla
Cholula
Mexico

 SAGE Periodicals Press *THOUSAND OAKS   LONDON   NEW DELHI*

The American Academy of Political and Social Science

3937 Chestnut Street   Philadelphia, Pennsylvania 19104

Board of Directors

ELIJAH ANDERSON   RICHARD D. LAMBERT
LYNN A. CURTIS   SARA MILLER McCUNE
FREDERICK HELDRING   MARY ANN MEYERS
KATHLEEN HALL JAMIESON

Editors, THE ANNALS

ALAN W. HESTON, *Editor*   RICHARD D. LAMBERT, *Editor Emeritus*
ERICA GINSBURG, *Managing Editor*   NEIL A. WEINER, *Assistant Editor*

Origin and Purpose. The Academy was organized December 14, 1889, to promote the progress of political and social science, especially through publications and meetings. The Academy does not take sides in controverted questions, but seeks to gather and present reliable information to assist the public in forming an intelligent and accurate judgment.

Meetings. The Academy occasionally holds a meeting in the spring extending over two days.

Publications. THE ANNALS of the American Academy of Political and Social Science is the bimonthly publication of The Academy. Each issue contains articles on some prominent social or political problem, written at the invitation of the editors. Also, monographs are published from time to time, numbers of which are distributed to pertinent professional organizations. These volumes constitute important reference works on the topics with which they deal, and they are extensively cited by authorities throughout the United States and abroad. The papers presented at the meetings of The Academy are included in THE ANNALS.

Membership. Each member of The Academy receives THE ANNALS and may attend the meetings of The Academy. Membership is open only to individuals. Annual dues: $59.00 for the regular paperbound edition (clothbound, $86.00). Add $12.00 per year for membership outside the U.S.A. Members may also purchase single issues of THE ANNALS for $12.00 each (clothbound, $16.00). Add $2.00 for shipping and handling on all pre-paid orders.

Subscriptions. THE ANNALS of the American Academy of Political and Social Science (ISSN 0002-7162) is published six times annually—in January, March, May, July, September, and November. Institutions may subscribe to THE ANNALS at the annual rate: $281.00 (clothbound, $332.00). Add $12.00 per year for subscriptions outside the U.S.A. Institutional rates for single issues: $49.00 each (clothbound, $57.00).

Periodicals postage paid at Thousand Oaks, California, and additional offices.

Single issues of THE ANNALS may be obtained by individuals who are not members of The Academy for $19.00 each (clothbound, $29.00). Add $2.00 for shipping and handling on all pre-paid orders. Single issues of THE ANNALS have proven to be excellent supplementary texts for classroom use. Direct inquiries regarding adoptions to THE ANNALS c/o Sage Publications (address below).

All correspondence concerning membership in The Academy, dues renewals, inquiries about membership status, and/or purchase of single issues of THE ANNALS should be sent to THE ANNALS c/o Sage Publications, Inc., 2455 Teller Road, Thousand Oaks, CA 91320. Telephone: (805) 499-0721; FAX/Order line: (805) 499-0871. *Please note that orders under $30 must be prepaid.* Sage affiliates in London and India will assist institutional subscribers abroad with regard to orders, claims, and inquiries for both subscriptions and single issues.

Printed on recycled, acid-free paper

THE ANNALS

© 1999 *by* The American Academy *of* Political *and* Social Science

Editorial Office: 3937 Chestnut Street, Philadelphia, PA 19104.

For information about membership* (individuals only) and subscriptions (institutions), address:

SAGE PUBLICATIONS, INC.
2455 Teller Road
Thousand Oaks, CA 91320

From India and South Asia, write to:		*From the UK, Europe, the Middle East and Africa, write to:*
SAGE PUBLICATIONS INDIA Pvt. Ltd		SAGE PUBLICATIONS LTD
P.O. Box 4215		6 Bonhill Street
New Delhi 110 048		London EC2A 4PU
INDIA		UNITED KINGDOM

SAGE Production Staff: ERIC LAW, LISA CUEVAS, DORIS HUS, and ROSE TYLAK
*Please note that members of The Academy receive THE ANNALS with their membership.
International Standard Serial Number ISSN 0002-7162
International Standard Book Number ISBN 0-7619-2032-3 (Vol. 565, 1999 paper)
International Standard Book Number ISBN 0-7619-2033-1 (Vol. 565, 1999 cloth)
Manufactured in the United States of America. First printing, September 1999.

Information about membership rates, institutional subscriptions, and back issue prices may be found on the facing page.

Advertising. Current rates and specifications may be obtained by writing to THE ANNALS Advertising and Promotion Manager at the Thousand Oaks office (address above).

Claims. Claims for undelivered copies must be made no later than twelve months following month of publication. The publisher will supply missing copies when losses have been sustained in transit and when the reserve stock will permit.

Change of Address. Six weeks' advance notice must be given when notifying of change of address to ensure proper identification. Please specify name of journal. **POSTMASTER:** Send address changes to: THE ANNALS of the American Academy of Political and Social Science, c/o Sage Publications, Inc., 2455 Teller Road, Thousand Oaks, CA 91320.

THE ANNALS

of The American Academy *of* Political
and Social Science

ALAN W. HESTON, *Editor*
NEIL A. WEINER, *Assistant Editor*

See page 2 for information on Academy membership and
purchase of single volumes of **The Annals.**

CONTENTS

BOOK DEPARTMENT CONTENTS

PREFACE

Civil society and the voluntary and nongovernmental associations that support it by building social capital are receiving increased attention as part of the democratization process: Fareed Zakaria (1995) comments,

In the world of ideas, civil society is hot. It is almost impossible to read an article on foreign or domestic politics without coming across some mention of the concept. . . . At the heart of the concept of civil society lie "intermediate institutions," private groups that thrive between the realm of the state and family. (1)

Fueling the discussion has been Francis Fukuyama's book *Trust* (1995), confirming his ability to sense what is going to be the issue of the hour—witness his *End of History and the Last Man* (1992). Fukuyama is an enthusiast for how democracy is sustained by what he calls "intermediate institutions" (Fukuyama 1995). Many others have also come forward to reemphasize the role of private associations in sustaining democracy, a point made by Alexis de Tocqueville (1988) more than a century and a half ago.

A central theme of those who feel that associationalism nurtures democracy is along the lines that political man cannot live by economics alone. This theme is perhaps partly a reaction to the prevalence of rational choice theory in the academy over the last few decades. After acknowledging the contributions of Milton Friedman, Gary Becker, and other partisans of rational choice, Fukuyama (1995) denies that the rational choice approach can be the whole story: "As Adam Smith well understood, economic life is deeply embedded in social life, and it cannot be understood apart from the customs, morals, and habits of the society in which it occurs. In short, it cannot be divorced from culture" (13). This is echoed by the interesting dialogue readers will discover between the articles, in the present volume, by Isidro Morales and Finn Laursen, which refer to deep integration arising out of economic integration and indicate that the economic debate is indeed sliding over into a more general cultural debate. The same idea is also emphasized in the article by José L. García-Aguilar.

Fukuyama (1995) further warns, "Not being content to rest on their laurels, many neoclassical economists have come to believe that the economic method they have discovered provides them with the tools for constructing something approaching a universal science of man" (17). He adds critically that "the political science departments of many major universities are now filled with followers of so-called rational choice theory, which attempts to explain politics using an essentially economic methodology" (17).

Scholarly interest in civil society and its nongovernmental organizations seems likely to increase; the attention is partly a consequence of the end of the Cold War:

The renewed interest in civil society first emerged in Eastern Europe after communism crumbled. Leaders like Vaclav Havel wanted to go beyond establishing new governments and create a culture that could sustain political and economic liberalism. They looked for help to those private groups beyond the reach of the state—citizens' associations, churches, human-rights chapters, jazz clubs—that had nourished dissident life. Around the same time, the victorious Western democracies found themselves confronting sagging economies, a fraying social fabric and the loss of national purpose. Here, too, the experts and statesmen agreed, revitalizing civil society would overcome our malaise. (Zakaria 1995, 1)

Interest in civil society has been accompanied by revived interest in political culture, and the background to this is discussed in the article by Paul Rich. It is evident as well in other contributions to this issue, including those of Marco A. Almazán, Corwin Smidt, Lorena Melton Young Otero, Olga Lazcano, Gustavo Barrientos, Guillermo De Los Reyes, and Antonio Lara in the strong section containing specific examples of social capital creation.

A political culture approach[1] places in better perspective the more ideologically bound discussions that sometimes characterized scholarship during the Iron Curtain era.[2] For example, during that period, not enough attention was paid to how democracy and voluntary associations were linked. We therefore all owe Robert Putnam (1995) a debt, even if we do not agree with him about "bowling alone," for reminding us of the role of volunteerism.

A healthy civil society is basic to democratization, and that is a theme that William Ratliff, Armando Cíntora, John S. Robey, and Andreas Schedler take up in the section of this *Annals* issue devoted to conditions for democratization. Writes Stephen Bailey (1976),

Even with the twentieth century's massive depreciation of Victorian rhetoric, millions of people have continued to find nourishment for the free self in fulfilling perceived obligations and in performing voluntary services. I remember my father donning his greatcoat on a blustery night of snow and wind preparing for a mile walk and saying, "I do not want to go to the meeting of the prudential committee of the church, but I ought to go!" Upon returning, he would smile and say simply, "Well, I have done my duty." (70)

In Latin America, the region of the world where several of the contributors to the present volume reside, the expansion of voluntary organizations[3] is reflected in the fact that a recent guide to nongovernmental organizations in the region cites 42 directories containing information about more than 20,000 groups, a doubling since 1990 (Evans 1995, 1). These societies and their influence on democratization are evidence for the arguments about civil culture encouraged by Fukuyama: "[Fukuyama's book *Trust* (1995)] could mark a turning point in the way we look at ourselves, usefully erasing the phony wall that has grown up between economics (which is hard and scientific) and culture (which is soft and studied often by men with beards). . . . Now we are discovering that many of the important things can't be captured by numbers, even in economics" (Brooks 1995).

The claim is made, notwithstanding Putnam, that "a striking upsurge is under way around the globe in organized voluntary activity and the creation of private, nonprofit or nongovernmental organizations" (Salamon 1994, 109). This constitutes a second or parallel world of large numbers of networks of people.[4] But Salamon has criticized the idea that this is a new phenomenon: "While recent years have witnessed a dramatic upsurge in organized voluntary activity, such activity has deep historical roots in virtually every part of the world." He warns that "careful efforts must thus be made to acknowledge the nonprofit sector's peculiar historical roots" (121), but he concludes,

The resulting surge of interest in nonprofit organizations has opened the gates to vast reservoirs of human talent and energy, even while it has created dangers of stalemate and dispute. While it is far from clear what must be done to keep these gates open, a crucial first step is a better understanding of the dramatic process under way and the immense new challenges it represents. (122)

The six different nationalities of the authors represented in the present volume are a good indication of the internationalization of civil society discussions. While the United States has a nonprofit sector, which is especially vigorous, the growth of volunteerism elsewhere has been marked for some years. An estimated 40,000 new private organizations were created in France in one year, 1986 (see Growth of Nonprofits 1990, 10). In the case of Britain, France, and Holland, "as nonprofit organizations step up their activism and lobbying, the governments will increasingly have to contend with groups that, like their American counterparts, take responsibility for influencing public policy, hold governments at all levels more accountable, and mount advocacy campaigns" (13).

The worldwide significance of the discussion of civil society is apparent,[5] as is the fact that it is virtually a universal proposition that social trust owes a great deal to the voluntary societies that create civil society. In the United States, that political associations are only one small part of the immense number of different types of associations found there has been noted for many years.

Americans of all ages, all stations in life, and all types of disposition are forever forming associations. There are not only commercial and industrial associations in which all take part, but others of a thousand different types—religious, moral, serious, futile, very general and very limited, immensely large and very minute. . . . In every case, at the head of any new undertaking, where in France you would find the government or in England some territorial magnate, in the United States you are sure to find an association. (Tocqueville 1988, 513)

The consequences of not having durable intermediate associations that stand between the family and state are devastating.[6] The Soviet Union and Eastern Europe, where civil society was destroyed, provide a prime example. However, the lack of volunteerism was not confined to former Communist states:

Many Latin Catholic countries like France, Spain, Italy and a number of nations in Latin America exhibit a saddle-shaped distribution of organizations, with strong families, a strong state, and relatively little in between. These societies are utterly different from socialist ones in any number of important ways, particularly with regard to their greater respect for the family. But, [as] in socialist societies, there has been in certain Latin Catholic countries a relative deficit of intermediate social groups in the area between the family and large, centralized organizations like the church or the state. (Fukuyama 1995, 55)

Of course, this discovery of the role of civil society and voluntary groups is not new and has been anticipated—for instance, by the work of Seymour Martin Lipset and in the influence of Masonic lodges during the seventeenth and eighteenth centuries, the Enlightenment. Jacob (1991) argues,

Modern civil society was invented during the Enlightenment, in the new enclaves of sociability of which freemasonry was the most avowedly constitutional and aggressively civic. The nature of Masonic sociability has not been understood because historians have seldom looked at actual Masonic practices. (15)

She believes that, "in the final analysis freemasonry, for all of its exclusivity, secrecy, and gender bias, transmitted and textured the Enlightenment, translated all the cultural vocabularies of its members into a shared and common experience that was civil and hence political" (224).

Voluntary associations, then, have been and are a mainstay of democracy (Cameron 1994, 4). But not all contributions of voluntary groups are helpful (Jennings 1995, 65).[7] Having made the case for the study of the place of voluntary associations, one has to ask many questions about how they individually affect situations, including those involving women and blacks.

In a society that is looking for alternatives to a way of life dominated by corporations and state, social movements suggest other choices. A network of organizations that encompass broad constituencies can change our understanding of what is possible and desirable. Little by little we can build a new political culture based on our own questions about the existing order. Meeting human needs neglected by the state and the market is the basis for social movements. By working together they promote positive change and stretch our understanding of democracy and justice. The values of the everyday world, including friendship, respect and concern for others, combined with shared hopes and aspirations, and healthy doses of courage and patience, characterize what is best about the culture of social movements. (Cameron 1994, 2; see also Sgambati 1995)

The present volume is in some ways a statement that, contrary to the claims of Putnam, who argues that civic life is collapsing and has popularized the phrase "bowling alone," volunteerism is still a strong force but a changing force. This is certainly clear in the articles presented in this *Annals* issue that concern the indigenous, rural society, and mining communities.

An estimated 70 percent of the American population belongs to at least one association, and 25 percent belong to at least four (Rauch 1994, 23). As Bailey (1976) relates about his years of residence in Middletown, Connecticut:

I came to know hundreds of people who found meaning and satisfaction in performing community services [as] volunteer firemen, members of library boards, organizers of community chests and United Fund drives, hospital aides, readers for the blind. These activities were frequently in addition to service on PTA committees or church boards and participation in service-club benefits for the crippled. . . . no reform of the bureaucratic and political system can possibly obviate the need for the intimate expressions of caring that are associated with the voluntary performance of works of obligation and service. (70)

Countries that have lacked a really viable civil society are now bent on acquiring it. The role of volunteerism in international relations is becoming increasingly important (Bermeo and Nord 1995, 6-9). This is true in Latin America and in the emerging nations of the former Soviet Union, where new organizations are taking the place of close communities and normative systems.[8] All this brings to mind Tocqueville's words: "Among laws controlling human societies there is one more precise and clearer, it seems to me, than all the others. If men are to remain civilized or to become civilized, the art of association must develop and improve among them at the same speed as equality of conditions spreads" (Tocqueville 1988, 517; see also Boyles 1997).

ACKNOWLEDGMENTS

This issue of *The Annals* is authored by the nationals of six different countries, which is appropriate because it reflects the worldwide role of learned societies such as the American Academy of Political and Social Science as the twenty-first century dawns. These days problems and solutions are more often than not international.

That is doubly true when it comes to the renewed attention to civil society and nongovernmental organizations and to their connection with democratization. Thus this volume is both a contribution to one of the major debates in contemporary and international social science and a pledge about the continued relevance of learned societies in the new millennium.

Civil society and democratization have been a major theme of discussions at the Congress of the Americas, the conference that the American Academy sponsors in cooperation with the Universidad de las Américas–Puebla, the Hoover Institution, the American Culture Association and Popular Culture Association, Phi Beta Delta, the Policy Studies Organization, and a number of other learned societies. The rector of the Universidad de las Américas–Puebla, Dr. Enrique Cárdenas, has been unfailingly supportive. So has Dr. John Raisian, the director of the Hoover Institution. Hoover not only sends its fellows to the Congress and makes a financial contribution but also has a book-publishing program in connection with the meetings.

The premier Mexican research institution, Consejo Nacional de Ciencia y Tecnología (CONACYT), supports the Congress and supports the civil society research under Grant 8244 of Messrs. De Los Reyes, Rich, and Lara. Support also comes from the research office of the Universidad de las Américas, which is headed by Dean Marco Rosales. We wish to especially thank Dr. Marcial Bonilla, director of scientific development at CONACYT. The William and Flora Hewlett Foundation is also a firm supporter; Dr. David Lorey is one of the program officers whose help has been enormously valuable.

All of the authors in this issue have been prominent participants in past Congresses. This is the second issue of *The Annals* arising from the Congress, the first being the March 1997 issue, *NAFTA Revisited: Expectations and Realities*. Professor Alan Heston, of the University of Pennsylvania, has represented the American Academy at the Congresses and has played a central and essential part in the relationship between the Academy and the other sponsors.

This issue of *The Annals* will be much in use at discussion groups at the Fourth Congress of the Americas, to be held at the Universidad de las Américas–Puebla, Cholula, Mexico, 30 September to 2 October 1999. The Congress has been a valuable meeting place for political and academic leaders as well as for business and diplomatic interests, providing a forum for considering the consequences of NAFTA, the future of the North American community, and the countervailing trends of globalization and regionalism as well as the tensions caused by free trade and neoliberalism.

ISIDRO MORALES
GUILLERMO DE LOS REYES
PAUL RICH

Notes

1. For a representative example of the comparative and political culture approach, now gaining renewed favor, see Almond and Powell 1988.

2. As for cultural studies emerging from a defensive position, after some years of rational choice dominance in the academy, see Green and Shapiro 1994.

3. For helpful discussion of anomic, nonassociational, institutional, and associational groups, see Almond and Powell 1988, 68-70.

4. The proliferation of electronic networks via the Internet, including those operated by individual members of such secretive organizations as the Masonic and Opus Dei societies, gives added value to the concept of networking.

5. These arguments were anticipated by Coleman 1993.

6. We are grateful to Dr. Henry Rowen, a fellow at the Hoover Institution, Stanford University, for discussion of whether the absence of this intermediary layer of voluntary organizations is a reason for the lack of movement toward democracy by Arab states.

7. Nor, of course, are voluntary organizations in other countries always enlightened. "The same 'communities' of like-minded neighbors that care for and protect their own have also historically shunned outsiders, blackballed misfits, and persecuted minorities . . . one alternative to the law court is the parish visiting committee; another is the lynch mob" (Jennings 1995, 61).

8. "We fail to recognize that the social capital on which primordial social organization depends is vanishing; we fail to recognize that societies of the future will be constructed, and that we should direct our attention to designing those social structures. We need not mourn the loss of the supports for the social controls of primordial social organization. As anyone who was raised in a small close community knows, normative systems have many unpleasant aspects: They operate more via constraints and coercion than via incentives and rewards" (Coleman 1993, 10).

References

Almond, Gabriel A. and G. Bingham Powell, Jr. 1988. *Comparative Politics Today: A Worldview*. Glenview, IL: Scott, Foresman.

Bailey, Stephen. 1976. *The Purposes of Education, Phi Delta Kappa*. Bloomington: Indiana University Press.

Bermeo, Nancy and Philip Nord. 1995. Civil Society Before Democracy. *European Studies Newsletter* 25(1-2):6-9.

Boyles, Ann. 1997. The Rise of Civil Society. *One Country* 2(Jan.-Mar.):25-36.

Brooks, David. 1995. Why Nice Folks Build Bigger Businesses. *Wall Street Journal*, 11 Aug.

Cameron, Duncan. 1994. Civil Society: Building a Better Canada. *CUSO Forum* 12(3):1-4.

Coleman, James S. 1993. The Rational Reconstruction of Society. *American Sociological Review* 58(Feb.):1-15.

Evans, George A. 1995. *A Guide to NGO Directories*. Arlington, VA: Inter-American Foundation.

Fukuyama, Francis. 1992. *The End of History and the Last Man*. New York: Free Press.

———. 1995. *Trust: The Social Virtues and the Creation of Prosperity*. New York: Free Press.

Green, Donald P. and Ian Shapiro. 1994. *Pathologies of Rational Choice Theory: A Critique of Applications in Political Science*. New Haven, CT: Yale University Press.

Growth of Nonprofits in Europe, The. 1990. *Transatlantic Perspectives* (German Marshall Fund of the United States) Spring(21):10.

Jacob, Margaret C. 1991. *Living the Enlightenment: Freemasonry and Politics in Eighteenth-Century Europe*. New York: Oxford University Press.

Jennings, Lane. 1995. Restoring Community in 21st-Century America. *Futurist* July-Aug.:50-61.

Putnam, Robert D. 1995. Bowling Alone: America's Declining Social Capital. Available at http://muse.jhu.edu/demo/journal_of_democracy//v006/putnam.html
Rauch, Jonathan. 1994. The Hyperpluralism Trap. *New Republic*, 6 June, 22-23.
Salamon, Lester M. 1994. The Rise of the Nonprofit Sector. *Foreign Affairs* 73(4):109.
Sgambati, Albert. 1995. Helping Others the United Way. *Mexico City News*, 28 Aug.
Tocqueville, Alexis de. 1988. *Democracy in America*. Ed. J. P. Mayer. Trans. George Lawrence. New York: Harper Perennial.
Zakaria, Fareed. 1995. Bigger Than the Family, Smaller Than the State: Are Voluntary Groups What Make Countries Work? *New York Times Book Review*, 13 Aug., 1.

American Voluntarism, Social Capital, and Political Culture

By PAUL RICH

ABSTRACT: Robert Putnam has suggested that membership in American voluntary associations has declined in recent decades. The contention now has been challenged by various writers. The historical evidence indicates that associations come and go, reflecting changes in society. Using specific examples to prove there is a malaise that threatens democracy is a risky business. Some associations have simply failed to meet the needs of a better-educated, more discriminating public and have paid the price. A Darwinian process of selection goes on all the time among the many thousands of American groups. Different kinds of voluntarism are constantly being invented. For example, the Internet and World Wide Web have created a whole new voluntary world, which is just beginning to find its voice. This underlines the need for a more detailed examination of the issues and the data than has been the case.

Paul Rich is Titular Professor of International Relations and History, Universidad de las Américas–Puebla, Mexico, and a fellow at the Hoover Institution, Stanford University. He is endowment chair of the American Culture Association and the Policy Studies Organization, recipient of the Cameron and James Carter awards for social science research, and fellow of the Royal Historical Society. Among his books are Chains of Empire *and* The Invasions of the Gulf. *The support of Consejo Nacional de Ciencia y Tecnologia (CONACYT) for Dr. Rich's research is gratefully acknowledged.*

T O understand America, it is necessary to recognize the significance of civil society (Almond 1996) and of the luxuriant voluntarism that is its lifeblood.[1] During his famous visit to the United States of 1831, Alexis de Tocqueville was especially impressed by the plethora of voluntary associations and decentralized institutions. America's associations—including religious societies, civic organizations, school boards, fraternal orders, and philanthropic groups—are lifelong training grounds for citizenship and leadership, and they create crucial communication networks (Fowler 1991, 36).[2] This pattern of voluntarism, still much more common in America than elsewhere, assumes global significance in the post–Cold War era.[3]

Literature seeking to explain the failure of democratic efforts in the 1920s and 1930s turned Tocqueville's analysis on its head in propagating the theory of mass society. These analyses, ably systematized by William Kornhouser, discussed the absence of voluntary groups in relation to polities in which individuals were relatively isolated—a mass society, one in which there were few institutions mediating between the state and the citizenry (Kornhouser 1959). On the positive side, social scientists like Peter Berger, Richard Neuhaus, Seymour Martin Lipset, Martin Trow, and James S. Coleman sought to extend the Tocquevillian approach with reference to the conditions fostering democracy in private governments like unions and parties in the larger polities (Lipset 1996, 276). They documented the way voluntary associations provided a source of new opinions independent of the state and a means of communicating these new suggestions to a large section of the citizenry, as well as training men and women in the skills of politics and promoting their actual participation in political organization (Lipset 1956, 85).

Nevertheless, until recently there has been far more written about the state than about civil society. "When it comes to civic life," complains Claire Gaudiani (1996), "we are like visitors to a strange city without a map. The phrases 'civil society,' 'social capital' and 'civic virtue' sound as strange to most of us today as price/earnings ratio, ego and biodiversity must have sounded 50 years ago" (38).

Now a change is under way. There has been a markedly increased use of such terms, popularized by Francis Fukuyama and Robert Putnam, among others. The space in a nation-state occupied by civil society,[4] social capital,[5] and their supporting organizations is increasingly spotlighted by political scientists, recalling Geertz's phrase that "the politics of a country reflect the sense of culture" (1992, 262). Partly because of a revival in political culture studies accompanied by an increased empiricalism in defining their influence,[6] voluntarism and associationalism as components of democracy have become popular topics.[7] With the end of the Soviet Union, scholars are interested in seeing how the former totalitarian states can be kept in the democratic camp, realizing that this is not only an economic issue (Rich and De Los Reyes 1998; Alonso 1993). As Ronald Inglehart (1988) warns,

There is no question that economic factors are politically important, but they are only part of the story. I argue that different societies are characterized to very different degrees by specific syndromes of political culture attitudes; that these cultural differences are relatively enduring, but not immutable; and that they have major political consequences, being closely linked to the viability of democratic institutions. (1203; cf. Seligson 1966)

Writing in the 1970s, Alex Inkeles (1979) reported a continuing belief among American historians of a high level of community participation and a corresponding high degree of interpersonal trust, which contrasted favorably to the circumstances in other countries. Continued searching for the conditions nurturing a democratic political culture (for example, Diamond 1997; Hodgson 1993; Packenham 1992; Sowell 1994) has produced a "renaissance" (Inglehart 1988) or, at least, a "return to political culture studies," as Gabriel Almond (1993) puts it.[8]

Recently, though, scholars and political commentators have called attention to evidence from survey research and electoral data of a decline in confidence and interpersonal trust and a decline in electoral participation. The latter has fallen to 50 percent of the eligible electorate in presidential contests and to much lower levels in state and local elections and party primaries. Concern for the implications of such findings for the operation of the democratic process has led many to feel the need for research on the conditions fostering strong civic cultures. Seemingly all is not well in the relationship between civic society and democracy. The Saguaro Seminar and National Workshop on Civic Engagement, both promoted by Robert Putnam, and Theda Skocpol's project on voluntary associations—all Harvard-based—as well as the Aspen Institute's Nonprofit Sector Research Fund, the Center for the Study of Philanthropy and Voluntarism at Duke University, forums sponsored by the Pew Foundation, and a plethora of other projects emphasize the resurgent interest in the nongovernmental sector as part of this problem, focusing on voluntarism (Sorman 1990, 198). This has become an international concern (Metzger 1998; Peschard 1996).

SOMETIMES BOWLING ALONE

Doubts about the health of American civil society were expressed prior to the current controversy. Debates over whether voluntarism in America really is in decline are not new (Lipset 1956, 16, 82-86). For some time it has been apparent that individual associations rise and fall and that no complex society has discovered the secret of organizational equilibrium when it comes to particular ones maintaining their stability and social gains (Lipset 1950, 82, 332).

But a loud alarm has been sounded by Robert Putnam based on the assumption that the republic is in danger as the number of couch potatoes grows, as watching television replaces civil participation (Putnam 1995). Cliché makers have taken up the cry, muttering about a nation of strangers, a land of the disinvolved, a growth in the politics of mistrust, and the emergence of a society in which indeed people bowl alone (Heller 1996). The suggestion has been made that those bowling alone not only are less likely to be involved in politics but also are more prone to illness than those on teams: "People with few social ties were two to three times more likely to die of all causes than those with more extensive contacts." This has "ominous implications . . . [since] social capital is declining in America" (Kawachi, Kennedy, and Lochner 1997, 56).

An aspect of the initial debate was, somewhat tongue-in-cheek, actually about the decline of bowling leagues, abetted by photographs of Putnam incongruously squatting, alone, in the middle of a darkened bowling lane (Heller 1996). What should have been noted immediately was brought to the fore by Nancy Ammerman: "Knowing that people are not bowling in leagues does not tell us that they are necessarily bowling alone. They may be bowling with informal friendship groups, their families, or their Sunday school classes. The decline in one form of associational participation—while disconcerting to those with an economic investment in that form—does not necessarily signal a decline in association, as such" (Ammerman 1996). In retrospect, the idea was inherently strange that a new generation of silent bowlers, eating their pizzas in gloomy isolation, had replaced gregarious groups.[9]

Moreover, there have been other changes in bowling culture that might be investigated. As reported by the Billiard and Bowling Institute, an expansion of 11.4 percent occurred in the number of participants between 1987 and 1997, particularly among persons with incomes over $50,000. There was an increase in the number of young people bowling and a decrease in the number of elderly bowlers (Billiard and Bowling Institute 1998). Recent findings amend past perceptions of the sport as a blue-collar avocation. This change may be as significant as any possible move from league play to bowling alone.[10]

It would be an interesting twist to the bowling-alone thesis if it turns out that television affects bowling by not giving enough time and publicity to the game. Bowling exposure on television appears to have induced some people to take up the game, just as more extensive treatment of golf on television allegedly increased interest and participation in golfing (Wright 1996, 1997). As for the growth in voluntary spirit among bowlers, the new Bowl for Kids' Sake organization, aiding the Big Brother and Big Sister mentoring programs, involves more than 2 million bowlers a year and has produced more than $125 million.[11] The argument could be made that Bowl for Kids' Sake members do not share beers as readily as do members of company teams, but proving that would be a challenge.

Voluntary organizations are not exempt from social change. There is a Darwinian process of selection going on (Kaufman 1991, 91-96). Research is needed on the effect of extensive social mobility on the stability of social groups. Taking part in civil society is a continual, dynamic, and sometimes problematic process of interaction between individuals and the associations linked to their interests and values. In America, improvement in the respective positions of individual people strengthens the bonds of civil society more than it weakens them, and fosters the myriad of voluntary associations and their mutations (Lipset 1996, 276-77).

Whether voluntarism has grown or declined depends on one's conception of the subject.[12] It would be most peculiar if the changes in American society over the last 30 years had not affected the character of voluntarism. Changes in the way in which people wish to serve as volunteers seem more likely than a decline in voluntarism (Schudson 1996). For example, the conventional raison d'être of the women's auxiliary was to cook dinner for the men's group, a role now considered ludicrous by many.

Arguments about growth or decline in voluntarism have to come to terms with a variety of contrary or conflicting data. Countering Putnam, Gallup polls have found that the proportion of people reporting that they volunteered for charitable, "social service," or "non-profit" organizations has doubled between 1977 and the 1990s. Ethnic organizations have increased their total membership in percentage terms (Lipset 1996, 280-81). Margaret Conway, Alfonso Damico, and Sandra Damico (1996), using a large data set (22,652 initial interviews in 1972, with follow-up surveys in 1974, 1976,

1979, and 1986), indicate that baby boomers in the high school graduating classes of 1972, who were traced across their early adult years, showed "a pattern of increasing community engagement." They conclude, "Putnam's data overlook a variety of other types of civic activity" (8).

WHITE MALE SHRINERS

The bowling-alone thesis heavily relies on statistics showing declines in membership of several familiar civic organizations. An early-morning shave with Occam's razor is suggested. Some well-known groups may have declined because of changes in constituency and failure to innovate rather than from any general lack of altruism and public spirit (Charles 1993, 11).[13] Everett Ladd (1998) remarks,

Unless one is prepared to argue that a particular organization is uniquely valuable in civic terms, what is one to make of its losing ground? Why should we care that the Benevolent Protective Order of Elks (BPOE) has fewer members now than in the 1950s? Putnam offered no evidence—nor have other civic-decline-thesis proponents—that the loss of Elks and Jaycees has not been matched, or even surpassed, by increases in other groups equally attractive in their so-cial/civic reach.

A number of organizations have not been able to meet economic and social challenges, such as failing to adopt to increased levels of education and changing tastes (Inkeles 1998, 86).[14] Skocpol (1997) notes,

Better-educated Americans, in short, have pulled out of broad community groups in record numbers since the mid-1970s, sometimes leaving behind people with a high school education or less. America's largest cross-class associations have withered. The best-educated people are still participating in more groups overall, but not in the same groups as their less well-educated fellow citizens.

Putnam does admit that gender and race have had an influence, suggesting that "the pace of disengagement among whites" reflects the fact that joining traditionally male Anglo-Saxon Protestant movements is no longer attractive in an increasingly pluralistic society (Putnam 1995, 672). Some of the groups he mentions, like the Caucasian or George Washington Masons (as distinct from the Prince Hall or black Masons), although reforming in desperation to avoid collapse, have long been perceived as stuffy white male bastions. A more sophisticated America is less content with listening to endless minutes of past meetings or sitting through lengthy and artery-clogging dinners. The sources of the increasingly ecumenical and educated tastes of Americans when it comes to food may also be reflected in a changing taste in leisure activities (Nessman 1997). Adequate discussion requires attention to the almost endless variety of new voluntary activities arising in the last 20 years.

The initial praise given to Putnam's description of American society, attention that benefited from the interest created by the work done by Francis Fukuyama on trust and so-

cial capital, now has given way to a chorus of reservations. Skocpol (1997) writes,

Perhaps unintentionally, Putnam largely ignores the cross-class and organizational dynamics by which civic associations actually form and persist—or decay and come unraveled. An association may decline not only because people with the wrong sorts of individual traits proliferate in the population, but also because opportunities and cultural models for that association (or type of organization) wither in the larger society and polity. An association may also decline because the defection of crucial types of leaders or members makes the enterprise less resourceful and relevant for others.

The whole subject is indeed more complicated than the initial bowling-alone discussions made out. Skocpol announced at the American Political Science Association meetings in Boston in 1998 that she had just taken the initial ritual degrees in the Grange or Patrons of Husbandry lodge in an effort to extend her understanding of the little researched American fraternal world—which, in fact, is changing rapidly. Claiming that Putnam has missed the growth of small local organizations that are now the significant and preferred venue for voluntary service, Wattenberg and Wattenberg (1998) comment, "In a demassifying America, it is a mistake to derive sweeping conclusions about our civic health from the fate of an unrepresentative sample of mass organizations."

Francis Fukuyama himself has developed reservations about the decline of associations. "It is not clear," he writes, "that either the number of groups or group memberships in civil society declined overall in this period, as the political scientist Robert Putnam has suggested." Instead,

despite the apparent decline in trust, there is evidence that groups and group membership are increasing. . . . Rather than taking pride in being a member of a powerful labor federation or working for a large corporation, or in having served in the military, people identify with a local aerobics class, a New Age sect, a co-dependent support group, or an Internet chat room. (Fukuyama 1999, 60, 71)

Regardless of the qualifications now being added to the argument, Putnam's case for decline in voluntary activity still rests partly on numerical evidence that

fraternal organizations have . . . witnessed a substantial drop in membership during the 1980s and 1990s. Membership is down significantly in such groups as the Lions (off 12 percent since 1983), the Elks (off 18 percent since 1979), the Shriners (off 27 percent since 1979), the Jaycees (off 44 percent since 1979), and the Masons (down 39 percent since 1959). In sum, after expanding steadily throughout most of this century, many major civic organizations have experienced a sudden, substantial, and nearly simultaneous decline in membership over the last decade or two. (Putnam 1995, 672)

These reports sound very alarming until one realizes that the decline is not limited to the last decade or two. Some of these organizations have been suffering severe membership losses since the 1920s.[15] Research by Brent Morris (1993) shows the last year of growth for several once proud and large organizations: Knights of Pythias (1921), Odd Fellows (1923), Grotto (1925), Knights Templar (1926), Royal Arch Masons (1926), Shrine (1926), Royal and Select Master Masons (1927), Freemasons in general (1928), and Scottish Rite Masons (1929).[16] He observes,

By the 1920's, fundamental changes in American society were beginning to cause changes in fraternities. . . . It is important to note that nearly all had experienced declining membership before 1929, and in fact had only insignificant increases before their last year of growth. By this time, many of the needs formerly filled by fraternal orders either were not pressing or were met by other groups. (23 passim)

Thus the decline of some of these familiar organizations is not an alarming development of the last decade or two. Many of these societies were dealt a fatal blow by the fact that their insurance benefits were no longer as competitive as those offered by insurance companies as simple business propositions with no secret handshakes required (Lipset 1996, 179).

In any case, the decline of an organization may not be regarded as bad for American democracy. It might even be positive.[17] Blacks or women or Jews or Catholics, who were formerly excluded from some of those organizations that are now fighting for existence, will not think that the overall quality of American voluntarism or civic culture has also fallen as a consequence.[18] The still-overwhelmingly white male Shriners is not essential to democracy, nor is the resolutely white Order of the Eastern Star of irreplaceable value to maintaining American democracy in the coming millennium.[19] The decision of the Elks in 1995 to admit women might seem a little late. So does the decision of the white Masons and the white Shriners to accept blacks, a policy change that is far from unanimous. The onus is on such organizations to change or decline, and sympathy for a plight largely of their own making is misplaced. Many of the organizations now in trouble misread the changes in American society.

Commenting on the supposed bowling-alone malaise, Claire Gaudiani (1996) notes,

American democracy did not really establish the possibility of democratic civil society until relatively recently when equal opportunity became explicit law. We are not the same people we have been. The United States has never been as culturally, ethnically, racially and religiously diverse as it is today. Never before has so large a percentage of our population experienced as much higher education. Never before has such a large percentage of African Americans participated in or been above the middle income group. Never before have so many women entered the professions, just to name a few of the successes of the last 30 years. There were no "good old days"—no golden age for democratic civil society during which we were all at the same table.

VOLUNTARISM IS
ALIVE AND WELL

In a leaky, drafty former VFW hall on Milwaukee's northwest side, Pastor Gerald Saffold is busy rebuilding civil soci-

ety. Of course, that's not how he would describe what he's doing. He would say that he's bringing souls to Christ—using his immense gift for music to draw inner-city teens into his "Unity in the Community" Choir, where former gang leaders and drug dealers help him write the songs and choreograph the dances that they then perform all over the city. Nonetheless, this is an unmistakable act of civic renewal, and under the least hospitable circumstances imaginable. Where before there were inner-city gangs of angry teens, there is emerging today a cohesive community, united in common endeavor, mutually developing skills of cooperation, leadership, and citizenship. Yet sadly, we as a society do not seem inclined to celebrate this simple gospel choir as a significant civic event. (And this, ironically, in the very face of Putnam's now famous discovery of the link between active choral societies and civic health.) Instead, we seem to be scanning the horizon for larger, more sweeping countrywide movements. Those who accept Putnam's argument and seek to revitalize civil institutions tend to focus their concerns on a limited range of major national non-profits like the PTA or the Red Cross. (Schambra 1998)

It is not only the growth of such alternative religious groups that suggests that American voluntarism is alive. Even such time-honored pursuits as stamp collecting have developed new groups. Since 1980, among the new philatelic societies that have been founded are those for studying stamp and postal history related to aviation, birds, malaria, Christopher Columbus, cats, moths, golf, rainbows, lighthouses, and petroleum. There is no evidence that the Lighthouse Stamp Society will be less of a contributor to American associational life in the future than the Order of Buffaloes was in the past. The fact is that new clubs see the light of day all the time, and others disappear. In fact, the Moth Stamp Society already has evidently come too close to the candle and perished (Chronology 1999).

The PTA is one of Putnam's concerns. Everett Ladd (1998) has effectively put the issue of its decline to rest. He notes that while the national PTA membership is considerably below its high point, reached in 1962, the loss does not reflect a decline in enrollment at the local level. The drop-off resulted from the secession of many local chapters from the national organization. The latter now includes only one-quarter of all schools. The overwhelming majority of parent-teacher groups are no longer affiliated with the national body. But the proportion of parents of public school children who report having attended a "PTA meeting," as a generic term, actually rose from 36 percent in 1983 to 49 percent in 1992. Ladd also reports that in "1965, just 16 percent of all parents told Gallup that they had attended a school board meeting, [whereas,] in 1995, 39 percent said they had."

As Ladd documents in detail, the story of increased parental participation in educational affairs is characteristic of a host of voluntary activities. The evidence also indicates that the plethora of voluntary associations in America, which so impressed Tocqueville, Weber, and other foreign observers as one of the distinctive American traits, is still linked to the uniquely American system of "voluntary religion" (Lipset 1996, 61). As a result, Tocqueville

contended that Americans are among the most religious peoples in Christendom. They still are, but the functions of many churches have changed and broadened. Churches and synagogues have been "reinventing" themselves in order to attract members and may offer more civic involvement to their members than two or three memberships in single-purpose organizations (Schudson 1996).

In sum, many of the pessimistic generalizations inspired by the bowling-alone discussion fail to consider the constant change and enormous variety of American organizations. As another example, while fewer Americans are joining the Odd Fellows and their ilk, every day more are involved in college alumni groups if only because more are going to college. The voluntary-organization scene has become more varied and complicated than has been appreciated by bowling-alone enthusiasts, and it is understudied. Thus Masons and Elks are not confined to the category of white men's groups whose declining members are cited by Putnam. There are black and female Elk organizations, female and black Masons and co-Masonic organizations, black Shriners, and other black and female organizations that have grown precisely because white male organizations excluded blacks and women (Rich 1997). Like associations that attract minorities and women, the Catholic Knights of Columbus has shown a constant growth. Whatever a thorough examination of the fortunes of all of these groups will uncover, the time has passed when the health of American voluntarism could be judged by examining the success or failure of white male Protestant organizations.

Putnam has responded to some of the positive findings by asserting that many, if not most, of those groups that have shown recent growth are "passive," that is, they do not require or even allow opportunities to meet. But passive membership is not a new phenomenon. There were many passive member organizations, such as the National Geographic Society, in the past. Strangely, it is only the new large groups such as the Sierra Club and the American Association of Retired Persons that are cited as "mailing list" and "checkbook" associations, and therefore not relevant to the civic culture. Moreover, while making a financial contribution is not the same as serving in an office, it can be an efficient exercise of citizenship, possibly more so than attending a meeting (Schudson 1996).

Furthermore, the argument that belonging to the organizations mentioned by Putnam has come to mean little more to members than a magazine subscription is contradicted by the people-centered activities of the groups he singles out. The American Association of Retired Persons has more than 4000 local chapters, most of which are involved in community service such as blood drives, hospital visitation, and other civic activities. One affiliate, the National Retired Teachers' Association, is meeting a pledge to provide 45 million volunteer service hours for 1.5 million young people by the end of the year 2000.

The causal connections between American voluntarism and political behavior are more complicated than the bowling-alone arguments make out. Judith Cohen (1998) points to the artificiality of

the distinction made between local, "secondary" associations like the Elks Club which are said to be in decline—and the new "tertiary," mass-membership organizations, from the National Organization for Women to the American Association of Retired Persons. Putnam and others have argued that whereas the traditional groups offered opportunities for face-to-face interactions, these new associations rely on abstract impersonal ties of people to common symbols, texts, leaders, and ideals. . . . Other evidence, however, does not support this conclusion. For example, a recent study by Sidney Verba and his colleagues indicates that the falloff in voter turnout is not part of a general erosion in voluntary activity or political participation. They report *increases* in certain forms of civic activism, such as membership in community problem-solving organizations.

Another troubling matter is that the expansion of university-connected organizations has been discounted by Putnam on the grounds that universities, including their alumni activities, are run by bureaucrats. But consider the case of Putnam's university, Harvard. It has generated almost endless examples of voluntarism such as the Harvard Mountaineering Club, the Harvard Music Association, the Harvard Unitarian Universalist Ministers' Association, the Friends of the Arnold Arboretum, the Harvard Business

School Club of Hong Kong, and so on. Universities breed such voluntary organizations with the fecundity of a rabbit. Hundreds of Harvard clubs raise millions for scholarships. There are a vast and increasing number of special Harvard alumni groups, ranging from those for computer zealots to those for cookbook enthusiasts. These societies have their own elections, their own policy disputes, and their own experiences in democracy. The increase of alumni-based groups is but one of the ways that the enormous growth in higher education has contributed to civil society.

MISTAKING CHANGE FOR DECLINE

People still bowl together, but they also do other things together. Optimism about American voluntarism is clearly warranted (Smith 1997, 472). The number of groups listed in Gale Research's *Encyclopedia of Associations* has grown from 5000 in 1956 to more than 20,000 in the 1990s, and it is not in any way a complete list. (Nor indeed has this encyclopedia ever been a complete list.) Reporting on a survey taken in Philadelphia, Andrew Kohut (n.d.) of the Pew Research Center reports trying to

explore further and in considerable depth the principal concepts in this social trust/civic engagement debate . . . we found that overwhelmingly people said whether they were playing in softball leagues or doing e-mail or in self-help groups that they were meeting people who became important to them. In another follow-up question, we asked, Do you meet people in these activities that you could turn to in time of help. And the answer was 70 percent yes in most cases. So we were trying to push this Putnam thesis that people are not engaged in activities and have become social isolates, and that's not the case.

In rejecting "bowling alone," Robert J. Samuelson (1996) points out that softball leagues now claim 40 million participants, in contrast with only 27 million in 1972. Another critic, Diana Eck (1997), discusses how the American penchant for volunteerism has influenced the behavior of religious groups comprising new immigrants who lacked such experience back home. There are Hindu groups that adopt a highway and an organization called Sikhs Serving America, which tries to help street people. There has been a proliferation of "voluntary associations based on democratic, and not necessarily Christian, principles" (3). The academic debate has had little to say about such new religious movements as the Iron Man bands and the Promise Keepers, which are not groups that faculty join (cf. Dunn 1996, 47; Berger 1971). It seems that only organizations that were part of Main Street are to be considered in determining the alleged decline.

As for international voluntarism, Ann Boyles (1997) is impressed not by decline but by increase: "the sudden efflorescence of countless . . . organizations . . . at local, regional, and international levels." She adds, "This blossoming of civil society, as represented by non-governmental organizations, community-based groups, academic institutions, and others, is significantly reshaping the international agenda" (34). The rapidly growing international side of voluntarism is encouraged by the Internet. If one area is to be singled out for discussion, it should be the ultimate effect on political and social life of this worldwide explosion in communication (Rich and De Los Reyes 1997). I am impressed by the animated discussion, lobby, and support groups that have sprung up via the Net. A new cyber generation is connecting people in ways only partly understood. Attention needs to be paid to the ways that these e-mail–stimulated chat groups, which now involve millions of people, contribute to sustaining democratic political systems, as well as to creating international pressure groups.[20] People with common interests may come together from all over the world.[21] A striking example may be found in the fact that indigenous peoples from Australia to Siberia to Canada have been able to develop a consciousness of kind and the ability to communicate and work together. Democracy everywhere is taking new and different forms (Nye and Owens 1996, 19).

OLIGARCHIC CONTRIBUTORS
TO DEMOCRACY

Of course, the debate that Putnam has helped promote is of immense value, and there are many questions that have long gone unanswered that may now get attention. The thesis that voluntary organizations contribute to the health of democracy has been criticized on the grounds that few large associations are themselves internally democratic (Smith 1997, 478-80). There is considerable documentation that Robert Michels's neglected theory of organizational oligarchy (1949) is valid for groups as diverse as trade unions, professional associations, Internet groups, fraternal orders, veterans' bodies, and so on. The oligarchy theory asserts that most large associations are inherently dominated by their leadership and bureaucracy. The leaders and bureaucrats control communication with the membership, have a monopoly on political skills, and can therefore generally determine policy and remain in office with little or no opposition. As Michels asserted, how can groups, which themselves are not democratic, enhance democracy? The answer to the conundrum is simple. A voluntary organization must represent its members to some degree if the association is to retain their support. Members have the option to leave or to stop contributions. Thus voluntary organizations must fulfill representative functions. They also, of course, may carry out the role, which Tocqueville assigned to them, of linking the citizenry to the polity.

Discussion and argument about the rule of voluntary organizations in democracies will continue. The effort started by Tocqueville to understand them still requires much more information. But, at the moment, all we safely say is that they are not declining. We do note with satisfaction that the bowling-alone debate shows that political culture and civil society are getting the attention they have always deserved and, for a time, were irrationally denied (Verba 1965;

Almond and Verba 1963; Kavanah 1972; Rosenbaum 1975; Brint 1994.[22] The heightened interest in how a healthy political culture might be sustained has become almost synonymous with an increased interest in the conditions fostering democracy (Diamond 1992, 116-20).

The considerable research over the past three decades documenting the importance of economic development to democracy stands. However, if economic growth helps nation-states trying to democratize, it is not as certain that it alone is going to solve political problems. Much is needed from the nongovernmental sector.[23] Without organized parties and organized groups independent of the state, there can be no democracy. For example, the promising changes as far as democracy is concerned in Mexico primarily result from developments outside the formal government structure (Alonso 1993, 7-10). Indeed, understanding of the new Mexican politics requires insight into the decision making now taking place in the informal spheres (Alonso 1993; Berger 1971). The Mexican political commentator Juan Ruiz Healy (1998) claims, "The NGOs are already as powerful as the Church and the Army."

CONCLUSION

In *The Politics of Unreason* (1970), Lipset and Raab analyzed how the fortunes of political organizations varied over time. They suggested as a useful concept "selective support." The ability to attract members is a function of the ability of an organization to keep up with change in the needs and wants of its constituency and to maintain effective leadership. In this respect, the bowling-alone excitement, as Alex Inkeles has suggested to me in a letter (26 July 1996), does not involve discovery of an alarming fatal illness but simply a rediscovery of the basic fact that the health of voluntary organizations waxes and wanes: support is selective.

I agree with Robert Putnam about the need to focus on the health of intermediate organizations. I would never suggest complacency. Yet some of the remarks made in the current debate about voluntarism have been wide of the mark. There are other reasons for current problems in American political life.[24] I am optimistic about American civil society (Smith 1997, 472). The essayist Samuel McChord Crothers, after a long-winded Harvard commencement, was asked by his wife how the speeches had gone. He dryly remarked that evidently the world had been in great danger, but now all would be well! Possibly there is wisdom here for the bowling-alone alarmists. America leads the world when it comes to richness of organizational life and inventing new forms of voluntarism. So it did, to Tocqueville's bemusement, in the early nineteenth century—and, fortunately for democracy, it still does.

Notes

1. I wish to thank my colleagues at the Hoover Institution, including Alex Inkeles, Larry Diamond, Seymour Martin Lipset, and Henry Rowen, for discussions about the role of civil society in democratization. Needless to say, my views are not necessarily theirs.

2. "One of the frustrations of studying the policy literature on civil society is the large scale unwillingness to look at the dynamics within. This was certainly the whole point of Gramsci's contributions: understanding the forces within civil society was the key to emancipation. Without differentiation, analysis, picking good-and-bad guys, the idea of civil society loses any explanatory value—either as theory, or as a tool for policy decisions" (Van Roony 1997, 6).

3. "Some of the recent literature seems to place the leadership responsibility for civil society functions in Africa on voluntary associations in Tocquevillean terms. By virtue of their existence, their performance of civil society's norm-setting functions is tacitly assumed" (Harbeson 1994, 17). See also Stiles 1997.

4. "As a first approximation, civil society may be defined as all social interests not encompassed by the state or the economy. In its political aspects it also excludes private life, although recent attacks by feminists and others on the public/private distinction make this boundary less clear.... Prominent examples of civil society in action would include the early bourgeois public sphere discussed by Habermas, the insurgent 'free spaces' in U.S. political history constituted by women, blacks, workers, farmers, and others, the democratic opposition in Eastern Europe prior to 1989, and, in the West, feminist, antinuclear, peace, environmental, and urban new social movements. . . . Civil society is a heterogeneous place, home to the Michigan Militia as well as the movements I have mentioned" (Dryze 1996, 481). "Almond and Verba argue that the distinctive property of a 'civic culture' is not its participant orientation but its mixed quality" (Diamond 1993, 14). See also Diamond 1996.

5. "Professor Rahn noted that contemporary social scientists are actually trying to refine an insight from Alexis de Tocqueville's *Democracy in America*. Tocqueville had wanted to know why some communities prosper, possess effective political institutions, have law-abiding and satisfied citizens, while others do not. The success of the American experiment, he concluded, could not be explained by geography, or circumstance, or even good laws. Rather, it derived from what he called the mores of the American people—by which he meant the habits of thought, the patterns of behavior, that came as second nature to most American citizens. It is these attitudes and behaviors that are described, in modern parlance, as social capital" (*Newsletter of the National Commission* 1998).

6. "But the development of a stable and effective democratic government depends upon more than the structures of government and politics: it depends upon the orientations that people have to the political process—upon the political culture. Unless the political culture is able to support a democratic system, the chances for the success of that system are slim" (Almond and Verba 1963, 498). "Until recently rather little attention has been directed to how political culture affects the possibilities for democracy in the less developed world and the newly transforming polities of the former communist bloc" (Diamond 1993, 15). "To say that political culture involves the important ways in which people are subjectively oriented toward the basic elements of their political system is an accurate but not yet satisfactory definition . . . so many different formulations have been offered (twenty-five by one count) that one might think he was grappling with the riddle of the Sphinx" (Rosenbaum 1975, 5).

7. "In an article of 1956, Gabriel Almond, building upon conceptions of culture created by such sociologists and anthropologists as Clyde Kluckholm, Ralph Linton, and Talcott Parsons, defined a specifically political area of culture that, in collaboration with Sidney Verba, he proceeded to study empirically in five democracies. The findings were published in 1963 in *The Civic Culture* (Princeton, NJ: Princeton University Press, 1963). A few years earlier, working independently of Almond, Samuel Beer and Adam Ulam presented a somewhat different definition of the concept in a comparative government text of 1958 (*Patterns of Government*, New York: Random House, 1958)" (Bluhm 1974, xii).

8. Certainly to describe as Inglehart does a renaissance in political culture implies that there was a previous hiatus, and that seems to have been the case for political culture as rational choice theory became intensely popular. "To speak of a return to political culture implies that there was an earlier time when political culture studies were here at hand and prospering, that this was followed by a time in which the approach declined, and these studies are once again prospering" (Almond 1993, ix).

9. "Questions can be asked about the General Social Survey (GSS) on which he chiefly relies. The GSS asks respondents about 'types' of organizations to which they belong, not concrete group memberships; as groups have proliferated within certain categories, the extent of individuals' involvement may well be undercounted. What is more, newer types of involvement—such as parents congregating on Saturdays at children's sports events, or several families going together to the bowling alley (just visit one and look!)—may not be captured by the GSS questions. As many fathers and mothers have pulled back from Elks Clubs and women's clubs, they may have turned not toward 'bowling alone' but toward child-centered involvement with other parents" (Skocpol 1996).

10. "And yet, there are some who still look down on bowling, as if it were somehow beneath them. These are the people of which we must be aware! In a world of fascist, bourgeoisie [sic] golfers, bowling is the game of the proletariat—THE PEOPLE'S GAME! So embrace it! Cast off the shackles of class struggle, and unite in the spirit of fun and fair play! From ancient Egypt to the German monks to 'Another Fine Brunswick Family Recreation Center,' the legacy of the world's oldest sport lives on in all of us! Grab your ball! Put on those funky shoes! and BOWL! BOWL LIKE THE WIND!" (Berk 1998).

11. "The Bowl for Kids' Sake provides funding to support continued operation of the Jewish Other Big Sister Association. Last year's sponsors helped us raise over $60,000 from our one day event. Please think about what you are able to do to help many local kids" (Bedford Bowl 1998).

12. "Putnam's measures may, in fact, overlook several types of civic activity. . . . According to the San Diego Union, of 800,000 licensed motorcyclists, 10,000 are now members of the American Brotherhood Aimed Toward Education (ABATE), which has been credited as decisive in several races for the state legislature. Members do not meet on a regular basis, but they do periodically mobilize in local political contests to advance their one legislative purpose. Would Putnam's data pick up on this group? What about the intense but brief house-building activity for Habitat for Humanity? Fourth, Putnam notes but leaves to the side the vast increase in Washington-based mailing list organizations over the past 30 years. He ignores them because they do not require members to do more than send in a check. This is not Tocquevillian democracy, but these organizations may be a highly efficient use of civic energy. The citizen who joins them may get the same civic payoff for less personal hassle. This is especially so if we conceive of politics as a set of public policies. The citizen may be able to influence government more satisfactorily with the annual membership in Sierra Club or the National Rifle Association than by attending the local club luncheons" (Schudson 1996).

13. I recall an elderly lady of my acquaintance who was a stalwart member of the Widows of World War I and constantly bemoaning an inability to find new recruits.

14. The Grange could not sustain growth as the farming population decreased, but, in reduced size, it is still a lively organization. While the United Commercial Travelers still maintains a lodge system for lonely salesmen, air transportation makes it possible to be home for the weekend, and the organization has had to meet falling membership by reinventing itself and finding new purposes. United Commercial Travelers lodges have become a sponsor of the Special Olympics for the retarded, of a Junior Golf Tournament, cancer education, an International Safety Poster Contest, and a Hugs Drugs program for families dealing with drug problems (United Commercial Travelers 1996).

15. After a long period of decline, there was an increase in fraternal membership immediately after World War II, partly attributed to the fact that those who served in the war had not been able to join and now were making up for lost time. Other reasons included a desire to fulfill a promise made to join if one survived and to reaffirm a family tradition as a legacy member. The death of many who joined then but were never active members is another reason for the present sharp membership decline. See Morris 1993 for an exhaustive treatment of this subject.

16. The Odd Fellows started to disappear in the 1920s, and the decline from 1920 to 1935 exceeded all its growth from 1900 to 1920. In 1920, the Odd Fellows had 1.7 million members. In 1940, they had 666,000 members. Morris documents in detail how other, now nearly vanished organizations such as the Pa-

triarchs Militant, Rebekah, and Knights of Pythias also peaked around 1920 and then began to disappear (Morris 1993 passim).

17. Beauty is in the eye of the beholder: "We like intermediate institutions when they have good effects and dislike them when they have bad ones. What we want, it would seem, is not civil society, but civic—what the Romans called civitas; that is, public-spiritedness, sacrifice for the community, citizenship, even nobility. But not all of civil society is civic minded" (Zakaria 1995, 15). See also de Guerra 1995.

18. For example, the contribution to democracy of the many parent-teacher associations (PTAs) at all-white schools during the 1950s and 1960s is debatable. The PTA has had a mixed record in facing many of the changes that the country at large has faced. Nationally, the largely white PTA merged with the National Congress of Colored Parents and Teachers only in 1970. In 1977, after years of procrastination, the word "church" finally was stricken from its list of objectives and "house of worship" substituted in deference to non-Christians. As for membership figures, they began to rise after 20 years of decline in 1983 and as some of the autonomous regional and local groups affiliated or reaffiliated. See PTA History 1999.

19. When I interviewed the executive secretary of the Grand Eastern Star Chapter of New York in 1996, she expressed the view that the absence of black members was not a problem, although perhaps the time would come for having a single black chapter for "exceptional cases"!

20. The most important issue is not total activity but the quality of participation, especially with regard to issues that affect the whole community. "In July 1994 the Minnesota Council of Nonprofits Board began developing a long term project focusing on new ways nonprofit organizations could increase citizen participation, including voter turnout. In early 1995 MCN sponsored a series of discussions included in the Civic Engagement Project, to assess what nonprofits are currently doing to enhance civic participation, and to explore how an association of nonprofits such as MCN could support and promote the role of nonprofits in this area" (Gillespie 1999).

21. "The infection cyberspace spreads today is far more virulent than the bubonic plague. Anathema to government, the 'net carries the virus of freedom" (McCullagh 1996, 33).

22. "There is something spectacular and perhaps ironic about the way in which civil society has burst into social sciences literature in recent years after lying dormant for so long. An important component of Western political thought, the concept was neglected in the West for most of the twentieth century, while it gained more common use in Marxist terminology and some of its derivatives (Gramsci used the term in opposition to the oppressive fascist state). Its new surge, however, occurred just as socialism declined and a capitalist market-oriented socioeconomic order began to spread throughout the world" (Azarya 1994, 85).

23. "The development of a stable and effective democratic government depends upon more than the structures of government and politics: it depends upon the orientations that people have to the political process—upon the political culture. Unless the political culture is able to support a democratic system, the chances for the success of that system are slim" (Almond and Verba 1963, 498).

24. "While the evidence now available does not permit firm conclusions about the overall condition of associational life in America, it appears that voluntary activities are on balance healthier than are formal political institutions and processes. Indeed, many citizens—particularly the youngest—seem to be shifting their preferred civic involvement from official politics to the voluntary sector" (National Commission on Civic Renewal 1998).

References

Almond, Gabriel. 1993. Forward: The Return of Political Culture. In *Political Culture and Democracy in Developing Countries*, ed. Larry Diamond. Boulder, CO: Lynne Rienner.

Almond, Gabriel A. 1996. The Civic Culture? Prehistory, Retrospect, and Prospect. Available at the site of the Center for the Study of Democracy, University of California, Irvine: http://hypatia.ss.uci.edu/democ/papers/almond.htm

Almond, Gabriel A. and Sidney Verba. 1963. *The Civic Culture: Political Attitudes and Democracy in Five Nations*. Princeton, NJ: Princeton University Press.

Alonso, Jorge. 1993. Introducción. In *Cultura política y educación cívica*, ed. Jorge Alonso. Mexico City: Grupo Editorial Miguel Angel Porrúa, and UNAM.

Ammerman, Nancy. 1996. Bowling Together: Congregations and the American Civic Order. Seventeenth Annual University Lecture in Religion, Arizona State University, 26 Feb. Available at http://www.asu.edu/clas/religious_studies/home/1996lec.html

Azarya, Victor. 1994. Civil Society and Disengagement in Africa. In *Civil Society and the State in Africa*, ed. John W. Harbeson, Donald Rothchild, and Naomi Chazan. Boulder, CO: Lynne Rienner.

Bedford Bowl for Kids' Sake. 1998. Web page available at http://www.dynamicsonline.com/bowlforkids

Berger, Peter L. 1971. *Para una teoría sociológica de la religión*. Barcelona, Spain: Editorial Kairós.

Berk, Scott. 1998. An Introduction to Bowling. Available at http://www.cardhouse.com/x06/intro.html

Billiard and Bowling Institute Report 1987-1997. *Bowling Participation: Popular and Stable*. 1998. Available at http://www.sportlink.com/press_room/ 1998_releases/bbia98-03.html

Bluhm, William T. 1974. *Ideologies and Attitudes: Modern Political Culture*. Englewood Cliffs, NJ: Prentice Hall.

Boyles, Ann. 1997. The Rise of Civil Society. *One Country* 2(Jan.-Mar.):25-36.

Brint, Steven. 1994. Sociological Analysis of Political Culture: An Introduction and Assessment. In *Research on Democracy and Society*, ed. Frederick D. Weil. Vol. 2. Greenwich, CT: JAI Press.

Charles, Jeffrey A. 1993. *Service Clubs in American Society*. Chicago: University of Illinois Press.

Chronology of American Topical Association Affiliate Chartering. 1999. *Topic Time* 50(2):51-52.

Cohen, Judith. 1998. American Civil Society. Institute for Philosophy and Public Policy. Lecture. Available at http://www.puaf.umd.edu/ippp/summer98/american_civil_society_talk.htm

Conway, M. Margaret, Alfonso J. Damico, and Sandra Bowman Damico. 1996. "Bowling Alone" or Civic Participants? Patterns of Community and Political Participation. Paper presented at the meeting of the American Political Science Association.

de Guerra, Regina Nowicki. 1995. Neighborhood Associations and Substantive Democracy. Paper presented at the meeting of the Latin American Studies Association.

Diamond, Larry. 1992. Economic Development and Democracy Reconsidered. In *Reexamining Democracy: Essays in Honor of Seymour Martin Lipset*, ed. Garry Marks and Larry Diamond. Newbury Park, CA: Sage.

———. 1993. Introduction: Political Culture and Democracy. In *Political Culture and Democracy in Developing Countries*, ed. Larry Diamond. Boulder, CO: Lynne Rienner.

———. 1996. Is the Third Wave Over? *Journal of Democracy* 7(3):20-37.

———. 1997. Consolidating Democracy in the Americas. *The Annals* of the American Academy of Political and Social Science 550(Mar.):12-41.

Dryze, John. 1996. Political Inclusion and the Dynamics of Democratization. *American Political Science Review* 90(1):475-87.

Dunn, Elizabeth. 1996. Money, Morality and Modes of Civil Society Among American Mormons. In *Civil Society: Challenging Western Models*, ed.

Chris Hann and Elizabeth Dunn. New York: Routledge.

Eck, Diana. 1997. Comments at the symposium The Democratic Soul. *Religion and Values in Public Life* (Harvard Divinity School) 6(1):3.

Fowler, Robert Booth. 1991. *The Dance with Community: The Contemporary Debate in American Thought*. Lawrence: University Press of Kansas.

Fukuyama, Francis. 1999. The Great Disruption: Human Nature and the Reconstruction of Social Order. *Atlantic Monthly* 283(5):55-80.

Gaudiani, Claire L. 1996. Our Ailing Civil Society. *Boston Globe*, 3 Apr. Available at http://camel2.conncoll. edu/ccadim/gaudiani/writings/ailing. html

Geertz, Clifford. 1992. *La interpretación de las culturas*. Barcelona, Spain: Editorial Gedisa.

Gillespie, Jennifer. 1999. Civil Engagement Project. Available at http://www. mncn.org./civ_eng.html

Harbeson, John W. 1994. Introduction. In *Civil Society and the State in Africa*, ed. John W. Harbeson, Donald Rothchild, and Naomi Chazan. Boulder, CO: Lynne Rienner.

Healy, Juan Ruiz. 1998. Nongovernmental Organizations: A Political Weapon. *Mexico City News*, 11 Mar.

Heller, Scott. 1996. "Bowling Alone": A Harvard Professor Examines America's Dwindling Sense of Community. *Chronicle of Higher Education*, 1 Mar., A10.

Hodgson, Marshall G. S. 1993. *Rethinking World History: Essays on Europe, Islam and World History*. New York: Cambridge University Press.

Inglehart, Ronald. 1988. The Renaissance of Political Culture. *American Political Science Review* 82(Dec.):1203-30.

Inkeles, Alex. 1979. Continuity and Change in the American National Character. In *The Third Century: America as a Post-Industrial Society*, ed. Seymour Martin Lipset. Stanford, CA: Hoover Institution Press.

———. 1998. *One World Emerging? Convergence and Divergence in Industrial Societies*. Boulder, CO: Westview Press.

Kaufman, Herbert. 1991. *Time, Chance, and Organizations: National Selection in a Perilous Environment*. 2d ed. Chatham, NJ: Chatham House.

Kavanah, Dennis. 1972. *Political Culture*. New York: Macmillan.

Kawachi, Iichiro, Bruce P. Kennedy, and Kimberly Lochner. 1997. Long Live Community: Social Capital as Public Health. *American Prospect* 35(Nov.-Dec.):56-59.

Kohut, Andrew. n.d. Remarks presented to the National Commission on Civic Renewal, First Plenary Panel on Social Trust and Civic Engagement. Available at http://www.cpn.org/sections/ new_citizenship/nccr-jan2.html

Kornhouser, William. 1959. *The Politics of Mass Society*. Glencoe, IL: Free Press.

Ladd, Everett Carill. 1998. Bowling with Tocqueville: Civic Engagement and Social Capital. American Enterprise Institute for Public Policy and Research. Bradley Lecture, 15 Sept. Available at http://www.aei.org/ bradley/b1091598.html

Lipset, Seymour Martin. 1950. *Agrarian Socialism: The Cooperative Commonwealth Federation in Saskatchewan*. Berkeley: University of California Press.

———. 1956. *Union Democracy*. Garden City, NY: Anchor Books.

———. 1996. *American Exceptionalism: A Double-Edged Sword*. New York: W. W. Norton.

Lipset, Seymour Martin and Earl Raab. 1970. *The Politics of Unreason: Right-Wing Extremism in America, 1790-1970*. Chicago: University of Chicago Press.

McCullagh, Declan. 1996. Plague of Freedom. *Internet Underground* 1(9):1-17.

Metzger, Thomas A. 1998. *The Western Concept of the Civil Society in the Context of Chinese History.* Stanford, CA: Hoover Institution on War, Revolution and Peace.

Michels, Robert. [1911] 1949. *Political Parties.* Reprint, Glencoe, IL: Free Press.

Morris, S. Brent. 1993. *A Radical in the East.* Ames: Iowa Research Lodge No. 2.

National Commission on Civic Renewal. 1998. Final Report. Available at http://www.puaf.umd.edu/civicrenewal

Nessman, Ravi. 1997. Rate of Volunteering Has Been on the Rise. *Miami Herald*, 25 Apr.

Newsletter of the National Commission on Civic Renewal. 1998. Available at http://www.puaf.umd.edu/civicrenewal/fon.html

Nye, Joseph S., Jr. and William A. Owens. 1996. America's Information Edge. *Foreign Affairs* 75(2):19-29.

Packenham, Robert A. 1992. *The Dependency Movement: Scholarship and Politics in Development Studies.* Cambridge, MA: Harvard University Press.

Peschard, Jacqueline. 1996. *Cultura política: Congreso Nacional de Ciencia Política.* Mexico City: Colegio Nacional de Ciencias Políticas y Administración.

PTA History and Milestones. 1999. Available at http://www.pta.org/apta/index.html

Putnam, Robert D. 1995. Tuning in, Tuning out? The Strange Disappearance of Social Capital in America. *PS: Political Science & Politics* 28(4):664-83.

Rich, Paul. 1997. Female Freemasons: Gender, Democracy, and Fraternalism. *Journal of American Culture* 20(1):105-10.

Rich, Paul and Guillermo De Los Reyes. 1997. Internet Insurrection: Chiapas and the Laptop. In *Mapping Cyberspace: Social Research on the Electronic Frontier*, ed. Joseph E. Behar. New York: Dowling College Press.

———. 1998. Democracy, Gnosticism, and Eric Voegelin. *Contemporary Philosophy* 20(1):61-66.

Rosenbaum, Walter A. 1975. *Political Culture.* New York: Praeger.

Samuelson, Robert J. 1996. Why It Doesn't Matter If You Bowl Alone. *Mexico City News*, 12 Apr.

Schambra, William A. 1998. Remarks presented to National Commission on Civic Renewal, First Plenary Session, Panel Four: National Community and Civil Society. Available at http://www.cpn.org/sections/new_citizenship/nccr-jan4.html.

Schudson, Michael. 1996. What If Civic Life Didn't Die? *American Prospect* 25(Mar.-Apr.). Available at http://www.epn.org/prospect/25/25-cnt1.html

Seligson, Mitchell A. 1966. Agrarian Inequality and the Theory of Peasant Rebellion. *Latin American Research Review* 31(2):140-57.

Skocpol, Theda. 1996. Unraveling from Above. *American Prospect* 25(Mar.-Apr.). Available at http://www.epn.org/prospect/25/25-cnt2.html

———. 1997. America's Voluntary Groups Thrive in a National Network. *Brookings Review* 15(4). Available at http://www.brookings.org/pub/review/fall97/build.html

Smith, Rogers M. 1997. *Civic Ideals: Conflicting Visions of Citizenship in U.S. History.* New Haven, CT: Yale University Press.

Sorman, Guy. 1990. *The New Wealth of Nations.* Stanford, CA: Hoover Institution Press.

Sowell, Thomas. 1994. *Race and Culture: A World View.* New York: Basic Books.

Stiles, Kendall. 1997. Civil Society, Empowerment and Multilateral Doors. Paper delivered at the meeting of the International Studies Association.

United Commercial Travelers. 1996. Available at http://uctfraternal.org/programs.html

Van Roony, Alison. 1997. The Civic Society Agenda. Paper delivered at the meeting of the International Studies Association.

Verba, Sidney. 1965. Comparative Political Culture. In *Political Culture and Political Development*, ed. Lucian W. Pye and Sidney Verba. Princeton, NJ: Princeton University Press.

Wattenberg, Ben and Danille Wattenberg. 1998. The Age of the Minnies. Oct. Available at American Enterprise Institute, http://www.aei.org/oti/oti9645.html

Wright, Donald. 1996. Bowling, the Wright Way. 3 July. Available at http://www.treasuresoftware.com/dw12.html

———. 1997. The Good and the Bad in 1997. Available at http://www.treasuresoftware.com/dw12.html

Zakaria, Fareed. 1995. Bigger Than the Family, Smaller Than the State: Are Voluntary Groups What Make Countries Work? *New York Times Book Review*, 13 Aug., 1.

NAFTA: The Governance of Economic Openness

By ISIDRO MORALES

ABSTRACT: Although the rule-based regime of the North American Free Trade Agreement (NAFTA) has instituted the empowerment of private actors vis-à-vis government bureaucracies, and of transstate institutions at the regional level, it is contended in this article that NAFTA should be envisioned as a hybrid model of economic governance. Under the agreement, some issue areas still remain under the administration of state-centered authorities, and other ones, such as investment, trade remedy policies, and labor and environmental issues, under the surveillance and fragmented authority of nonstate actors. This transfer of authority to private or civil society actors is, in fact, a major trait of the NAFTA policy mechanism. It is also argued in this article that, contrary to what some authors have suggested, NAFTA's hybrid institutional machinery is provoking deep integration in the region, in spite of the absence of supranational institutions or the homogenization of national legislation.

Isidro Morales is chairman of the International Relations and History Department at the Universidad de las Américas–Puebla, in Mexico. He has mainly pursued an academic career, within national and international institutions, combining both teaching and research. He has coauthored two books and published several articles in specialized journals, dealing mainly with energy- and trade-related topics. He is currently writing a book about the present and future of regionalism in North America.

NOTE: This article was written thanks to financial support from the Consejo Nacional de Ciencia y Tecnología and a grant provided by the Canadian Studies Program, administered by the Canadian Embassy in Mexico.

THE North American Free Trade Agreement (NAFTA) was conceived not only to increase trade and investment flows between the partners; it was also devised as a rule-based regime aiming to reduce nontariff and nontrade barriers affecting cross-border trade and investment decisions. In other words, NAFTA has established a rule-based trade and investment regime under which economic openness and the mobility of both trade and capital are to be maintained and activated at the trilateral level. By so doing, this regime has instituted the empowerment of market actors vis-à-vis government bureaucracies, and of institutional actors at the supra-state level (namely, panels and NAFTA-based institutions). The latter play a major role for building confidence and facilitating conflict resolution between private parties and government agencies. The common denominator of these alternative dispute settlement mechanisms is that they attempt to protect the rights and interests of private actors, mainly firms involved in trade or business across the region, against discretionary or unjustified policies that are enacted by public agencies and that could breach or impair the agreement. This was highly desired by Canada and Mexico due to market access problems they traditionally have had in the United States. But this was also particularly relevant for the United States vis-à-vis Mexico, mainly concerning the pre-NAFTA investment and trade regimes that prevailed in the latter country, which were highly unpredictable for U.S. investments.

Although NAFTA's rule-based regime has instituted the empowerment of private actors vis-à-vis government bureaucracies, and of trans-state institutions at the regional level, I contend in this article that NAFTA should be envisioned as a hybrid model of economic governance. Under the agreement, some issue areas still remain under the administration of state-centered authorities, and other ones, such as investment, trade remedy policies, and labor and environmental issues, under the surveillance and fragmented authority of nonstate actors. This transfer of authority to private or civil society actors is, in fact, a major trait of the NAFTA policy mechanism. I also argue in this article that, contrary to what some authors have suggested, NAFTA's hybrid institutional machinery is provoking deep integration in the region, in spite of the absence of supranational institutions or the homogenization of national legislation. The first three parts of this article aim to develop my first argument, while the last one is devoted to the second idea.

NAFTA AND FACILITATION OF
THE GOVERNANCE OF CROSS-
COUNTRY ECONOMIC OPENNESS

NAFTA was created around a major normative goal: the foundation of a free-mobility area in commodities, services, and financial flows in order to increase efficiency, productivity, and welfare in the economies of the three participating countries. Hence NAFTA aims to maintain the openness in those areas in order to increase the opportunities and gains of market actors. Those areas in which integration must be accomplished have defined key level playing fields of which some are ruled and administered at the trilateral level, and some, at the national level. Figure 1 depicts those issue areas that I consider most important, though the list is not exhaustive and is intended just to illustrate the scope and interplay of the functional areas encompassed by this regime.

The first issue area embraces those rules and norms regulating the creation of free trade in commodities and services during a 15-year span. It also embraces those specific sectors in which each country has made particular accommodations to the deregulation process, such as the fields of automobiles, energy, and agriculture. The issue area also includes the rulings on other trade-related issues such as government procurement, the enforcement of property rights, and phytosanitary and standard policies. The second issue area depicted in Figure 1 is that covered by chapter 11 of NAFTA, concerning the rights of NAFTA-based firms and their investments within North America. The third one is that particularly covered by chapter 19 of the agreement, concerning the use of trade remedy laws by state members in the realm of dumping and subsidies. The remaining issue areas are those regulating environmental and labor issues in North America. The special nature of these areas is that changes in labor and environmental matters in each country's legislation are required. That is,

they are the only NAFTA issue areas the rules and norms of which are not framed at the cross-country level.

This classification is neither hierarchical nor exhaustive. It just pretends to illustrate that NAFTA could be understood, by the way it rules and works, as a cluster of functional areas conforming to a trade and investment regime operating at a trilateral level. Though the term "regime" has become misleading when analyzing trade and investment issues, I keep it as an analytical tool provided that some other key conceptual issues are clarified. NAFTA is a regime, or a cluster of regimes, according to Stephen Krasner's classical definition of it, that is, as "sets of implicit or explicit principles, norms, rules, and decision making procedures around which actors' expectations converge in a given area of international relations" (Krasner 1983, 186). If we consider principles as arising out of reality, we could say that free trade, economic openness, and other market-oriented principles are the major principles guiding this venture. Those principles are explicitly stated in the foreword of the agreement. If we consider norms as standards of behavior defined in terms of rights and obligations, and rules as prescriptions or proscriptions for or against action (see Kratochwil 1991, 59), the 22 chapters composing the agreement, as well as its seven annexes and two side agreements, constitute the body of norms, rules, and decision-making procedures so characteristic of international regimes.

The question of the convergence of expectations of those participating in

FIGURE 1
NAFTA'S ISSUE AREAS AND REGIME MAINTENANCE

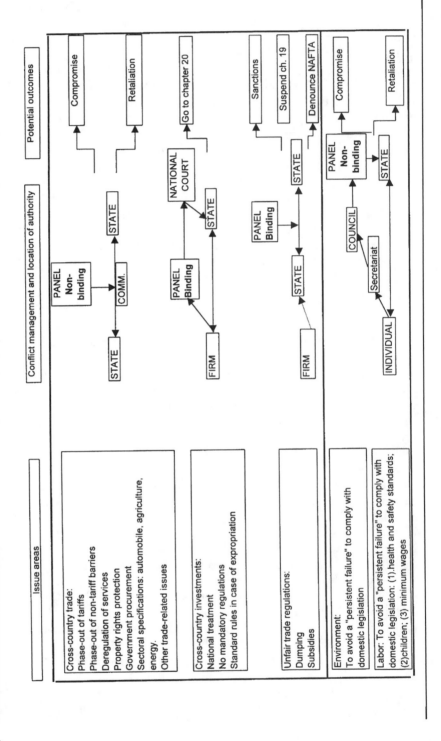

a regime is also important. As a whole body of literature has extensively explained, regimes can be created only if the participants have the need or the will to cooperate and hence adjust their individual policies in a certain issue area under the expectation that collective gains in the long term will overcome unilateral short-term gains.[1] That is, regimes define issue areas to be maintained in the long term, which could become eventually transformed, renovated, or adapted according to changing circumstances. Furthermore, regimes also become the locus around which other regimes could be nested. In the case of NAFTA, the span of the game, so to speak, has been settled at 15 years, at least for the construction of a free-trade area. In other fields, like investments and property rights, the duration of the agreement remains open. NAFTA has already become the locus in which two other agreements were nested, one addressing environmental issues and the other focusing on labor issues. These agreements were negotiated after the negotiations of the main agreement were over, as a condition of the Clinton administration for obtaining the congressional support for NAFTA. These two agreements were the product of a domestic compromise between the White House and powerful environment and labor associations. However, they do not reflect an interstate consensus mainly because they were not a priority for the Mexican government. That is why they rather reflect a transitional instrument of "soft law"[2] anticipating newly formed laws to be settled once

the political consensus is reached over time.

However, NAFTA is more than a regime and much less than a supranational body for regulating trade and investment issues between partners. Though many authors still conceive it as a free-trade area, the fact that it prescribes the liberation of investment flows, the enforcement of property rights, the deregulation of government procurement, and the enforcement of national policies on other trade-related issues makes it difficult to classify NAFTA among the classical stages leading toward a common market. That is why I prefer to approach the integration drive within North America with the analytical tools of the institutionalist and regime schools. As some authors have already suggested, institutional regimes most of the time derive from international law, that is, from international agreements. Those agreements are already a formal institution around which signing parties agree to adapt their policies and behavior on a certain issue area (Chayes and Chayes 1995, 2). In the case of NAFTA, the different issue areas are fully regulated by explicit rules that together constitute an international treaty.

Treaties are not just juridical forms to which signatory parties have the discretionary capacity to comply. They are institutions in themselves, with practical and political consequences. First, they increase the efficiency in the making of policy options for states, because they do not have to recalculate their policy options each time they must make a decision in those areas already governed by the agreement. In this sense, as Kratochwil has correctly asserted, rules and norms guide choices; or as Keohane stated it, regimes create a patterned behavior (Kratochwil 1991, 43; Keohane 1984, 97). Regimes and treaties embody an economy of procedural decisions and choices.

The second point to be addressed is that treaties, agreements, and regimes are not politically neutral; they are the product of political bargaining and undertakings that reflect the interests of states. This point is one of the most controversial issues in regime and institutions theory. It is well known that some authors, such as Gilpin (1987), maintain that regimes could be created and maintained only by hegemons, that is, superpowers that devise the regimes and multilateral institutions as a tool for maximizing and legitimizing their hegemony. In this sense, regimes are the extension of the power of the hegemon, either as a way to legitimize its supremacy in a certain field or as a cost-sharing device for reducing the burdens of its leadership (see Nye 1990, 253-61). For other authors, however, regimes and institutions have a dynamic in themselves that permits them to be maintained yet transformed as long as the different actors recognize that mutual gains over time still exist (Keohane 1984). There is, however, a common ground in this discussion that highlights the political dimension of all agreements, in the sense that they reflect, to some extent, the accommodation of the interests of the negotiating parties (Chayes and Chayes 1995, 4). As a body of

literature is already suggesting, the accommodation of divergent and/or contending interests is being done at a two-level game of negotiation, the first one being that of interstate negotiation, the second one being that between national bureaucracies and local constituencies (see Milner 1997).

In the case of NAFTA, it is clear that the core of rules and norms around which state actors have made a compromise is to the benefit of market actors, mainly firms and transnational companies. The core of the consensus between the three countries is consequently to build a more transparent and predictable environment for market actors, in order to increase the efficiency of cross-country trade, services, and investment transactions. NAFTA has built some key issue areas around that major goal, such as the creation of a free-trade area in a span of 15 years, the use of trade remedy laws by governments, the explicit enforcement of property rights, the regulation of a new code for cross-country investment, and so on. This leads us to think that this is where mutual expectations of the three partners are located so that even if short-term opportunistic gains are possible, they will in the long run comply in these basic areas. Conversely, due to the way they were devised and implemented, the labor and side agreements were conceived to work as discussion forums through which nongovernmental organizations and other civic groups could put forward their claims on specific issues. The studies, discussions, and decisions coming from this issue area could eventually shape a new agenda for better implementation of labor and environmental standards in the coming years, when the competing and shared interests of the actors involved make feasible a better-defined undertaking. Labor mobility and social issues were kept out of the agreement, suggesting that a political will within the region is still missing for addressing these issues at the transstate level.

Finally, the third point to be addressed concerning regimes and agreements is the level of compliance with and enforcement of norms. As Chayes and Chayes (1995) have correctly suggested, if norms are clear, unambiguous, and reflect well the political interests involved, there is a high propensity to comply with them (3-17). The opposite is also valid when rules are ambiguous and poorly reflect the interests at stake. States sometimes agree to broad and vaguely defined principles in order to avoid international surveillance in areas that they consider as remaining under their national jurisdiction. There is a time lag between those principles and the will to abide by them; this gap could nonetheless be narrowed in a series of agreements negotiated in different rounds of negotiation.

However, what gives strength to a regime is not only the clarity of the norms but, most of all, how they become incorporated into authoritative decisions that establish what the law is (Kratochwil 1991, 63). In the case of NAFTA, this is mainly accomplished by the alternative dispute resolution mechanisms (ADRMs) provided by the agreement. That is,

the way economic openness is ensured and maintained by NAFTA goes beyond the economic normativeness of the agreement. Openness is being provided, overseen, and enforced by complex institutional machinery working at two levels of jurisdiction. In most of the cases, the goal of the ADRMs is not necessarily the enforcement of agreed-upon rules. They rather work as facilitators in government-to-government negotiations when dealing with conflicts stemming from most of the issue areas in which economic integration is taking place. This is especially the case with the ADRM in NAFTA's chapter 20 covering any conflict that threatens or actually challenges any stipulation of the agreement—except those directly covered by the other ADRMs—as well as those conflicts arising from the interpretation of the agreement itself. This is also the case with the ADRMs instituted by the side agreements, that is, the agreements dealing with environmental and labor issues.

A second level of rule enforcement was instituted by chapters 11 and 19 of the agreement, dealing with investors' rights and the administration of anti-dumping and subsidy laws by national trade agencies, respectively. Only in these cases, ADRMs are entitled to award quasi-adjudicative decisions, that is, decisions taken by neutral panels and that are mandatory. Hence, according to the nature of the conflict and the issue area in which it is grounded, panel decisions are mandatory or not, highlighting the regime's two levels of enforcement and compliance. Figure 1 attempts also to depict these two levels of rule enforcement and their nuances throughout the five main issue areas encompassed by NAFTA.

Last but not least, the NAFTA regime, with its clusters of issue areas, institution-building process, and two levels of rule enforcement, is redefining the governance of trade and investment exchanges within North America. If we understand governance to mean the exercise of political, economic, and administrative authority within different spheres of human activity (see Rosenau 1997, 145), it is clear that NAFTA is relocating the loci of authority within trade and investment matters from the national-based level to the transstate, yet substate levels. I use the term "transstate" in order to avoid the term "transnational." The latter applies to supra-state institutions that are still nonexistent within NAFTA. Authority has been transferred to the substate level because firms and other nonstate actors participating in the civil society have been empowered by NAFTA normativeness in some key issue areas such as trade remedy laws, investments, and, to a lesser extent, labor and the environment. Authority has been transferred to transstate institutions—the Trade Commission and NAFTA panels—mainly in those areas covered by chapters 11 and 19. Figure 1 depicts this double way in which the transfer of state-centered authority is being made by the NAFTA regime.

Hence, it is clear that arbitral panels are a new juridical figure, not only a new institutional actor, mediating between states, even between firms and states. Panels are entitled to assess whether a breach of the agreement or a threat not to comply with it has been committed by one party. The fact that panel determinations are normally not politically motivated, but rather technically based and rule-framed, entitles the panels to build the general framework under which confidence building and conflict resolution are implemented between partners. Even in those areas in which state-to-state negotiations remain important to the maintenance of the regime, the role of NAFTA's normativeness, institutions, and dispute resolution is no less important, provided they facilitate policy options and the mutual adjustment of state's preferences.

NAFTA'S FUNCTIONAL AREAS
GROUNDED IN NEGOTIATION
AND COMPROMISE

NAFTA's chapter 20 and labor and environmental agreements are enforced under the formula of negotiation and compromise. This section will review the major features of that formula.

NAFTA's ADRMs addressing a breach, impairment, or nullification of the overall agreement

Chapter 20 institutes a resolution mechanism covering any conflict—except those directly covered by the other ADRMs—that is considered to be inconsistent with the agreement, that threatens to cause impairment or nullification of any right or concession, or that arises from the interpretation of the agreement itself. The creation of a panel under chapter 20 takes place once consultation between the conflicting parties and conciliatory actions of the Trade Commission are unsuccessful in helping the parties to reach a compromise. Conflicts under this chapter must be handled mainly on an interstate cooperative basis. As stated in article 2003, "The Parties shall at all times endeavor to agree on the interpretation and application of this Agreement, and shall make every attempt through cooperation and consultations to arrive at a mutually satisfactory resolution of any matter that might affect its operation."

Under chapter 20, panels also play a conciliatory role. They first draft a preliminary decision or a so-called action plan in order to get the opinion of the contending parties. In this first report, panelists are bound to state whether an action is not compatible with the agreement (or suppresses the expected benefits of it), and, if necessary, they draft a recommendation in order to solve the conflict. Once panelists have submitted their preliminary position to the contending parties, they elaborate a final decision. According to article 2018 of the agreement, "the disputing Parties shall agree on the resolution of the dispute, which normally shall conform with the determinations and recommendations of the panel."

That is, final decisions are not binding. However, they frame policy options for the disputants in order to make them negotiate a mutually satisfactory solution. If there is no solution that is mutually satisfactory to the disagreeing parties, the complaining party may suspend against the nonabiding party the benefits of "equivalent effect" in order to compensate for the damage. Retaliation could be accomplished in the same sector in which the damage is being done or, in case this does not have any effect, in another sector (cross-sector retaliation). That is, drawing from the General Agreement on Tariffs and Trade (GATT) experience and from most of the trade agreements of the sort, NAFTA institutes unilateral retaliation as a compensatory measure and as a tool of last resort in order to make partners play by the rules. However, it is understood that unilateral retaliation is the second best of all desirable outcomes. The role of states, the commission, and panel decisions is precisely aimed to facilitate the accommodation of conflicting interests. The potential of achieving unilateral retaliation could eventually be used as a bargaining tool to reach a mutual agreement.

Chapter 20 of NAFTA is a slightly improved version of chapter 18 of the Canada-U.S. Free Trade Agreement (CUFTA) signed in 1988.[3] At the time, the dispute resolution mechanism instituted by chapter 18 of CUFTA constituted a step forward compared to the settlement of disputes that prevailed under GATT. In fact, both chapter 18 and its revised version under chapter 20 of NAFTA gave to a disputant party the option to settle a dispute either under the coverage of the trilateral trade regime or under article XXII.2 of GATT. Prior to the creation of the World Trade Organization (WTO) and the setting of the WTO

Understanding on Rules and Procedures Governing the Settlement of Disputes (WTO Understanding), chapter 20 of NAFTA was still more efficient and attractive than the dispute settlement mechanism that prevailed under GATT. The major disadvantage of the GATT mechanism compared to that of CUFTA and NAFTA was the dominance of the positive consensus formula. Under GATT, all members, including the disputing parties, should agree by consensus to establish a panel, to formulate recommendations, or to work out an eventual solution, and, worst of all, to decide about the adoption of panel reports and the use of retaliatory measures in order to compensate a grievance. Though many reports were adopted by the Council of GATT, many others were shelved because a disputing party eventually used its "veto power" guaranteed by the positive consensus formula. Furthermore, panel resolutions lacked transparency, and the dispute resolution process was slow and uncertain (see Komuro 1995, 17-37).

The WTO Understanding replaces the GATT dispute settlement mechanism and, consequently, since 1996, it has been the new ADRM competing with that of chapter 20 of NAFTA. The gap in terms of rapidness and effectiveness between the two mechanisms has been narrowed considerably mainly due to the conversion of the positive consensus formula of the GATT system to a negative consensus mechanism now dominating the WTO Understanding. That is, the veto power that a disputant previously had under the former mechanism has been lifted by requiring now a consensus of all members for preventing the functioning of the dispute mechanism. A consensus is needed if members agree that a panel should not be established to deal with a dispute, if they consider that a panel decision must not be adopted, or if retaliation should not proceed. This has made the WTO Understanding more expeditious and less uncertain. However, according to some authors, final decisions could take four times longer than under NAFTA, the time frame of which is theoretically no more than six months, with eight months to be allowed to implement unilateral retaliation (Reisman and Wiedman 1995, 22).

The time frame difference between the two mechanisms could be explained by some procedural differences. The WTO Understanding establishes an appellate body that does not exist in NAFTA chapter 20. Once a panel report is concluded, the Dispute Settlement Body (DSB) of the WTO establishes a "reasonable" period of time for the implementation of a solution. Chapter 20 of NAFTA set that time limit as 30 days after the complaining parties received a final report. This is a substantial difference due to the fact that the DSB decides what a "reasonable" period of time is under the formula of the positive consensus. Because the complaint parties are also part of the DSB, any decision around this matter could eventually be blocked. The WTO establishes that in this case the period of time is decided through binding arbitration. Consequently, the implementation of final decisions could take much more time if a conflict is settled under the WTO than under the NAFTA mechanism (Komuro 1995, 57-58). This reflects what Reisman and Wiedman (1995) have called a difference in the "contextual imperatives" of these two ADRMs. Independent of the clarity and the level of formality of the two agreements, they become functional and effective, taking into account the political environment in which they are nested. Consequently, as a multilateral and wide-open agreement, the WTO Understanding provides more time for disputing actors to reach a negotiated compromise than the more focused and selected-members approach of NAFTA.

Moreover, retaliation is never unilateral if it stems from a WTO-framed conflict, contrary to what prevails in NAFTA. In the case of the WTO, retaliatory measures are always under the approval and surveillance of the DSB. Retaliation could be parallel, if it is accomplished in the same sector where nullification or impairment was found; it could be cross-sector if it is done in a different sector; or it could be cross-agreement if retaliation is carried out under a different agreement covered by the WTO (Komuro 1995, 60).

Finally, both the WTO Understanding and chapter 20 of NAFTA envisage an arbitral mechanism if a party finds that the level of retaliatory measures exceeds the level of the impairment or nullification.

As of February 1999, around 12 conflicts have been handled under chapter 20, though only 3 have activated the panel mechanism. Two cases are already terminated, confirming by unanimity in each case the Canadian[4] and Mexican positions.[5] The fact that 9 of 12 conflicts were terminated before going to a panel might suggest that chapter 20 is working according to the goal it was originally anticipated to meet, that is, to induce intergovernment negotiations in order to solve conflicts. Further research, however, should be undertaken in order to clarify that hypothesis. Nonetheless, we should remember that the controversial Helms-Burton Law was one of the cases discussed under chapter 20, prompting the Trade Commission to mediate between the parties. The extraterritorial faculties of this law have been suspended, however, due to the discretionary powers of the White House to decide the final implementation of the law. Did NAFTA and the WTO—a forum where the Helms-Burton Law was also strongly criticized—help to contain U.S. trade measures that played against the new trading system, or did NAFTA and these new trade mechanisms help the American president to contain strong protectionist pressures coming from the U.S. Congress? Though further research on this point is necessary, we should stress that both Canada and Mexico were very cautious in bringing the problem up to the panel level. In some way, they realized that this law was the product of strong domestic pressures (coming mainly from the Cuban American lobby) demanding a political response from the White House in an electoral year. In this sense, the so-called two-level game approach for international agreements is true in a double sense:

international agreements, in this case NAFTA, are the product of a compromise between the interests of domestic actors and government agencies; however, this compromise may challenge the agreement, if domestic interests can prevail, even for a short while, over international commitments. However, the example of the Helms-Burton Law may suggest that international commitments may be used to temper the excesses of parochialism.

So far, all the conflicts handled by either chapter 18 of CUFTA or chapter 20 of NAFTA have focused on technicalities or on the interpretation of the agreement. This is the case with the two disputes already resolved under NAFTA panels. To the present, the settlement mechanism has been a success because it has been expeditious. Once appointed, the panels issued their determinations quite promptly (in 4-6 months, except one that took 9 months), faster than GATT panels that have issued reports, and far faster if disputes were referred to a national court for adjudication.[6] According to some authors, panel decisions were thorough and of high quality (see Davey 1996, 65-68).

NAFTA's ADRMs addressing the domestic enforcement of labor and environmental issues

As stated in the first part of this article, the so-called side agreements covering trade-related labor and environmental issues were not part of the core concerns of the White House and U.S. Congress with respect to gaining the voting support

for NAFTA. That is why these agreements instead reflect anticipated fields in which international ruling could eventually evolve throughout time. These agreements do not provide for transstate norms or principles by which parties must abide. They just stress that each state's own environmental and labor legislation must be properly enforced in order to deter environmental and labor dumping[7] in North America's free-trade area. It was clear that these agreements were designed to deter an anti-NAFTA movement stressing the relocation of highly polluting or low-technology industries from the United States to Mexico.

The fact that these agreements were nested at the U.S. domestic level, and thereafter negotiated at the interstate level as a compromise formula for facilitating the passing of NAFTA by the U.S. Congress, explains their genetic deficiencies. As Reisman and Wiedman (1995) have asserted, they were designed not to work (30). First of all, the possibilities for activating a panel review are considerably vague and limited. A topic might be reviewed by a panel if a country witnesses a "persistent pattern of failure"—never defined by the two agreements—to effectively enforce its environmental law or labor legislation in specific areas. The issues raised must be submitted to ad hoc secretariats and councils in order to assess whether there really is a persistent failure to comply with a domestic law. The respective councils (one for labor and another for environment) are integrated by cabinet-level members of each state and must convene to the activation of a panel by two-thirds of the vote. That is, the activation of a panel under these two agreements is not automatic, as in the rest of NAFTA's ADRMs, giving the possibility that a pertinent issue could become eventually blocked by the council. Furthermore, in the case of labor issues, a panel review proceeds only if there is a persistent failure to comply with legislation covering health and safety standards, children's work, or minimum wages.

The role of panels is to find whether, in fact, there was a violation of labor or environmental laws taking into account the restrictions already mentioned. Panels are not entitled to review the adequacy of those laws or any amendment to them, as is the case within chapter 19 of NAFTA. If a panel's finding is positive, states and not private actors should normally negotiate a mutually satisfactory solution, as in the case of chapter 20. In case a mutually satisfactory solution is not reached, the novelty of these agreements is that they envisage a monetary enforcement award (MEA), or a fine, that panels can impose on a nonabiding party. However, an MEA cannot exceed 0.007 percent of the total trade between the parties, and it could take more than two years for a panel to decide that this measure be used. In case a complained-against party does not comply with the MEA, an annual fine can be collected— though it should not exceed the original MEA—through the suspension of benefits by the complaining party. But this final solution could take three years to be implemented (see Reisman and Wiedman 1995, 32-33).

It is worth noting, however, that these side agreements empower advocacy groups and other civic organizations—even individuals—to agitate for an investigation directly with the ad hoc council. Nonetheless, all remedial negotiations derived from a panel award are handled strictly by states. Though the chance for a private initiative to become a final panel award is not high, these side agreements have already proved that they can work as a real forum in which different environmental organizations, research institutes, human rights groups, lawyers' associations, and other groups of the civil society can put forward their claims concerning specific environmental or labor issues. Their claims have spurred the making and publication of several ad hoc studies, the organization of ministerial-level consultations, and the monitoring of some cases by the administrative body created by the side agreements. Though no submission under these agreements has activated a panel so far, claims coming from civic associations have sometimes succeeded in putting pressure on state agencies to solve a qualifying case. This is what happened, for instance, when the U.S. National Labor Relations Board ruled that a plant closing was prompted for anti-union reasons, after a submission was made by private groups at the Mexican National Administrative Office created by the side agreement on labor cooperation.[8]

NAFTA'S FUNCTIONAL AREAS GROUNDED IN QUASI-ADJUDICATORY DECISIONS

In contrast with the issue areas in which conflict resolution is guaranteed by mediation and negotiation, NAFTA embraces two major fields where dispute resolution is handled by panels on a quasi-adjudicative basis. These fields cover the domain of cross-country private investments coming from a party, regulated by chapter 11, and trade remedy laws targeting dumping and subsidies, regulated by chapter 19. Within these areas, there is little room for states to negotiate their differences, except in those cases where negotiation is allowed. Furthermore, within those two areas, market actors have the possibility of substituting local tribunals for a panel review. However, in neither case are panels to be considered as supranational bodies. Under chapter 11, final awards are to be enforced by a domestic court. Under chapter 19, panels cannot judge or abrogate final decisions coming from national administrative agencies; they are allowed only to decide whether those final decisions are consistent with national legislation, and, if this is not the case, they remand this decision in part or in full for reconsideration by the appropriate agency.

Regulating conflicts in the field of capital mobility

Chapter 11 does not truly institute a new ADRM; it rather provides that any conflict arising from the issues covered by that chapter (trade-related investment measures) as well as by articles 1502 and 1503 of the agreement (concerning state monopolies and government-owned enterprises) must be handled by arbitrage procedures regulated either by the World Bank's International Center for the Settlement of Investment Disputes (ICSID) or the United Nations Commission on International Trade Law Arbitration Rules (UNCITRAL). However, the ICSID Convention works for a panel if both the disputing party and the party of the investor are parties of the convention. The United States is currently the only signatory of the ICSID Convention, which means that no panel, under present circumstances, can be invoked under those rules. However, chapter 11 provides that the Additional Facility Rules of ICSID could be eventually invoked, if the disputing party or the party of the investor, but not both, is a party of the ICSID Convention. Hence, these rules will regulate arbitration activities under any dispute arising between the United States and either of the other two members. Due to the fact that neither Mexico nor Canada is a signatory of the ICSID Convention, the arbitration of disputes stemming from this chapter will be regulated under UNCITRAL arbitration rules.

An important feature of the chapter 11 arbitral provisions is that market actors could activate a panel dispute against a state without having to go through their own governments. No other ADRMs within NAFTA empower private actors as this one does. This is not the case under chapter 20 disputes, under which government-to-government conflicts are framed and negotiated. Furthermore, according to the broad definition of the "origin" of the investor provided by this chapter, the investor does not have to be a citizen of any NAFTA country but can be any enterprise with a "significant business presence" in any of the party members. However, once a private actor activates a panel under this chapter, he or she waives rights to address the same conflict in a domestic court.

Final awards of arbitrated panels activated under chapter 11 are binding, but they are to be enforced by domestic courts. Alternatively, the investor may choose the remedies available in the host country's domestic courts. In case final awards are not enforced or are neglected by governments, the complaining party has the option to activate a panel mechanism under chapter 20. The fact that there is a possibility that government agencies could ultimately neglect the final implementation of the award, notwithstanding the mediation of a domestic court, could severely restrain the scope of the ADRM under chapter 11. The mechanism is conceived to put legal pressure on governments in case they breach investors' rights under chapter 11 of the agreement. But governments could ultimately fail to correctly enforce arbitrated awards. In such a circumstance, private investors have the option of activating a panel mechanism under the rules of chapter 20. However, as previously seen, disputes under this chapter are handled by states, not by market actors against states, and final solutions are not necessarily rule-based but, rather, the result of political compromise.

Chapter 11 did not exist under CUFTA, so in many ways it could be envisioned as a device for deterring Mexico's discretionary policies concerning nationalization and foreign investment policies. In many ways, this chapter has meant a challenge to Mexico's and in some way Latin America's state-centered law paradigm regarding the treatment of foreign investments. Chapter 11 draws from the settlement mechanism for disputes between investor and host state established in U.S. bilateral investment treaties signed with some Latin American countries but that Mexico traditionally refused to sign (Taylor 1996-97; Manning-Cabrol 1995, 1200). The reason for this is that Mexico was attached, for historical reasons, to the principles of the Calvo Doctrine. This doctrine has established, since the end of the nineteenth century, the absolute equality between sovereign states and the equal treatment between nationals and foreigners. Consequently, when a foreign investor was involved in a dispute, he could not claim the diplomatic protection of his own government and had to submit claims under local tribunals. Though enacted by an Argentinean magistrate, the Calvo Doctrine became very popular in Mexico and in most Latin American countries seeking to protect themselves against potential military invasions coming from Europe or the United States, alleging the defense of their nationals in disputes concerning their investments in the host country.

That is why the Mexican Constitution still inserts a Calvo clause under its chapter 27, requiring foreign investors to be treated as nationals, and if such an investor invokes diplomatic protection, his or her property is ceded to the Mexican state (Manning-Cabrol 1995, 1188). Hence, the Calvo-based Mexican paradigm, as in most of Latin America, compelled foreign investors to be treated as nationals, renouncing the privileges of diplomatic protection. This approach reached its height in the late 1930s, when the Mexican government nationalized foreign oil companies, following local criteria enacted by national tribunals. Though diplomatic protection was invoked by those companies, Mexico made clear that the conditions of the expropriation were settled by national tribunals.

This approach was completely opposed to the international minimum standard that the U.S. government has traditionally required all states to comply with when dealing with foreign investments. According to the U.S. view, even if a state does not provide its own nationals with minimum international rights, it may not escape international responsibility to guarantee minimum standards to nationals of other countries (Manning-Cabrol 1995, 1177). Though Latin American countries, including Mexico, have moved progressively from the national-centered paradigm to that of the "minimum international standard" approach, chapter 11 of NAFTA is a turning point in this regard. Under NAFTA, Mexico is accepting not only that foreign arbitration could

substitute for national tribunals in conflicts arising with foreign firms, including the case of expropriation, but also what Stephen Zamora has called the increasing internal heterogeneization of state regulation, that is, the emergence of a new form of plurality of legal orders featuring the existence of partial legal fields constituted by discrepant logics coexisting in the same state legal system (Zamora 1997).

The case of the Calvo clause is a good example of this so-called heterogeneity of legal orders coexisting in the same territorial space. NAFTA has put an end to the Calvo clause if a conflict involving foreign investments could be claimed under its jurisdiction. What about those investors that could not eventually prove their origin as North American investors (that is, they do not have significant business activities in the region)? In principle, the Calvo clause remains valid for them, as far as this clause remains a part of the Mexican Constitution. To make things more complex, we should remember that Mexico has negotiated NAFTA-like investment agreements within the Organization for Economic Cooperation and Development and with Germany, and they will certainly be included if Mexico signs a free-trade agreement with the European Union. This means that the "minimum international standard" legal space accepted under NAFTA is being extended to other partners. What about those countries remaining outside those overlapping agreements? Furthermore, by accepting international arbitration in conflicts arising with foreign investors, the Mexican government is contradicting, ironically, one of the principles of the Calvo Doctrine: the equality between national and foreign individuals. Mexican investors remain attached to the logic of the state-centered legal system, while their NAFTA and other foreign partners have the option either to submit their disputes to local tribunals or to address them under international arbitration. This shows well how the nation-state is losing, according to Stephen Zamora, coherence as a unified agent of social regulation, becoming a network of "microstates," each one managing a partial dimension of sovereignty or of the loss of it with a specific regulatory logic (Zamora 1997).

In my view, what chapter 11 and its spin-offs are confirming is exactly what I asserted in the first part of this article: the relocation of authority competencies from state-centered actors to nonstate actors. Moreover, this relocation of authority is being done to both the upper and lower levels. At the upper level, authority is being transferred from the state level to the international level, considering that national tribunals may be substituted by the former. At the lower level, authority is being transferred from the state to the individual, as long as private investors or firms may directly activate a dispute against a state. This transfer of authority to the individual actor could eventually become completed, at least in the field of investments, when national investors realize that the principle of equality is being contradicted by the proliferation of NAFTA-like agreements. This time, however, the principle of equalization will move in the opposite way, at least in Mexico and other Latin American countries, from the state-centered paradigm to the international-centered.

Consequently, chapter 11 of NAFTA is proving that trade regimes are not only fragmenting sovereign faculties of states in their own territories, as Stephen Zamora suggests, by creating new spheres of authority at the trans- or subnational level; they are also providing for new spaces of convergence in complex issue areas where multiple and differentiated actors have a stake. In that sense, NAFTA is facilitating economic governance in a system that is moving from the nation-state as the most important actor of that system, to a multi-actor international system in which firms, civil-society organizations, and multilateral institutions are playing a salient role (see Manning-Cabrol 1995, 1171).

Finally, it is important to stress that chapter 11 is, in fact, a compromise between the two types of ADRMs encompassed by NAFTA. It prescribes that disputes concerning this chapter should be addressed by rule-based resolution mechanisms, that is, adjudicative decisions. Nonetheless, it envisions the use of a policy-oriented mechanism in case the adjudicatory mechanisms fail to redress the problem in a satisfactory way. This two-tier formula devised by chapter 11 reinforces the idea that NAFTA is not instituting supranational bodies compelling states to abide by supranational rules. NAFTA strengthens the role of arbitrage panels in order that both governments and market actors frame the scope and nature of a conflict, and it puts pressure on those parties that fail to comply with the principles and rules instituted at the trilateral level. A wider consensus, and consequently more time, is still needed in order for the idea to mature that transnational bodies and rules are necessary to improve the governance of this issue area. So far, some cases have been activated under this chapter, though no final decision has been awarded in any of them.

Administration and surveillance of trade remedy laws under chapter 19 of NAFTA

Chapter 19 is the most sophisticated of the ADRMs instituted by NAFTA. It could also be considered as a self-contained agreement, due to the fact that this chapter applies only to the interpretation and implementation of trade remedy laws concerning antidumping (AD) and countervailing duties (CVDs) of each member party. NAFTA does not institute any common body of rules concerning dumping and subsidies to be observed by the three countries. Contrary to that, each country maintains its own body of rules, laws, and procedural practices concerning the activation of AD and CVD mechanisms. However, in order to deter the use of those remedy laws for protectionist purposes, a major concern shared by both Canada and Mexico when this chapter was negotiated with the United States, chapter 19 institutes four ADRMs in order to review final decisions of administrative agencies and to ensure the actual enforcement of final awards. Two of these mechanisms are entitled to award quasi-adjudicative decisions, in the sense that awards are binding and leave no room for negotiation. The two other mechanisms work on a basis similar to chapter 20's in the sense that they frame the conflict in order to facilitate a mutually satisfactory solution for the disputant parties. However, in case a mutually satisfactory solution is not reached, this chapter allows a complaining party to apply the most severe of the retaliatory measures envisioned in the agreement. Retaliation ranges from the softest to the toughest actions, that is, from the mere suspension of benefits, to the dismissal of chapter 19 or the denunciation of the whole agreement. Complaining parties have the discretional faculties to choose from this myriad of retaliatory measures, giving them bargaining tools for inducing the complained-against party to reach a compromise. Consequently, even chapter 19, presumably the most accurate chapter for dealing with trade conflicts, is a mixture between adjudicative and negotiation-based mechanisms.

The first mechanism is activated under article 1904, when a party requests a panel in order to review a final determination (only concerning the implementation of AD and CVDs) of an administrative agency of another party. Contrary to chapters 20 and 11, there are no consultations between contending parties prior to the establishment of a panel. Market actors are entitled to request a panel, but they have to do it through the representation of their own governments; that is, they have no jurisdiction to call for a panel by themselves, as is the case within chapter 11. However, private actors have the right, within the first 30 days of an administrative agency's issuing of a final determination, to call for a panel following the trade authorities of their own country. Normally, official authorities cannot refuse this claim.

The scope of action of panels called under article 1904 is to work as an alternative device to domestic tribunals reviewing final decisions of administrative authorities. However, arbitrage panels do not have the same faculties that domestic tribunals have when reviewing those final decisions. The faculties of panels are severely restrained by the normative frame mandated by chapter 19. They are not entitled to judge or change the domestic legislation of the noncomplying country, but only to review whether AD or CVD final determinations were enacted in compliance with domestic legislation and procedures. In other words, their goal is to countercheck whether trade remedy laws were applied appropriately, that is, according to domestic legislation.

In no event are panels entitled to activate a new investigation concerning the application of AD or CVDs. They work as a corrective mechanism to deter any judicial or procedural anomaly coming from a public authority. Hence, final awards of these panels confirm final decisions or remand part or the totality of those decisions in order that the government authority adopts a final decision consistent with the arbitrated award. Panel decisions are binding, as in chapter 11, though, within chapter 19, panels establish a deadline for administrative agencies to comply with the final award, in case of a remand. After that deadline, the same panel reviews whether the administrative authority has implemented a decision according to the final award. If this is the case, the dispute is settled, but if not, the decision is once again remanded. In principle, decisions on remand can be remanded many times, but panels have the explicit faculty of finalizing all cases, that is, of issuing a final decision saying that the concerned administrative authority has modified its final decision according to the last remand decided by the panel.[9] No other chapter contains this important provision, giving authority to a panel to urge a party to abide by an award. Those mechanisms grounded in negotiation and compromise do not need this finalization process, because panel awards are intended to frame the bargaining positions of disputant parties. If disputes are to be considered politically sensitive, final or intermediate solutions are reached by the parties on the grounds of negotiation, normally before they reach the stage of panel activation. However, in those situations where panel awards are binding, as in chapter 11, panels do not have the faculties for finalizing disputes either.

The second arbitrage mechanism instituted under chapter 19 is the so-called Extraordinary Challenge Committee (ECC). In contrast with other chapters, chapter 19 allows a party to challenge a final arbitrage award. However, the possibility of a challenge is severely restricted to causes of impropriety or "gross panel error" that could threaten the integrity of the process (article 1904.13). Up to now, no ECC has been activated under NAFTA. This was not the case under CUFTA, where the ECC was activated three times, in very controversial cases reviewing U.S. measures against Canadian pork, live swine, and softwood lumber (for a review of these cases, see Davey 1996, 225-51). In all cases, the ECC confirmed the panel's final decisions. In two of these cases, the U.S. authority challenged the faculties of panels for finalizing cases. In the two cases, the ECC unanimously upheld that finalizing a case was part of the faculties of the panels reviewing AD or CVD decisions (see also Mercury 1995, 544-45).

In order to avoid a never ending remand process between panelists and administrative authorities, the third arbitration mechanism instituted by chapter 19 aims to safeguard the faculties and decisions of panels activated under article 1904. Article 1905 states that a three-member special committee may be established to review allegations of one party that the application of another party's domestic law has prevented the operation of the panel system. According to some authors, this mechanism has been devised against the *amparo* regime prevailing in Mexico, under which a private party can challenge a decision of an authority. If the final award of the committee states that a party is actually impairing the correct operation

of the panel mechanism, the contending parties will attempt to reach a mutually satisfactory solution. If the final award of the committee states otherwise, the complaining party has two options: either to suspend article 1904 vis-à-vis the noncomplying party (that is, the essence of the review mechanism under chapter 19) or to suspend benefits according to the circumstances (see Figure 2). Here once again we find a hybrid model for managing trade conflicts. If a country is blocking the implementation of a final award, a special panel should decide whether this is consistent with the agreement. If the implementation of a final award is being blocked, panels are not allowed to administer the remedies; the matter is handled through the "good offices" and political negotiations of the governments involved. However, NAFTA gives them the bargaining tool for not only suspending comparable benefits but for dismissing chapter 19 in its entirety. Up to now, since the ruling of CUFTA and its continuation through NAFTA, no panel under these circumstances has been activated. However, it is worth stressing that chapter 19 gives to a disputant party the opportunity to negotiate, with a complaining party, the noncompliance of a panel resolution if the former finds that it is politically costly (perhaps in terms of a domestic constituency) to abide by the rules.

Finally, and due to the fact that each party maintains its respective domestic trade remedy laws and, consequently, the right to modify them, chapter 19 establishes a fourth panel mechanism in case any

FIGURE 2
CHAPTER 19 OF NAFTA

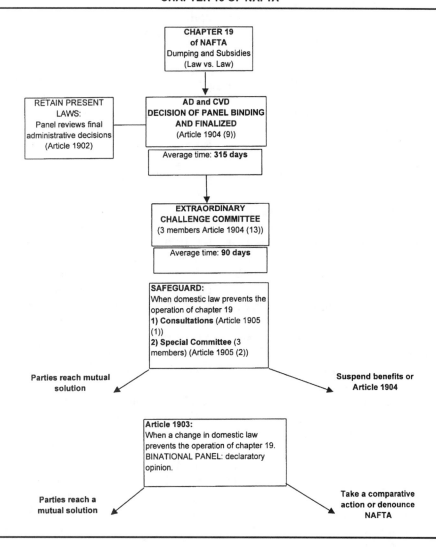

modification impairs a prior panel decision or is not consistent with article 1902. If the final award determines that the legal reform is not consistent with the agreement, contending parties start consultations in order to reach a mutually satisfactory solution. If this is not possible, the complaining parties have two options: either to adopt similar legal or administrative measures or to denounce the integrity of NAFTA vis-à-vis the noncomplying party. Though in principle any party can denounce the agreement whenever it wants, this is the only case in which

NAFTA clearly indicates that denouncing the agreement could become a legitimate retaliation measure when a party does not play by the rules. So far, this possibility has remained hypothetical.

The ECC safeguard and the panel mechanisms instituted under articles 1904.13, 1905.2, and 1903 reinforce each other and are devised for making panels work effectively under article 1904.4. So far, the historical record of both CUFTA and NAFTA proves that this has been the case, though the efficiency and fairness of panel decisions show mixed outcomes. During the lifespan of CUFTA (five years), 49 cases were considered by panels, of which 35 were finalized by them; 12 were terminated before a final decision was issued, either by the request of a participant or by mutual consent; and 2 remain active because a panel order stayed the proceeding pending a final resolution by the U.S. Court of International Trade.[10] In all cases, when a final award terminated the case, national authorities complied with the award at the first, second, or third remand. Of 35 finalized cases, 20 were remanded in part or in their entirety, most of them against U.S. authorities. The fact that panels should normally work with explicit time frames and that their decision-making could rarely become blocked guarantees that once a case has been activated, a final decision would come within a reasonable time (theoretically, 315 days). In case the decision is a remand, the time for finalizing a case could become longer, depending on the time it takes for an administrative authority to make a decision on remand, and the number of times that decision is remanded by panels. But as shown in the CUFTA experience, most panel disputes under chapter 19 were terminated in one way or another. In other words, the fact that 12 conflicts were resolved before the final award of a panel could be also considered as a systemic effect of chapter 19 for settling disputes. Either the complainant realized that it was not worth waiting for a final resolution or the disputants preferred to negotiate a mutually satisfactory solution. In both cases, we could assert that chapter 19 helped the conflicting parties to reach a solution.

In terms of time frames, the efficiency of panel procedures under CUFTA was less than anticipated. According to John Mercury (1995, 542), the average duration of a panel review was 511 days, far above that theoretically anticipated but still less, according to him, than if the conflict had had to be handled by the U.S. Court of International Trade, as was the case under CUFTA.[11] However, most of the time, delay is to be explained by the great number of cases that were remanded. Consequently, some highly controversial cases that were remanded more than once, such as those dealing with softwood lumber, carbon steel, and tufted carpets, took between 697 and 797 days to be finalized. The average time elapsed, for instance, in all cases remanded to the U.S. authority was 612 days, as against 498 for the Canadian cases.[12]

Last but not least, although the quality and professionalism of panel decisions under CUFTA were good, there are still some doubts about their fairness. From a sample of 30 finalized cases, 11 were not reached by unanimity; panelists either dissented from the majority or gave concurring opinions or views. Some experts have diagnosed that the way chapter 19 was designed and operates provokes an asymmetry of favorable outcomes to the benefit of Canada. This asymmetry results because, among other things, panels normally are bound to apply and respect the standard of review of each country, the Canadian being more deferential to trade authorities in some cases than that of the United States. Furthermore, as shown in a thorough analysis by John Mercury on panel decisions under CUFTA, the manner in which panels formulated and applied each country's standard of review was also decisive in explaining the asymmetry of outcomes. Panelists were severely strict when interpreting the U.S. standard of review and considerably soft when applying Canada's (Mercury 1995, 552-53).

Due to the fact that NAFTA's chapter 19 is in many ways a copy of the same chapter under CUFTA, its performance since 1994 has been very similar. As of February 1999, 44 cases had been submitted, of which 11 were terminated by request of the participants and by mutual consent; 18 were finalized; and 15 remain active (data are from Mexico's NAFTA Secretariat). However, the ECC has not been activated, suggesting that the United States has accommodated itself to the new rules. The fact that conflicts are still resolved before a full panel review is

terminated suggests that chapter 19 still helps the disputant parties to anticipate probable outcomes. All final decisions have been accepted, including those dealing with trade in steel and cement between the United States and Mexico and final decisions not favorable to the Mexicans.

In terms of time efficiency, NAFTA panels seem to improve the record of CUFTA. Six cases have been terminated in substantially less than or in approximately 315 days, that is, the time average provided by the agreement if administrative decisions are not remanded. The panels in two other matters issued their opinions 50 days above the theoretical average. In six other cases, the panels took roughly 425 days or more to issue final decisions, the most delayed one being that concerning flat coated steel, which took 769 days (Lopez 1997, 205).

As anticipated, chapter 19 of NAFTA inherited the genetic problem of CUFTA that affected the interpretation and procedures of the so-called standard of reviews. This time the Mexican standard, practices, and legislation had to be added to the process. So far, seven awards were not decided by unanimity, panelists either dissenting with the majority or presenting concurring opinions or views. The Mexican cases concerning imports of flat coated steel products (MEX-94-1904-01) and imports of cut-to-length plate products (MEX-94-1904-02) from the United States have been the most controversial. Though the two cases presented similar features—review of AD determination by the Mexican administrative agency—and the complaining companies argued their points on similar bases, the final award in each case was quite different. In the first case, terminated long after the second one, panelists remanded in part the Mexican decision but affirmed unanimously that the Mexican authority imposing dumping duties was legally constituted. By contrast, in the second case, the panel decided by majority that the Mexican decision was against its Constitution, because the Mexican authority lacked the authority to impose the duties. Yet the terms of the award were not such that Mexico's Trade Ministry had to remand in totality its decision; rather, it had to abrogate the decision, as the Fiscal Federation Tribunal—the domestic tribunal substituted by the panel—would have done had it reached the same decision. The two dissenting votes opposing the majority highlighted that panelists were exceeding their faculties strictly framed by chapter 19.[13]

The case of steel and Mexico's AD determinations reinforces John Mercury's hypothesis in the sense that the differences in the standard of review and the different manner in which they are interpreted could create a bias in a panelist's decisions in the wrong way, that is, to the detriment of a fair position that loses its legitimacy by skillful manipulation of the law by a complaining party. The contrary could be argued, in the sense that panelists still are learning from this process and that the more predictable their procedures become, the more reliable panels under chapter 19 will be. The problem here is

that panels do not create any precedent or jurisprudence. This is, in fact, a real limitation of the whole mechanism.

HOW DEEP COULD NAFTA EVENTUALLY GO?

The final topic this article aims to address is how NAFTA, conceived as it was in previous pages, that is, as a cluster of regimes encompassing a hybrid model of rule enforcement, is or is not promoting a deep integration in North America. Hence the key term to clarify here is what we understand as deep integration. Conventional wisdom defines deep integration in contrast to a shallow integration process. Shallow integration is mainly understood as what some economists call negative integration, that is, the suppression of tariffs and other trade barriers while nation-states maintain their autonomy on trade policy matters. For these authors, GATT was in many ways the very best example of a shallow integration process undertaken at the multilateral level (see Lawrence, Bressand, and Takatoshi 1996). Deep integration is located at the other extreme. The best example of it yet is the European single market, the European monetary union, where harmonization of sectoral policies takes place and the relocation of state-centered authority goes to the supra-state level dealing with sub-state issues. Defined this way, it is comprehensible that some authors have categorized NAFTA as a rather shallow integration process rather than the opposite. The major sign of this, they argue, is that NAFTA does not call for any harmonization of legislation or policies (see Taylor 1996-97).

Those authors stressing the lack of harmonization policies and legislation in NAFTA have a point. But to derive from this that NAFTA is promoting just shallow integration is far from being accurate. As I have stressed in this article, NAFTA establishes much more than a mere free-trade area. The abatement of tariffs throughout North America started long before NAFTA. Mexico, being the most protectionist country, began to reduce its trade tariffs in 1986, when the country finally decided to join GATT. From then on, trade between Mexico and the United States has increased dramatically, in spite of the fact that the liberalization process remained a government-centered commitment. Hence, shallow integration started long before NAFTA, and it will continue while NAFTA is in force and beyond.

As some authors have correctly suggested, the redefinition of governance at the local, state, and global levels is being done at multiple differentiated levels. No single jurisdictional level is right for all types of governance (Lawrence, Bressand, and Takatoshi 1996, 45). This observation supports the manner in which I have approached NAFTA, that is, as a cluster of issue areas in which governance among the actors involved is being reconfigured at different and distinctive levels. A common thread of this reconfiguration is that state-centered authority has

been modified in the NAFTA regime, in spite of the absence of transnational institutions or regulatory bodies seeking to harmonize legislation or policies. This fact already negates the assertion that NAFTA is promoting just shallow integration.

As a regime clustering different issue areas in which governance is shaped in a differentiated manner, NAFTA is mainly a product of a political compromise between state interests and local constituencies. In this sense, the three parties agreed to encourage the economic integration process that started previously and to maintain economic openness as a shared mutual principle for increasing the welfare of the region. However, in order to attain this commitment, the parties did not have either the will or the political capital to negotiate powerful transnational institutions promising the benefits of a deep integration process in the long term. By contrast, they pragmatically negotiated spheres of economic activity in which the relocation of government authority was feasible. NAFTA issue areas show that this relocation is uneven across the areas and in some of them is practically unchanged.

In some ways, it could be said that NAFTA is introducing within its institutional machinery, though still very roughly, the notion of subsidiarity for the governance of specific fields in which the parties involved have a stake. Understanding the term "subsidiarity" as the principle of keeping governance as local as possible, we could say that NAFTA is still centering the governance of the regime at the state level. The state level is what the three parties agreed is the "most local" level for maintaining integration and economic openness throughout the region. This could explain the nature of chapter 20, which aims to cope with any problem affecting the wide breadth of the regime and which is grounded on interstate negotiation and political compromise. This also explains why some authors have characterized NAFTA as an integration process in which sovereign faculties are not challenged.

However, the fact that the nation-state remains under NAFTA the "most local" level for governing integration does not mean that NAFTA has canceled other levels of authority that can be activated if states fail to maintain their commitments. This is mainly the case in the realm of investments. As stated earlier in this article, if a state fails to comply with the rights bestowed by NAFTA to firms in terms of investments and capital mobility, firms can directly call for a panel in order to attempt to redress the conflict. In other words, NAFTA gives authority to a private actor to call for a transstate authority, in this case the panel, to redress a problem. This has been a significant change in countries like Mexico, where the dominance of the state-centered paradigm regarding foreign investments put the primacy on the authority of local tribunals over a dispute. Chapter 19 of NAFTA could be understood in a similar way. Trade remedy laws remain shaped and administered at the national level. However, if an administrative agency presumably applies national laws unfairly, private actors, through their governments, may call for a panel—in any event a nonstate actor—to redress the problem. In those two cases, when state authority fails, authority is being transferred both to the private and the transstate levels.

This happens, though on a minor scale, with overall broad disputes concerning chapter 20. Those disputes are handled at the two-level game of interstate negotiations. If no mutually satisfactory solution is reached, and if it is politically feasible to stop the conflict at the panel level, a rule-based solution will be preferred. The eight cases handled under chapter 18 of CUFTA and chapter 20 of NAFTA seem to suggest this pattern. At the same time, other disputes that proved to be politically sensitive—mainly vis-à-vis domestic constituencies, such as disputes concerning Mexican tomatoes or the Helms-Burton Law—never went beyond the level of consultations. Government authorities realized the costs of escalating the conflict, as in the case of the Helms-Burton Law, or, in some instances, private actors realized that informal undertakings proved to be less costly. In those instances, it could be suggested that NAFTA institutions provoked a systemic effect for defusing conflict and/or reaching second-best compromises.

NAFTA's side agreements are in some way a better example of an issue area where shallow integration remains. States remain absolutely sovereign regarding their respective labor and environmental legislation. They could even change it in such a way as to make it less restrictive, without any concern of provoking any grievance, as is not any more the case in the dumping and subsidies legislation. NAFTA's side agreements institute the oversight of nationally based legislation at the trilateral level, via the creation of ad hoc secretariats and councils. Those institutions could eventually call for a panel, if a claim is filed by a state or individual, only if the complained-against state had failed to systematically enforce its own environmental legislation or some very specific points of its labor legislation. But even if a panel is activated (it needs, under both agreements, two-thirds of the council votes), the possibility of getting a remedy or a monetary fine remains fairly difficult. However, NAFTA's side agreements are accomplishing their functions, in the sense that they either defuse or gauge the environmental and labor concerns of nongovernmental organizations or interest groups. They could become the loci for elaborating a better-structured agenda in labor and environmental matters that could eventually mature, when the political momentum is reached, in a deeper issue area.

Hence, the perception of NAFTA as a cluster of areas with multilevel governance is highly appropriate for understanding the major trends and transformation that this regime is encompassing. In some areas, states remain sovereign, though under the surveillance of trilateral institutions; in other areas, when states

fail, authority is relocated to non-state actors, either market actors, such as firms, or institutional actors, such as trilateral bodies or panels. The flexibility of this multilevel governance approach aims to maintain cohesion in a region in which a high density of interdependence prevails and other multilevel governance regimes overlap.

However, the most decisive manner in which NAFTA will affect the future of integration in the region lies in the daily operation of its institutions and the new problems to overcome. As noted previously, the operation of panels under chapter 19 under both CUFTA and NAFTA have shown some genetic problems. Final awards risk becoming biased depending on the way panelists apply or interpret each country's standard or review. There is already a whole body of literature addressing the redress of the problem, suggesting either the creation of a permanent tribunal or the abrogation of nationally based trade remedy laws in order to replace them with a harmonized system of competition policies overseen by an international tribunal (Davey 1996; Boddez and Trebilcock 1993). All this already suggests that the working and eventual maturing of chapter 19 will end with the creation of a new demand for deeper integration that could gain momentum when the political and economic conditions make it feasible. The same could happen in the rest of the issue areas already clustered by the agreement, or those that will be nested around it.

Another area in which deep integration could become possible is the area that Sidney Weintraub calls the "micro"-institution level of integration, that is, the daily operation of local institutions dealing with trade and investment matters, in which local government agencies, as well as business associations and professionals, are involved. The cross-country interaction of these local groups is urgently needed in order to abate the red tape and multiple nontariff and other barriers that still hamper trade and investment flows (Weintraub 1994).

Figure 3 captures how I envisage the tensions attendant on the deepening of integration in North America. The more that dense and complex issue areas become shared by the three countries, the higher the demand for relocating authority from the state to the transstate level for better governance of the field in question. This is the trend not only for trade and investment matters, as previously discussed, but also for monetary issues as the current debate in Mexico concerning the establishment of a monetary board clearly shows. The governance of migration (both legal and illegal), illegal trade in narcotics, and social inequalities are also becoming hot issues of a cross-boundary agenda between the three partners. The emergence, however, of high-density issue areas between the countries is not enough to spur deeper integration. Figure 3 also illustrates the emergence of what I call a cross-boundary public sphere in which political activism, competing ideas, and social action take place. This will be the privileged place in which a thriving cross-boundary civil society will press for the creation of new institutions that reflect a better representation of their interests and that could eventually help to mediate between state and transstate authorities. Within this sphere, the integration process wins or loses legitimacy according to the societal and political articulation of strategies backing or denouncing the integrative move.

Last but not least, states still have a major stake in promoting or deterring the integrative move. They must have the will and the ability to articulate the political support for building and/or improving the institutional devices of those new spheres in which a multidifferentiated level of governance will take place. So far, the integration drive in North America has been highly dominated by a trade and investment agenda, clearly putting forward at the regional level what the United States is promoting at the multilateral level. However, as the impasse on the voting of the fast-track authority and the reluctance of the U.S. Congress to expand NAFTA to Chile have suggested, Washington is not willing to go further than a NAFTA-like agenda on integration matters. It is up to Mexico and perhaps Canada to convince the Congress that the governance on conflicting issue areas between the three countries will be more efficient and better accomplished if a deeper institutional approach, similar to that pursued by the European Union, is enhanced progressively during the twenty-first century.

FIGURE 3

THE NAFTA REGIME AND THE DEMAND FOR DEEPER INTEGRATION

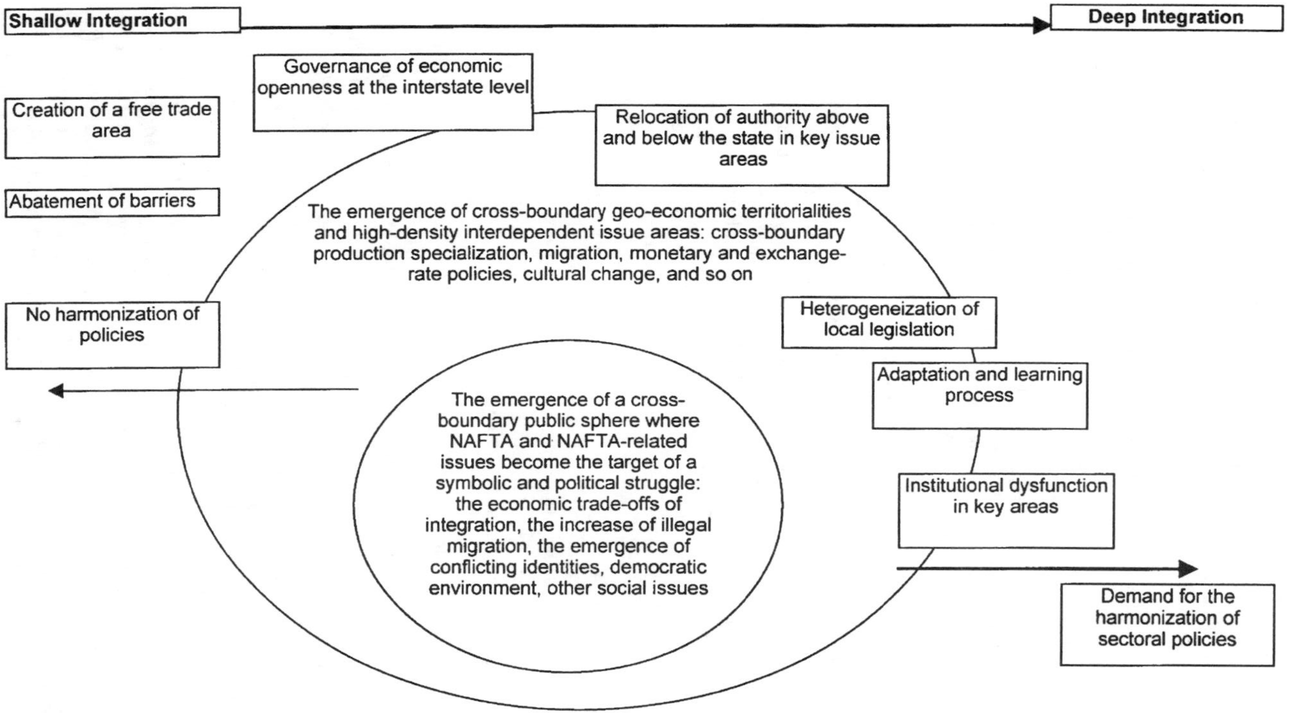

Shallow Integration

Creation of a free trade area

Abatement of barriers

No harmonization of policies

Governance of economic openness at the interstate level

Relocation of authority above and below the state in key issue areas

The emergence of cross-boundary geo-economic territorialities and high-density interdependent issue areas: cross-boundary production specialization, migration, monetary and exchange-rate policies, cultural change, and so on

The emergence of a cross-boundary public sphere where NAFTA and NAFTA-related issues become the target of a symbolic and political struggle: the economic trade-offs of integration, the increase of illegal migration, the emergence of conflicting identities, democratic environment, other social issues

Heterogeneization of local legislation

Adaptation and learning process

Institutional dysfunction in key areas

Demand for the harmonization of sectoral policies

Deep Integration

Notes

1. The classical study on this issue belongs to Keohane (1984, 1989). See also Gilpin 1987 and Chayes and Chayes 1995 for an updated discussion of the matter.

2. I mean by "soft law" the intentional fuzziness of a provision's normative statement, which highly contrasts with the "bright-line" precision of a hard normative statement. See Reisman and Wiedman 1995, 7.

3. In CUFTA, the establishment of a panel under chapter 18 required mutual consent. Binding arbitration was also envisaged, if it was considered appropriate by the Trade Commission or when disputes arising from the Escape Clause (emergency and safeguard measures) were to be considered. The procedures for selecting panelists evolved: instead of choosing from one's own roster, as CUFTA mandated, parties must choose under NAFTA from each other's roster, thereby giving to panels increased impartiality. Finally, NAFTA gives to the complained-against party the right to activate a panel if it considers that the suspension of benefits exceeds the level of the grievance (Reisman and Wiedman 1995, 19-21; Davey 1996, 26-27).

4. The panel determined that the application of customs duties by the government of Canada to U.S.-origin agricultural products conformed to the provisions of NAFTA. See In the Matter of Tariffs.

5. The panel decided that the safeguard measures put in force by the U.S. government against broomcorn brooms coming from Mexico failed to provide "reasoned conclusions on all pertinent issues of law and fact" and constituted consequently a "continuing violation of United States obligations under NAFTA." See In the Matter of the U.S. Safeguard Action.

6. Under the new WTO Understanding, panel reports must be issued within six to eight months of the selection of the panelists. If the dispute is referred to the U.S. Court of Justice, an adjudicatory decision could take more than two years. See Davey 1996, 65.

7. That is, the relocation of polluting or labor-intensive industries from countries where legislation is strictly enforced and costly (that is, the United States and Canada) to countries where legislation is loosely respected (that is, Mexico).

8. For a wider insight into the activities undertaken by both the labor and the environ-mental agreements, visit their respective home pages at www.naalc.org/ and www.cec.org/.

9. This is clearly stated in article 1904.8: "If review of the action taken by the competent investigating authority on remand is needed, such review shall be before the same panel, which shall normally issue a final decision within 90 days of the date on which such remand action is submitted to it."

10. The record is according to data collected from NAFTA's Mexican Secretariat home page at http://www.sec-tlcan-mex.org.

11. In this case, the time elapsed was 734 days on average, and up to 1210 days if decisions were appealed. See Mercury 1995, 542.

12. We should highlight that, of the five cases remanded to the Canadian authorities, only one, compared to eight in the case of the United States, was remanded more than once (Mercury 1995, 543). This would seem to indicate that U.S. authorities were more reluctant to adapt to the new international ruling established by CUFTA. The fact that the three ECCs were activated by the U.S. confirms this reluctance.

13. See the dissenting votes on Imports of Cut-to-Length Plate Products from the United States of America (MEX-94-1904-02), at the NAFTA Secretariat Web site at http://www.sec-tlcan-mex.org.

References

Boddez, Thomas M. and Michael Trebilcock. 1993. *Unfinished Business: Reforming Trade Remedy Laws in North America*. Policy Study 17. Toronto: C. D. Howe Institute.

Chayes, Abram and Antonia Handler Chayes. 1995. *The New Sovereignty: Compliance with International Regulatory Agreements*. Cambridge, MA: Harvard University Press.

Davey, William J. 1996. *Pine and Swine, Canada and United States Trade Dispute Settlement: The FTA Experience and the NAFTA Prospects*. Ottawa: Carleton University, Centre for Trade Policy and Law, Carleton University.

Gilpin, Robert. 1987. *The Political Economy of International Relations.*

Princeton, NJ: Princeton University Press.

In the Matter of Tariffs Applied by Canada to Certain U.S.-Origin Agricultural Products (CDA-95-2008-01). North American Free Trade Agreement (NAFTA) Secretariat Web site http://www.sec-tlcan-mex.org

In the Matter of the U.S. Safeguard Action Taken on Broomcorn Brooms from Mexico (SA-97-2008-01). North American Free Trade Agreement (NAFTA) Secretariat Web site http://www.sec-tlcan-mex.org

Keohane, Robert. 1984. *After Hegemony.* Princeton, NJ: Princeton University Press.

———. 1989. The Demand for International Regimes. In *International Institutions and State Power,* ed. Robert Keohane. Boulder, CO: Westview Press.

Komuro, Norio. 1995. The WTO Dispute Settlement Mechanism: Coverage and Procedures of the WTO Understanding. *Journal of World Trade* 29(4):5-95.

Krasner, Stephen D. 1983. Structural Causes and Regime Consequences: Regimes as Intervening Variables. In *International Regimes,* ed. Stephen D. Krasner. Ithaca, NY: Cornell University Press.

Kratochwil, Friedriech V. 1991. *Rules, Norms, and Decisions: On the Conditions of Practical and Legal Reasoning in International Relations and Domestic Affairs.* New York: Cambridge University Press.

Lawrence, Robert Z., Albert Bressand, and Ito Takatoshi. 1996. *A Vision for the World Economy: Openness, Diversity and Cohesion.* Washington, DC: Brookings Institution.

Lopez, David. 1997. Dispute Resolution Under NAFTA: Lessons from the Early Experience. *Texas International Law Journal* 32(2):163-207.

Manning-Cabrol, Denise. 1995. The Imminent Death of the Calvo Clause and the Rebirth of the Calvo Principle: Equality of Foreign and National Investors. *Law and Policy in International Business* 26(4):1169-1200.

Mercury, John M. 1995. Chapter 19 of the United State–Canada Free Trade Agreement 1989-95. A Check on Administered Protection? *Northwestern Journal of International Law and Business* 15(3):525-605.

Milner, Helen V. 1997. *Interests, Institutions, and Information: Domestic Politics and International Relations.* Princeton, NJ: Princeton University Press.

Nye, Joseph S. 1990. *Bound to Lead: The Changing Nature of American Power.* New York: Basic Books.

Reisman, Michael and Mark Wiedman. 1995. Contextual Imperatives of Dispute Resolution Mechanisms: Some Hypotheses and Their Applications in the Uruguay Round and NAFTA. *Journal of World Trade* 29(3):5-37.

Rosenau, James. 1997. *Along the Domestic-Foreign Frontier: Exploring Governance in a Turbulent World.* New York: Cambridge University Press.

Taylor, Cherie O'Neal. 1996-97. Dispute Resolution as a Catalyst for Economic Integration and an Agent for Deepening Integration: NAFTA and Mercosur. *Journal of International Law and Business* 17(850).

Weintraub, Sidney. 1994. *NAFTA: What Comes Next?* Westport, CT: Praeger.

Zamora, Stephen. 1997. Allocating Legislative Competence in the Americas: The Early Experience Under NAFTA and the Challenge of Hemispheric Integration. *Houston Journal of International Law* 19(615).

ANNALS, *AAPSS*, **565**, September 1999

Civil Society and
European Integration

By FINN LAURSEN

ABSTRACT: Nowadays, various processes, events, and changes are discussed under the heading of regional integration. Examples of regional integration include the European Union (EU). States increasingly deal with international interdependence through international policy coordination and integration. Joint decision making can be one way to deal with the negative externalities of interdependence. This article looks mainly at European integration. The question is whether European integration, an example of deep integration, has lessons for other integration schemes. Such lessons, if they exist, could possibly help policymakers in other parts of the world plan their efforts better and maybe avoid some mistakes. Even if many scholars have stressed that European integration is sui generis, it is the assumption of this article that lessons can be learned and that integration in different parts of the world can be compared.

Finn Laursen is professor of international politics at the University of Southern Denmark, Odense. He taught at the London School of Economics (1985-88) and the European Institute of Public Administration, Maastricht (1988-95) and directed the Thorkil Kristensen Institute at the South Jutland University Center, Esbjerg, Denmark (1995-98). He was a foreign professor at the University of Tsukuba, Japan (1998-99).

A number of processes, events, and changes are discussed under the heading of regional integration. Important examples of regional integration include the European Union (EU), the North American Free Trade Area, the Southern Common Market, the Association of South East Asian Nations, and the Asia-Pacific Economic Cooperation forum. States increasingly deal with international interdependence through international policy coordination and integration. Joint decision making can be one way to deal with the negative externalities of interdependence.

Much of what regional integration schemes do is to facilitate trade in goods. But they can also go further to include services, investments, and so on. In Europe, the internal market program gave intra-European trade and integration a new momentum in the late 1980s. The program was about securing four freedoms: free movement of goods, services, capital, and people. Some scholars have seen this as deep integration (Lawrence 1996; Baldwin 1997; Winters 1997). Other integration schemes are often limited to free-trade areas, a kind of shallow integration. But the dynamics of integration may well take these more shallow integration schemes toward deeper integration. In that case, will the European experience be relevant in other parts of the world?

For many years, regional integration was mainly a European phenomenon. There were some early efforts in other parts of the world, and they were studied by regional integration scholars at the time, but these efforts turned out largely not to be successful. Why then these renewed efforts of regional integration in the late 1980s and early 1990s? Why does it look as if they may be more effective this time?

Bhagwati has talked about a "Second Regionalism" and has suggested that "the main driving force for regionalism today is the conversion of the United States, hitherto an abstaining party, to Article XXIV" of the General Agreement on Tariffs and Trade (GATT) (Bhagwati 1994). This GATT article allows free-trade areas and customs unions to be exempt from the general most-favored nation principle. Frustration with the multilateral negotiations under GATT has also been mentioned as a cause of regionalism.

Other scholars have questioned these explanations. Baldwin, for instance, has developed a domino theory of regionalism. With respect to the Americas, the North American Free Trade Area created what Lawrence (1996) calls "powerful pressures for inclusion" (77). Mexican privileged access to the U.S. market had costs for other Latin American countries that sought similar access. This led to the Bush administration's Enterprise for the Americas Initiative in 1990 and various integration schemes in South America, the most important of these being Mercosur (Baldwin 1997, 870-71).

In this article, we will concentrate on European integration. The question is whether European integration, an example of deep integration, has lessons for other integration schemes. Such lessons, if they exist, could possibly help policymakers in other parts of the world plan their efforts better and maybe avoid some mistakes. Even if many scholars have stressed that European integration is sui generis, it is the assumption of this article that lessons can be learned and that integration in different parts of the world can be compared.

THE CONCEPT OF INTERNATIONAL INTEGRATION

There is much discussion in the literature on international integration on how to define the concept. Deutsch, for instance, defined integration as "the attainment, within a territory, of a 'sense of community' and of institutions and practices strong enough and widespread enough to assure, for a 'long' time, dependable expectations of 'peaceful change' among its population." When a group of people or states have been integrated this way, they constitute a security community (Deutsch et al. 1957, 5-6).

Early efforts to study regional integration concentrated on the European Coal and Steel Community and the European Economic Community. In Leon Lindberg's study of the early European Economic Community, *The Political Dynamics of European Economic Integration* (1963), political integration was defined as

(1) the process whereby nations forgo the desire and ability to conduct foreign and key domestic policies independently of each other, seeking instead to make *joint decisions* or to *delegate* the decision-making process to new central organs; and (2) the process whereby political actors in several distinct settings are per-

suaded to shift their expectations and political activities to a new center. (6)

It is questionable to what extent one can talk about a new center in regional integration schemes outside Europe, but those schemes all involve some joint decision making. One can also say that regional integration creates rules, norms, and procedures that constrain the national decision makers. Integration creates what is now commonly referred to as international regimes.

EARLY COMPARATIVE INTEGRATION STUDIES

In a study that compared regional integration in Europe with integration in other regions of the world, Haas (1961) suggested that one should study the environment in which the processes take place in order to understand the differences. He listed three sets of background factors that he considered important: social structure, economic and industrial development, and ideological patterns. With respect to social structure, Western Europe is dominated by pluralism, that is, the existence of "articulate voluntary groups, led by bureaucratized but accessible elites." With respect to economic and industrial development, Western Europe has a high degree of industrialization and urbanization. With respect to ideological patterns, there is a certain degree of homogeneity in Western Europe. According to Haas, "integration proceeds most rapidly and drastically when it responds to socio-economic demands emanating from an industrial-urban environment, when it is an adaptation to cries for increasing welfare and security born by the growth of a new type of society." On the other hand, "countries dominated by a non-pluralistic social structure are poor candidates for participation in the integration process" (375).

If it is true that we are witnessing a second regionalism today, one can, of course, ask whether there have been important changes in what used to be known as Third World countries in the factors mentioned by Haas. Indeed, much of the literature on integration in the Americas emphasizes the turn toward democratic regimes and liberal economic policies in Latin America during the 1980s. "Adjustment of the mid-1980s settled into a new economic orthodoxy around export promotion and deregulation of the economy," first in Chile, later in Mexico, and finally Argentina and Brazil (Grugel 1996, 138).

DIMENSIONS
OF INTEGRATION

Integration, then, is about joint decision making. Such joint decision making can be measured on various dimensions. In the classical literature on European integration, three dimensions were considered especially important: functional scope, institutional capacity, and geographical domain.

Functional scope refers to the issues included in the integration or cooperation schemes. With respect to the European Communities (EC), integration started with the coal and steel sectors in the European Coal and Steel Community in 1952. Atomic energy was included with EURATOM in 1958. But in the same year, a wider economic integration process started with the European Economic Community, which first of all set out to realize a common market, including a customs union. It emphasized common policies in four major areas: agriculture, transport, competition, and commerce. The latter was, of course, linked with the customs union. Beyond this, the Treaty of Rome foresaw the harmonization of other economic policies, and article 235 made it possible for the EC to adopt common policies by unanimity if such policies were considered necessary to get the common market to function. This made it possible for the European Economic Community to develop common policies in areas not foreseen in the Treaty of Rome, such as environmental policy. This expansion of scope continued with the Single European Act (SEA) in 1986, when new treaty provisions regarding environment, regional policy, and research and development were introduced. Next it continued with the Maastricht Treaty on European Union, signed in 1992 and in force since November 1993. This treaty includes new or improved treaty provisions concerning industrial policy, trans-European networks, consumer protection, public health, economic and social cohesion, environment, research and development, and education and culture. Most important, it outlines the stages of economic and monetary union.

This process of expanding scope has now reached a level where many people start wondering whether the EU will start interfering in too many aspects of daily life. Some see the principle of subsidiarity, which is explicitly mentioned in the Maastricht Treaty, as a way to stop further expansion, possibly even transferring some powers back from the central European level to the national or regional levels.

The second important dimension, institutional capacity, is first of all a question of decision-making capacity but taken in a broad sense, including capacity to implement and enforce decisions, so the whole question of legitimacy also enters here. We could also talk about capacity to solve common problems. The nature of common institutions is an important aspect of this dimension. In this connection, it is of central importance whether these institutions have supranational powers or remain purely intergovernmental. The EC/EU has introduced the so-called Community method, including at least three components: the Commission, which is independent and has the right of initiative; majority voting in some areas in the Council of Ministers; and a legal system, which has primacy and direct effect, including the Court of Justice, which can make binding judgments.

It is in respect to these components that the EC differs from classical intergovernmental organizations including other integration schemes around the world, where, normally, initiative belongs to the member states, where decisions usually require unanimity or consensus, and where decisions often remain recommendations because of weak surveillance and enforcement mechanisms.

The question of institutional capacity has been an important one in the history of European integration. The founders of European integration believed supranational institutions to be important. The United Kingdom and the Scandinavian countries, which did not take part in the integration process at the outset, believed that traditional intergovernmental institutions would be sufficient. Nor did General de Gaulle like supranational institutions. The first major institutional crisis in the EC in the mid-1960s between de Gaulle's France, on the one hand, and the Commission and the other five member states, on the other, centered on institutional capacity. The Luxembourg Compromise in January 1966, where the French insisted on having a right of veto whenever important national interests were at stake, for many years stopped the movement toward applying qualified majority voting in the Council even where this was clearly foreseen in the Treaty of Rome.

A unanimity approach means that decisions will be based on the lowest common denominator. The possibility of "upgrading the common interest" is increased if qualified majority voting is applied (Haas 1961).

The unanimity approach associated with the Luxembourg Compromise increasingly became a problem in the 1970s, when the energy crisis put pressures on the system and the membership had increased from six to nine. The SEA in 1986 addressed this issue of institutional capacity. By specifying that the legislation to complete the internal market normally should be adopted by qualified majority voting in the Council, the SEA increased the institutional capacity of the EC. This was an important element among the factors that gave the Community a new momentum from the mid-1980s. The importance of good institutions, then, could be mentioned as one of the lessons of European integration.

The Maastricht Treaty continued the effort to increase the Community's institutional capacity. It introduced majority voting in some of the new policy chapters. However, some issues remained controversial and sensitive. For such issues, unanimity was to remain the rule. Among the new policy areas, this included industry and culture. It also remained the rule for many institutional issues, taxation policy, and even sensitive aspects of environmental policy.

The third important dimension is geographical domain. Geographical domain is shorthand for the question of membership. The European integration process started with six countries. Through four successive enlargements, in 1973, 1981, 1986, and 1995, the EU has reached 15 members. There are now applications from Turkey and Cyprus as well as 10 Central and Eastern European countries. Indeed, enlargement is one of the main issues on the current EU agenda.

Each successive enlargement has changed the nature of the Community. The more members, the more difficult one should expect the decision-making process to be. Enlargement therefore should ideally proceed in parallel with steps to increase the decision-making capacity. The SEA coincided with the third enlargement, which brought Spain and Portugal into the EC. With Greece's joining in 1981 and Spain and Portugal's in 1986, economic differences increased. This led to a doubling of the funds available for regional and structural policies in 1988. Today about a third of the EU budget is spent on structural policies, helping poorer regions to catch up. "Economic and social cohesion" is the name used for this in the EU. Nothing similar exists in other integration schemes.

The Maastricht Treaty prepared the fourth enlargement, in 1995, in which Austria, Finland, and Sweden became members. The latest intergovernmental conference, which negotiated the Amsterdam Treaty in 1996-97, was partly called to prepare for the future Eastern enlargement. Whether it succeeded in doing so is currently a matter of debate in Europe. Given the difficulties of getting the Maastricht Treaty ratified, the policymakers had become very cautious.

If all this has a lesson for other regions, it suggests that the legitimacy of integration becomes an issue once the process starts touching upon sensitive issues of national autonomy. In the case of Maastricht, these sensitive areas included money, defense, and citizenship. This lesson started to become clear during the difficult process of the ratification of the Maastricht Treaty, and it affected the debate about the Amsterdam Treaty. Political leaders in the states where ratification of Maastricht had been difficult deliberately sought to include in the Amsterdam Treaty new measures that would increase the popular support for the process of integration. Further, the institutional winner in the Amsterdam Treaty is the European Parliament, with the codecision procedure introduced by Maastricht for some new policy areas and the internal market extended now to most policy areas. This gives the European Parliament, which is directly elected by the European peoples, a veto over much legislation. This can be seen as a step to deal with the so-called democratic deficit. In parallel, the role of the national parliaments has been enhanced in many member states.

WHY EUROPEAN
INTEGRATION?

When integration started in Europe in 1950 with the Schuman Plan, it was very much a political project, bringing former enemies France and (West) Germany together in a commitment to international cooperation. Economics was a means to this cooperation. Starting with the coal and steel sectors, the intention was gradually to establish a de facto solidarity between the participating states. Gradually new sectors would be drawn into the process.

The theory of European integration went through various phases. It was mainly American political scientists who contributed to early theoretical efforts in the 1950s. Haas wrote the classic *Uniting of Europe* (1958), which studied the European Coal and Steel Community. The main mechanism suggested was one of spillover, seen as the inherent logic of sector integration. Lindberg produced an important study of the early years of the European Economic Community. According to Lindberg, " 'spill-over' refers to a situation in which a given action, related to a specific goal, creates a situation in which the original goal can be assured only by taking further actions, which in turn create a further condition and a need for more action, and so forth" (Lindberg 1963, 10). When the European integration process experienced a crisis in the mid-1960s, however, many scholars raised serious questions about spillover. Haas himself now admitted that he had not foreseen "a rebirth of nationalism and anti-functional high politics" (Haas 1967, 325).

In a much-quoted article, Hoffmann (1966) argued that the national situations and role perceptions were still too diverse within the EC. In general, he argued, "Every international system owes its inner logic and its unfolding to the *diversity* of domestic determinants, geohistorical situations, and outside aims among its units" (864). He contrasted the logic of integration with a logic of diversity. The latter sets limits to the degree to which the spillover process can operate. "It restricts the domain in which the logic of functional integration operates to the area of welfare." Hoffmann advanced the suggestion that, "in areas of key importance to the national interest, nations prefer the certainty, or the self-controlled uncertainty, of national self-reliance, to the uncontrolled uncertainty" of integration (882). He referred to the latter areas as "high politics." Spillover was limited to the areas of "low politics."

Lindberg took a second look at integration with Scheingold. Together they reformulated integration theory to take account of political leadership—or lack of same. They made the theory less deterministic, more voluntaristic (Lindberg and Scheingold 1970), mentioning four mechanisms as important in a process of integration. Apart from functional spillover, they also looked at bargaining processes (log-rolling and side payments), actor socialization, and feedback. The latter mainly refers to the impact of decisions on the attitudes and behavior of the public at large. If the public finds the output from the system good and relevant, support for the system will increase. If the system is unable to produce relevant decisions, support for the system should be expected to decrease.

According to Lindberg and Scheingold, there was a "permissive consensus" in the earlier years of European integration. One way to look at the difficulties of the Maastricht ratification process is to say that this permissive consensus had ceased to exist by the early 1990s. The question of legitimacy became decisive for the continuation of the process (Laursen 1994).

That external events can be important variables in an integration process was underlined by Nye in the 1960s. He talked about "perceptual conditions," which included

the perception of external force. He defined it as follows: "the way that regional decision-makers perceive the nature of their external situation and their response to it" (Nye 1971, 84).

In this respect, the year 1989 was decisive for the Maastricht Treaty. That was the year that witnessed the collapse of the Soviet empire in Central and Eastern Europe. The following year Germany was united, much faster than anyone had predicted. These events played on a double front. The new governments in Central and Eastern Europe all turned to the West, especially the EC, for assistance in modernization, including development of market economies and pluralistic political regimes.

The other front was internal to the EC. German unification had profound effects on many EC member countries in their way of thinking about the role and importance of the EC. In a way, the original political rationale of European integration, stated explicitly in the Schuman Declaration in May 1950—namely, that of integrating the Federal Republic into a wider system, thereby making adventurous German policies impossible—had returned. Fear of a future independent role of a strong united Germany led integration skeptics in a number of countries to see further integration as the only guarantee of peace, security, and cooperation in Europe. In post–Cold War Europe, the EC had become the only guarantee of peace and stability. To make sure that the EC could continue to play that role, further deepening of integration was deemed necessary by a growing number of political leaders. Overall, this may have been the most important factor explaining the institutional reforms of the Maastricht Treaty. Wider international systemic events, which made German unification possible, thus affected the EC profoundly (Laursen 1992).

LESSONS OF THE INTERNAL MARKET

Regional economic integration efforts can be seen as an effort to overcome a fundamental problem in the system of classical international relations, namely, that of defection. According to classical international law, states are sovereign. They do not have to accept supranational authorities. They can, of course, conclude agreements with other states, bilaterally or multilaterally; but once they find that conditions have changed, they are no longer bound by such agreements.

History shows us how unstable and fragile international agreements and cooperation efforts can be as long as they are based on the classical notion of sovereignty.

Modern game theory discusses this in a formal deductive fashion. The famous Prisoners' Dilemma game illustrates the situation where individually rational actors, which could be states, arrive at suboptimal outcomes if they act independently. Further, the theory shows that agreements that should realize optimal outcomes will often be unstable because actors will be tempted to cheat or defect from the cooperative agreement in order to realize outcomes that are better for themselves in the short term.

Postwar efforts at international cooperation between industrialized countries in the economic area can be seen as a response to protectionism—and beggar-thy-neighbor policies—of the 1930s. Free trade, it can be argued, will normally be in everybody's interest. Yet it is not easy to realize. States have tried through the GATT—and now the World Trade Organization—to facilitate and increase international trade. Trade conflicts nonetheless remain an important aspect of relations between the industrialized countries.

The experience of the EC is instructive in this respect. The EC is, first of all, a customs union that should realize free trade between its members (and introduce a common tariff toward third countries). But once the customs union was put in place in 1968, it gradually became clear that a customs union was not sufficient to realize free trade. Member states could continue to protect their national industries through non-tariff barriers to trade. Some of these were technical barriers to trade like different national standards for products (Pelkmans and Winters 1988).

A number of curious cases followed. Many of these eventually were taken to the European Court of Justice, which called the bluff. There were cases like the alcoholic drink Casis de Dijon, which could not be exported to the Federal Republic of Germany because it did not have the alcohol content required by German law; pasta that could not be exported to Italy because it was made of soft wheat instead of durum wheat; bread that could not be exported to the Netherlands because it did not have the salt content required by Dutch law; and so on. The European Court of Justice played an important role in stopping this and in enunciating the principle of mutual recognition of standards.

The internal market project can be seen as a renewed effort to overcome Prisoners' Dilemma situations. The Commission under President Jacques Delors played an important leadership role. In the SEA, the member states accepted the use of qualified majority voting to complete the internal market.

If we compare the EC with other regional integration schemes, some institutional differences become apparent. None of them has created independent supranational bodies like the EC Commission; none of them has accepted anything resembling Community law, at least until European Free Trade Association (EFTA) countries felt compelled to do so in an effort to benefit from access to the EC's internal market (Laursen 1997a); none has accepted a real limit on its sovereignty in the form of binding majority decisions (see also Feld and Boyd 1980; Jamar 1982).

If we look at the situation in Europe, it is clear that the EC has become a pole of attraction. Some EFTA countries realized early that the neofunctionalist integration strategy of the EC was more dynamic than the more limited functionalism of EFTA, and they joined the EC: the United Kingdom and Denmark in 1973; Portugal in 1986; Austria, Sweden, and Finland in 1995. At least another 12 countries are now waiting to join. The European dominoes are falling.

Is this a vindication of the Monnet-Schuman strategy of integration? It seems to me that the answer has to be affirmative. If so, it must have some implications for other regions of the world and, ultimately, for the global system itself. If countries are serious about international cooperation, they must give the international organizations they create the necessary powers to carry out their functions. This seems to be an important lesson of European integration.

LESSONS OF
MAASTRICHT

The continuation of the process also has lessons. As the process deepened, the necessity of democratic accountability increased. Since 1979, the European Parliament has been popularly elected. The SEA increased its role slightly in connection with internal-market legislation, and Maastricht introduced the co-decision procedure, giving the Parliament a right of veto over some legislation. But was this enough?

The difficulties of getting the Maastricht Treaty ratified led to a lot of soul-searching in Europe (Laursen 1994, 1997b). In preparing for the intergovernmental conference that negotiated the Amsterdam Treaty, the governments and the Community institutions produced various reports. A report from the European Parliament suggested the need for "more efficient, open and accountable institutions and decision-making mechanisms" (European Parliament 1995, 6). Similarly the Commission suggested that "the Union must act democratically, transparently and in a way people can understand" (European Commission 1995, 4). The Reflection Group, established by the governments, said that "ways must be found of increasing citizens' confidence in the European institutions." Institutional reform, therefore, had to "be subjected to the test of more democracy, more efficiency, more solidarity and more transparency" (Reflection Group 1995, 7).

The Amsterdam Treaty was the outcome of this process of thinking about and negotiating a better treaty. It did increase the role of the European Parliament, making codecision the most common procedure. It tries to simplify and make the legislative process more open, and it gives citizens new rights of access to information. It adds and improves policy chapters in order to get the EU to deal more with issues that citizens are concerned about: jobs, labor market conditions, the environment, internal security, fraud, drug trafficking, and so on. So far it has not run into any surprises in the ratification process.

Of course, one can argue that much remains to be done. As long as the intergovernmental element in the Council of Ministers remains important, it is difficult to use the standards of national democracy. Efficiency and relevance are part of legitimacy, too. If the perception spreads that the EU contributes to creating jobs, its legitimacy will surely increase.

CONCLUSION

The EU is the deepest form of regional integration in today's world. It has gone through a process of gradual deepening and widening. It has had both economic and political causes as well as lessons.

Economically, Europeans learned that protectionistic forces remain strong and that it takes good institutions and leadership to counteract and overcome those forces. The Community method was invented for that. But as the process deepened and started touching areas of symbolic importance for sovereignty, the issue of legitimacy had to be confronted. The Amsterdam Treaty tries to do that by increasing the role of the European Parliament and creating the basis for new policies that will deal with important concerns of the people.

References

Baldwin, Richard E. 1997. The Causes of Regionalism. *World Economy* 20(7):865-88.

Bhagwati, Jagdish. 1994. Regionalism and Multilateralism: An Overview. In *Asia Pacific Regionalism: Readings in International Economic Relations*, ed. Ross Garnaut and Peter Drysdale. Pymble: Harper Educational.

Deutsch, Karl W., Sidney A. Burell, Robert A. Kann, Maurice Lee, Jr., Martin Lichterman, Raymond E. Lindgren, Francis L. Loewenheim, and Richard W. Van Wagenen. 1957. *Political Community and the North Atlantic*

Area: International Organization in the Light of Historical Experience. Princeton, NJ: Princeton University Press.

European Commission. 1995. Report on the Operation of the Treaty on European Union. SEC(95) final. Brussels, 10 May.

European Parliament. Committee on Institutional Affairs. 1995. Report on the Functioning of the Treaty on European Union with a View to the 1996 Intergovernmental Conference—Implementation and Development of the Union. Doc. A4-0102/95/part I.B, 12 May.

Feld, Werner J. and Gavin Boyd, eds. 1980. *Comparative Regional Systems: West and East Europe, North America, the Middle East, and Developing Countries*. New York: Pergamon Press.

Grugel, Jean. 1996. Latin America and the Remaking of the Americas. In *Regionalism and World Order*, ed. Andrew Gamble and Anthony Payne. Houndsmills: Macmillan Press.

Haas, Ernst B. 1958. *The Uniting of Europe: Political, Social, and Economic Forces 1950-1957*. Stanford, CA: Stanford University Press.

———. 1961. International Integration: The European and the Universal Process. *International Organization* 15(Autumn):366-92.

———. 1967. The Uniting of Europe and the Uniting of Latin America. *Journal of Common Market Studies* 5:315-43.

Hoffmann, Stanley. 1966. Obstinate or Obsolete? The Fate of the Nation-State and the Case of Western Europe. *Daedalus* 95(Summer):862-915.

Jamar, Joseph, ed. 1982. *Intégrations régionales entre pays en voie de développement*. Bruges: De Tempel, Tempelhof.

Laursen, Finn. 1992. Explaining the Intergovernmental Conference on Political Union. In *The Intergovernmental Conference on Political Union: Institutional Reforms, New Policies and International Identity of the European Community*, ed. Finn Laursen and Sophie Vanhoonacker. Maastricht: European Institute of Public Administration; Dordrecht: Martinus Nijhoff.

———. 1994. The Not-So-Permissive Consensus: Thoughts on the Maastricht Treaty and the Future of European Integration. In *The Ratification of the Maastricht Treaty: Issues, Debates and Future Implications*, ed. Finn Laursen and Sophie Vanhoonacker. Dordrecht: Martinus Nijhoff.

———. 1997a. European Integration and Trade Regimes: From the European Economic Area to the "Europe" Agreements. In *Free Trade Agreements and Customs Union: Experiences, Challenges and Constraints*, ed. Madeleine O. Hosli and Arild Saether. Maastricht: European Institute of Public Administration.

———. 1997b. The Lessons of Maastricht. In *The Politics of European Treaty Reform: The 1996 Intergovernmental Conference and Beyond*, ed. Geoffrey Edwards and Alfred Pijpers. London: Pinter.

Lawrence, Robert Z. 1996. *Regionalism, Multilateralism, and Deeper Integration*. Washington, DC: Brookings Institution.

Lindberg, Leon N. 1963. *The Political Dynamics of European Economic Integration*. Stanford, CA: Stanford University Press.

Lindberg, Leon N. and Stuart A. Scheingold. 1970. *Europe's Would-Be Polity: Patterns of Change in the European Community*. Englewood Cliffs, NJ: Prentice Hall.

Nye, J. S. 1971. *Peace in Parts: Integration and Conflict in Regional Organizations*. Boston: Little, Brown.

Pelkmans, Jacques and L. Alan Winters with Helen Wallace. 1988. *Europe's*

Domestic Market. Chatham House Papers no. 43. London: Royal Institute of International Affairs; Routledge.

Reflection Group. 1995. Progress Report from the Chairman of the Reflection Group on the 1996 Intergovernmental Conference. Doc. SN 509/95 (Reflex 10). Madrid, 24 Aug.

Winters, L. Alan. 1997. What Can European Experience Teach Developing Countries About Integration? *World Economy* 20(7):889-912.

ANNALS, *AAPSS*, **565**, September 1999

The Autonomy and Democracy of Indigenous Peoples in Canada and Mexico

By JOSÉ L. GARCÍA-AGUILAR

ABSTRACT: This article has two objectives. One is to explain how, in the current international relations environment, the trend of global democratization is producing, ironically, the opposite trend of ethnic fragmentation of the multinational state and how this tension is resulting in new sources of international conflict. The other is to analyze the way in which, as a result of the aforementioned trends, local conflicts within the nation-states are representing a challenge to the nation-state as we know it. Taking advantage of the democratization wave, ethnic groups have launched, some with violence, some peacefully, a quest for emancipation, which constitutes a threat to the idea of the unitary nation-state and asks questions about the nature of civil society.

José L. García-Aguilar is assistant professor in the International Relations Department, Universidad de las Américas–Puebla, Mexico. He is a Ph.D. candidate at the Paul H. Nitze School of Advanced International Studies, Johns Hopkins University, in Washington, D.C.

AS we enter the new millennium and we are still trying to understand what kind of international order we have, it is a fact in international life that, with the dissolution of the conflict of the bipolar system, different issues emerged in the international arena, divergent from the traditional security agenda proper of the Cold War period.[1] This trend—although not new, as Robert Keohane and Joseph Nye have argued since the 1970s (see Keohane and Nye 1977)—was more noticeable during the years in which the Berlin Wall fell, the Persian Gulf war started, and the Soviet Union finally collapsed and disappeared as a multinational state, giving birth to new nation-states. Those events were interpreted by some observers and practitioners as the signals of a "new world order," as former U.S. president George Bush suggested, or the "end of history," as Francis Fukuyama optimistically asserted, or the beginning of a perennial liberal international order. Others, more cautious, saw the situation from the perspective of disorder, in other words, that the world had entered a phase of adjustment and that, by the force of the facts, two main and opposite currents could be observed: globalization and fragmentation (Falk 1993).

Although both trends could be analyzed separately, in fact they coexist in today's world affairs. At the same time that we can see the effects of global financial crises that have somewhat crushed the expectations that international experts had with respect to globalization, we see the emergence of local conflicts—in Bosnia, Somalia, and Rwanda—that have had an impact in world affairs. All these conflicts have in common the element of ethnicity. It seems that the wave of democratization gave impulse to domestic conflicts that were in some way dormant during the Cold War. The indigenous uprising in Chiapas, Mexico, on 1 January 1994 is another example. It is not that the conflict was not there before. Mexico has a long history of indigenous resistance and conflict (Díaz Polanco 1992). But, taking advantage of the global trends and the deep transformations that Mexican society was undergoing, the Zapatistas gave voice to those who are and have been on the margins of development and history.

GLOBALIZATION AND DEMOCRACY

There is a substantial scholarly literature on democracy and democratization with respect to the Latin American experience during the decade of the 1980s (O'Donell, Schmitter, and Whitehead 1986; Sartori 1987; Diamond, Linz, and Lipset 1989). This resulted from the need to explain how these societies were in the process of moving from authoritarianism to democracy and to compare them with other cases, such as Spain. When Eastern European societies began their own democratization process, the literature started to analyze this phenomenon as a global feature (Huntington 1994; Linz and Stepan 1996; Horowitz 1993).

The most important aspect to consider is that the movements that foster such transitions come from below, that is, from forces that are only somewhat part of society and that do not belong to an institutional structure. In other words, those forces come from the civil society expressed as movements that are qualitatively different from the state and that encompass a wide range of organization, from political parties to churches, universities, unions, professional organizations, and social and political networks, among others. Martin Shaw (1994) defines civil society as "the framework through which society in general and groups within it are represented, in both [a] socio-cultural sense (within networks which remain within civil society) and more specifically [a] political sense (in relation to the state)" (649).

In this sense, civil society represents the milieu in which different organizations exchange and defend their visions and interests vis-à-vis the power of the state. Thus, those forces—like the Catholic Church, unions like Solidarity, human rights organizations like the Madres de la Plaza de Mayo in Argentina—that contributed to regime transitions (in countries such as Poland or Chile) were fundamental to the political change in those countries. Although civil society participation is not recent, it is clear that under its framework, participatory democracy has become more global, in the sense that civil society has passed the limits of the territorial borders of the state, establishing transnational links. These links are forged with other organizations either within other states or in the international realm at conferences such as the Earth Summit in Rio de Janeiro, the World Conference of Women in Cairo, or conferences that nongovernmental organizations hold parallel to the Davos Economic Conference, creating the foundations of a "global civil society" (Lipschutz 1992).[2]

Thus, with the vital participation of civil society, democratization has become a global issue, not only in terms of elections being held in various countries but also in terms of civil apportionment at the national or international level. However, recent experiences have shown that, in spite of the spread of democratization around the world, such a process can result in a situation in which democracy releases civil society forces that are not precisely democratic, giving way to the emergence of what Fareed Zakaria (1997) has called "the rise of illiberal democracy."

Indeed, as Zakaria argues, it seems that, as the expectations rose after the Cold War regarding the prospects of democracy in the world, few observers noted that democracy does not necessarily mean good government. In other words, democracy tends to be thought of as meaning liberal democracy, which involves a constitutional setting that provides control of political power, respect for legal order, and regard for human rights (22-23).[3] In cases such as Peru, Yugoslavia, and Ghana, however, democracy is the government formed by the will of the people, but it does not entail the guidance of liberal constitutionalism. The election of a democratic government might bring also a radical sense of nationalism and violent conflict because respect for the rule of law and responsible government is less intense than the popular mandate. People can elect, in fair elections, demagogues, political bosses, and inefficient politicians. In the end, in such cases, only the process will have been democratic (35).

At the heart of this situation lies the problem of popular sovereignty, which gives legitimacy to those who are elected (see Almond and Powell 1996). Democratically elected nondemocratic governments tend to centralize authority to the detriment of other social and political participants. Thus, ironically, democracy gives birth to a regime with authoritarian tendencies. If democracy also means tolerance and respect for the rights of others, under the aforementioned circumstances, democracy could result in the preservation of social inequities and political grievances.

STATE SOVEREIGNTY AND
INDIGENOUS AUTONOMY:
BRITISH COLUMBIA AND CHIAPAS

The concept of sovereignty in the theory of international relations is troublesome, especially under the current condition of globalization. Since mainstream theory of the discipline considers the nation-state as the main actor in international politics, the concept of sovereignty is often taken for granted. The concept has been left to international law scholars or political scientists interested in redefining the scope and limits of the state (Duverger 1970; de Jouvenal 1957). Contributing to this, politicians use the term "sovereignty" to justify policy actions but also misuse the concept to cover actions such as violations of human rights or electoral fraud that bring unwanted international attention (see Zartman et al. 1996).

Likewise, the term "globalization" has become a cliché to indicate trends present, in some fashion, in today's international relations that prematurely assume the obsolescence of the nation-state, given some tendencies toward regional integration or the futuristic prospects of recent technologies, such as the Internet, that are shrinking the world. This cliché certainly provides an optimistic view of the future of the world, but in a very limited fashion.

As a result, it is possible to see contradictory patterns in the world. On the one hand, there is a pattern of redefinition of the state's role in the economy and society, releasing internal forces that otherwise would be bound to the state. These liberated forces, such as extreme nationalism, religious fundamentalism, and genuine desires of emancipation and self-determination, have an impact on the international level, resulting in a fragmentation process that is more and more visible not only in world politics but inside the nation-state as well. On the other hand, technology and the advancements in electronic communications are showing that there are issues that concern all humanity, with the result that people are becoming truly global in their awareness (Rosenau 1997). Thus, we are living in an increasingly global economy that favors productivity, efficiency, and markets around the world. Today, human rights concerns, ecological considerations, international migration, the spread of diseases, poverty, and aspirations for justice and democracy are issues with a clear global connotation as well.[4]

These contradictory patterns of, on the one hand, the redefinition and consequent fragmentation of the state in the international arena and, on the other, the globalization of today's world affairs are part of an increasingly complex phenomenology of international relations. In this sense, the mainstream theory of international relations has been limited to explaining the complexities of today's world partly because the prevalent theoretical vision from neorealism and its derivatives has been unable to consider questions and issues beyond the structure of the international system and the role that actors besides the state, such as civil society movements, have in world politics. This implies that the notions of power or anarchy, so important in international analysis for realism, in the first place, and for neorealism and its by-products, in the second, are not enough to explain, in a satisfactory and inclusive manner, the increasingly complex nature of international relations (Waltz 1979).[5]

Other approaches focus on the indispensable conceptual properties that identify international relations as a field of study and as a socially constructed human activity. These approaches raise the following question: is the notion of power still relevant nowadays in international relations, or are there other concepts at the heart of the discipline, such as culture, identity, gender, and context, that have been disregarded in international theory? Is anarchy the concept that really defines the international system, structurally speaking, or is it better to conceptualize the world as a society? Is it possible to reconcile structure, process, and agents in world politics? Is there an international dynamic process in the systemic sense of the word, or are international affairs the manifestation of the interaction of a diverse group of actors under rules, norms, values, or institutions of a broad framework called international society? In other words, current international phenomena require a broader framework that should include the complexities of world politics at the end of the century. Clearly those that envision only structure and anarchy are not enough. Consequently, the concept of international society, which was developed by the late Hedley Bull, seems more suitable (Bull 1977, 13).

With the idea of international society, it is possible to observe international phenomena beyond the nation-state and the logic of anarchy in the international system. Exploring rules, norms, obligation, ethics, social identities, the beliefs of the elite, and socialization, the observer is able to have a more accurate picture of the complexities of today's world, a socially constructed world.[6] From this point of view, the interaction of sovereign states is only one expression of international life; even the term "sovereignty" is a social construct (Biersteker and Weber 1996) derived from history that enabled political participants in the revolt against the central authority of the emperor and the Catholic Church to decentralize the highly hierarchical system of the Middle Ages and to enter the post-Westphalian decentralized international system. Sovereignty, therefore, in combination with the emergence of the territorial nation-state, became the cornerstone of the modern international system of states (see Ruggie 1993). But, under the current international condition in which globalization has made other nonstate actors participate in the world arena and in which phenomena such as financial crises easily spread, the traditional notion of sovereignty becomes fuzzy.

Those nonstate actors are numerous. They participate as part of the civil society within the boundaries of the nation-state or under the auspices of international organizations, such as the United Nations, or even as nongovernmental organizations involving national representation, like the International Olympic Committee (Archer 1983; Mansbach, Ferguson, and Lampert 1976). Such a diversity of nonstate actors has persuaded some authors, such as Hedley Bull, to believe that we are in a situation of "neomediaevalism" (quoted in Lipschutz 1992, 390; see also Mattews 1997).

In this context, indigenous peoples have gained more attention and a larger presence in the international arena. Their efforts in international networking and the use of modern telecommunication technology to spread their vision are remarkable (Lipschutz 1992, 395). But it is also democracy that has made it possible for their voice, little by little, to be heard. Their activism is not new. During the 1920s, some Indian leaders went to the League of Nations claiming respect for the treaties they had signed with nonaboriginal countries. But it was during the 1970s that real transnational networking began, with the creation of the World Council of Indigenous Peoples and with the involvement of the United Nations, which called for a study about the situation of indigenous peoples around the world. This activism reached its pinnacle with the declaration of 1993 as the Year of the Indigenous Peoples (Wilmer 1993, 3).[7]

This activism is the result of a long struggle against colonization, poverty, and cultural oppression. Such indigenous activism resulted in the revision of the International Labour Organization Convention Concerning Indigenous and Tribal Peoples in Independent Countries in June 1989 and the Universal Declaration on the Rights of Indigenous Peoples, by the United Nations Working Group on Indigenous Population, in 1990-1991 (Wilmer 1993, 215-26).

It is clear that indigenous peoples have been very active in transnational politics, taking advantage of globalization. But, domestically, the response from the state has been dubious and often violent. As we said before, social movements that, under the framework of civil society, participate in the public arena often challenge the state, particularly when they question its legitimacy or its territorial integrity, in other words, its internal sovereignty (see Hinsley 1986).

The Convention Concerning Indigenous and Tribal Peoples in Independent Countries provides the legal setting, if adopted, to begin solving the problem of indigenous autonomy. Indeed, articles 6 and 7 of the convention read as follows:

Article 6

1. In applying the provisions of this Convention, governments shall:

(a) consult the peoples concerned, through appropriate procedures and in particular through their representative institutions, whenever consideration is being given to legislative or administrative measures which may affect them directly;

(b) establish means by which these peoples can freely participate, to at least the same extent as other sectors of the population, at all levels of decision-making in elective institutions and administrative and other bodies responsible for policies and programs which concern them;

(c) establish means for the full development of these peoples' own institutions and initiatives, and in appropriate cases provide the resources necessary for this purpose.

2. The consultations carried out in application of this Convention shall be undertaken, in good faith and in a form appropriate to the circumstances, with the objective of achieving agreement or consent to the proposed measures.

Article 7

1. The peoples concerned shall have the right to decide their own priorities for the process of development as it affects their lives, beliefs, institutions and spiritual well-being and the lands they occupy or otherwise use, and to exercise control, to the extent possible, over their own economic, social and cultural development. In addition, they shall participate in the formulation, implementation and evaluation of plans and programs for national and regional development, which may affect them directly.

2. The improvement of the conditions of life and work and levels of health and education of the peoples concerned, with their participation and co-operation, shall be a matter of priority in plans for the overall economic development of areas they inhabit. Special projects for development of the areas in question shall also be so designed as to promote such improvement.

3. Governments shall ensure that, whenever appropriate, studies are carried out, in co-operation with the peoples concerned, to assess the social, spiritual, cultural and environmental impact on them of planned development activities. The results of these studies shall be considered as fundamental criteria for the implementation of these activities.

4. Governments shall take measures, in co-operation with the peoples concerned, to protect and preserve the environment of the territories they inhabit.

Also, the Universal Declaration on the Rights of Indigenous Peoples expresses in part I, paragraph 1, the right to self-determination (Wilmer 1993, 220). National governments have provided a legal basis for recognizing indigenous rights, as in the case of Canada, whose constitution in its Part II includes a section on aboriginal rights.[8]

Following the legal percepts that the Canadian Constitution sustains regarding aboriginal rights, on 4 August 1998, the Canadian government signed a treaty with West Coast Indians, in New Aiyansh, in the province of British Columbia. Although this treaty has not yet been ratified by the provincial legislature or the federal Parliament, it has already caused a lot of debate, particularly because it grants a big portion of land to the Nisga'a people. Such grants of land are always a contentious issue regarding aboriginal rights. The other difficult problem is the question of self-government or autonomy, which is particularly delicate in Canada's case due to the precarious balance in the Canadian federation with respect to Quebec, which for a long time has sought more political autonomy or even independence. The treaty signed with the Nisga'a exemplifies the political and constitutional struggles that the search for indigenous autonomy can result in for a country. But the Canadian case also is an example of a liberal-democratic country that tries to address the grievances of a very important part of its population: the indigenous peoples.

Quite different has been the case of Mexico. The modern Mexican state has not recognized indigenous autonomy even though it has historical experience in dealing with the self-rule of indigenous people (see Díaz Polanco 1997).

The most dramatic event in recent times has been the indigenous uprising in the state of Chiapas on 1 January 1994, the same day that the North American Free Trade Agreement came into force. That day, the Ejército Zapatista de Liberación Nacional (Zapatista Army of National Liberation; EZLN) entered the city of San Cristóbal de las Casas, altering forever the relations between the indigenous people and the Mexican state.[9] Before this, Mexico had implemented an indigenous policy that had ranged from integration to bilingualism. Although Mexico has a mythical view of the Indians, the fact is that they have lived under conditions of extreme poverty, exploitation, and racism since Spanish colonial rule. Even with the reform of article 4 of the national constitution in 1990, the legal situation of the indigenous population is not clear. Several states have tried to implement some sort of reform in their local constitutions in order to cope with the problem of indigenous autonomy. The most recent case was in the state of Oaxaca, whose legislature approved a constitutional reform called Ley de Derechos de los Pueblos y Comunidades Indígenas (Law for the Rights of Indigenous Peoples and Communities) (Nahmad 1998, 11).

But Chiapas represents, by all accounts, the most challenging problem. There, the January rebellion put pressure on the federal government to respond militarily. Although the administration of Mexican president Carlos Salinas de Gortari ordered a cease-fire 13 days after the rebellion began, the military presence has been permanent, adding more tension to the conflict. Moreover, the political situation in 1994 was deteriorating quickly because 1994 was an election year and the presidential candidate of the official party, the Institutional Revolutionary Party, was assassinated. In December 1994, the new president,

Ernesto Zedillo, took office with the promise of trying to solve the Chiapas situation peacefully. But in February of 1995, the federal government launched a military and police operation in search of the leaders of the Zapatista army, particularly its most visible leader, the Subcomandante Marcos, who had become an international icon. Civil society was mobilized in order to avoid a bloody confrontation. The federal government agreed to negotiate and to reach some accords. These accords are known as the Acuerdos de San Andrés Larráinzar.[10] These accords would have been the foundation of a comprehensive constitutional reform that would enable Mexico to enter the twenty-first century as a modern country that recognizes the right of self-determination for its ethnic minorities. But, with arguments over legal technicalities, the Zedillo administration refused to comply with the accords, not only rejecting the notion of autonomy but also violating the International Labour Organization's Convention Concerning Indigenous and Tribal Peoples in Independent Countries, which Mexico had signed and ratified in 1990. Today there is no dialogue between the Zapatista army and the Mexican government.

CONCLUSION

As we have seen, the awakening of civil society has been more visible since the collapse of the Soviet Union. The forces of democratization, coming from the civil society, have been instrumental in installing democratic regimes or in expediting transitions to democracy. But, as we have shown, democracy could mean, paradoxically, the unleashing of undemocratic forces that encourage intolerance and resulting civil unrest. Globalization has allowed the aspirations of marginalized people, such as the indigenous, to be much better known, in the sense that the global process allows social and political networking beyond the borders of the traditional territorial nation-state. If democracy means tolerance, negotiation, and accommodation under the rule of law, some cases in international relations show that, even with electoral democracy, violence could emerge. The process by which the Nisga'a people were guaranteed autonomy, land, and cultural rights shows that, even with the inevitable tensions, it is possible to have coherence between democratic aspirations of marginalized peoples and the constitutional interpretations about the unity of the nation-state and its sovereignty, a concept that urgently requires revision. The case of Chiapas is paradigmatic of this tension. But the Mexican government is trapped in its own rhetoric of national unity at any cost. Coupled with that are the old interests of landlords, political bosses, and private armies that do not want to abandon either their privileges or their prejudices. The Chiapas case shows how civil society is helpful in supporting democratic causes, but it also demonstrates the perils of having an old and erroneous construct about what sovereignty means at the end of the twentieth century.

Notes

1. Human rights and the environment are issues that have grown in importance on the international agenda, contributing to the emergence of transnational movements. See Sikkink 1998, 517.

2. It is important to note that not only does the transborder phenomenon represent globality but it also expresses the notion of a growing consciousness about global issues (Lipschutz 1992, 399).

3. Zakaria makes a very interesting distinction between liberal democracy and liberal constitutions, arguing that the confluence of them is a historical accident. The theoretical response to Zakaria's arguments is developed in Plattner 1998.

4. For a good review of recent literature on globalization, see Mayal 1998.

5. For a neostructural elaboration, see Buzan, Jones, and Little 1993.

6. A new generation of theorists in the field of international relations has tried to move the theoretical focus of the discipline from neorealism to social constructivism. See Wendt 1987, 1992; Dessler 1989; Onuf 1989; Lapid and Kratochwil 1996; Onuf, Kubálková, and Kowert 1998.

7. Wilmer 1993 is one of the few books that considers the indigenous question in international relations. It includes a very interesting chronology of events related to indigenous issues, as well as an appendix of documents.

8. For a better discussion of aboriginal rights, see Berger 1987; Dickenson 1992. On the particular issue of self-government, see Brock 1998.

9. To better understand the origins of the indigenous rebellion in Chiapas, see Tello Díaz 1995; Montemayor 1998. The Catholic Church's involvement in the conflict is a particularly interesting issue; see, for example, Legorreta Díaz 1998; Womack 1998. For a more recent reflection, at the fifth anniversary of the Chiapas uprising, see *Letras libres* 1999; *Nexos* 1999.

10. For a good account of the developments and complexities of this process, see Montemayor 1998, 134-234.

References

Almond, Gabriel and G. Bingman Powell, Jr. 1996. *Comparative Politics Today: A World View.* 2d ed. New York: HarperCollins.

Archer, Clive. 1983. *International Organizations.* London: Allen & Unwin.

Berger, Thomas R. 1987. Native History, Native Claims, and Self-Determination. *B. C. Studies* 57 (Spring):10-23.

Biersteker, Thomas J. and Cynthia Weber, eds. 1996. *State Sovereignty as Social Construct.* New York: Cambridge University Press.

Brock, Kathy L. 1998. The Politics of Aboriginal Self-Government: A Canadian Paradox. *Canadian Public Administration/Administration Public du Canada* 34(2):272-85.

Bull, Hedley. 1977. *The Anarchical Society: A Study of Order in World Politics.* New York: Columbia University Press.

Buzan, Barry, Charles Jones, and Richard Little. 1993. *The Logic of Anarchy: Neorealism to Structural Realism.* New York: Columbia University Press.

de Jouvenal, Bertrand. 1957. *Sovereignty: An Inquiry into the Political Good.* Chicago: University of Chicago Press.

Dessler, David. 1989. What's at Stake in the Agent-Structure Debate? *International Organization* 43(Summer): 441-73.

Diamond, Larry, Juan Linz, and Seymour Martin Lipset, eds. 1989. *Democracy in Developing Countries.* Boulder, CO: Lynne Rienner.

Díaz Polanco, Héctor. 1997. *Indigenous Peoples in Latin America: The Quest for Self-Determination.* Boulder, CO: Westview Press.

————, coord. 1992. *El fuego de la inobediencia: Autonomía y rebelión india en el Obispado de Oaxaca*. Mexico City: Centro de Investigaciones y Estudios Superiores en Antropología Social.

Dickenson, Olive Patricia. 1992. *Canada's First Nations: A History of Founding Peoples from Earliest Times*. Norman: University of Oklahoma Press.

Duverger, Maurice. 1970. *Institutions politiques et droit constitutionnel*. Paris: Presses Universitaires de France.

Falk, Richard. 1993. In Search of a New World Model. *Current History* 92(573):145-49.

Hinsley, F. H. 1986. *Sovereignty*. 2d ed. New York: Cambridge University Press.

Horowitz, Donald. 1993. Democracy in Divided Societies. *Journal of Democracy* 4(4):18-38.

Huntington, Samuel. 1994. Democracy's Third Wave. *Journal of Democracy* 2(2):12-34.

International Labour Organization. 1989. Convention Concerning Indigenous and Tribal Peoples in Independent Countries. No. 169.

Keohane, Robert and Joseph Nye. 1977. *Power and Interdependence: World Politics in Transition*. Boston: Little, Brown.

Lapid, Yosef and Fiedrich Kratochwil, eds. 1996. *The Return of Culture and Identity in International Relations Theory*. Boulder, CO: Lynne Rienner.

Legorreta Díaz, Ma. del Carmen. 1998. *Religión, política y guerrilla en las Cañadas de la Selva Lacandona*. Mexico City: Cal y Arena.

Letras libres. 1999. 1(1).

Linz, Juan and Alfred Stepan, eds. 1996. *Problems of Democratic Transition and Consolidation: Southern Europe, South America, and Post-Communist Europe*. Baltimore: Johns Hopkins University Press.

Lipschutz, Ronnie D. 1992. Reconstructing World Politics: The Emergence of Global Civil Society. *Millennium: Journal of International Studies* 21 (3):389-420.

Mansbach, Richard W., Yale H. Ferguson, and Donald E. Lampert. 1976. *The Web of World Politics: Nonstate Actors in the Global System*. Englewood Cliffs, NJ: Prentice Hall.

Mattews, Jessica. 1997. Power Shift. *Foreign Affairs* 76(1):50-66.

Mayal, James. 1998. Globalization and International Relations. *Review of International Studies* 24:239-50.

Montemayor, Carlos. 1998. *Chiapas: La rebelión indígena de Chiapas*. 2d ed. Mexico City: Joaquín Mortíz.

Nahmad, Salomón. 1998. Del subterráneo a la realidad. In *Masiosare*, Sunday supplement, *La Jornada*, 19 July, 11.

Nexos. 1999. 21(253).

O'Donell, Guillermo, Philippe Schmitter, and Laurence Whitehead, eds. 1986. *Transitions from Authoritarian Rule: Comparative Perspectives*. Baltimore: Johns Hopkins University Press.

Onuf, Nicholas. 1989. *World of Our Making: Rules and Rule in Social Theory and International Relations*. Columbia: University of South Carolina Press.

Onuf, Nicholas, Vendulka Kubálková, and Paul Kowert, eds. 1998. *International Relations in a Constructed World*. Armonk, NY: M. E. Sharpe.

Plattner, Marc F. 1998. Liberalism and Democracy: Can't Have One Without the Other. *Foreign Affairs* 77(2): 171-80.

Rosenau, James. 1997. The Complexities and Contradictions of Globalization. *Current History* 96(613):360-64.

Ruggie, John Gerard. 1993. Territoriality and Beyond: Problematizing Modernity in International Relations. *International Organization* 47(1):141-76.

Sartori, Giovanni. 1987. *The Theory of Democracy Revisited*. Chatham, NJ: Chatham House.

Shaw, Martin. 1994. Civil Society and Global Politics: Beyond a Social Movements Approach. *Millennium: Journal of International Studies* 23(3):649-62.

Sikkink, Kathryn. 1998. Transnational Politics, International Relations Theory and Human Rights. *Political Science and Politics* 31(73):517-27.

Tello Díaz, Carlos. 1995. *La rebelión de las cañadas*. Mexico City: Cal y Arena.

Waltz, Kenneth. 1979. *Theory of International Politics*. Reading, MA: Addison-Wesley.

Wendt, Alexander. 1987. The Agent-Structure Problem in International Relations Theory. *International Organization* 41(Summer):335-70.

———. 1992. Anarchy Is What States Make of It. *International Organization* 46(2):335-70.

Wilmer, Franke. 1993. *The Indigenous Voice in World Politics: Since Time Immemorial*. Newbury Park, CA: Sage.

Womack, John, Jr. 1998. *Chiapas, el obispo de San Cristóbal y la revuelta zapatista*. Mexico City: Cal y Arena.

Zakaria, Fareed. 1997. The Rise of Illiberal Democracy. *Foreign Affairs* 76(6):22-43.

Zartman, I. William, Francis M. Deng, Sadikiel Kimaro, Terrence Lyons, and Donald Rothchild. 1996. *Sovereignty as Responsibility: Conflict Management in Africa*. Washington, DC: Brookings Institution.

Development and Civil Society in Latin America and Asia

By WILLIAM RATLIFF

ABSTRACT: Market reforms began in parts of Asia after World War II and led to macroeconomic policies and governance that brought rapid and fairly evenly shared growth, with an emphasis on promoting capable civil services, community involvement, and good basic education and health. For historical and cultural reasons, reforms began decades later in most of Latin America. To bypass ossified bureaucracies, operating under largely democratic governments with elements of civil societies, Latin American reforms were under strongmen, or *caudillos*, who undertook macroeconomic reforms due to conviction or expediency or both. The leaders used teams of technocrats who operated alongside and above preexisting bureaucracies. Reforms began first and went furthest in Chile. After case studies of Chile, Argentina, Peru, Mexico, and Venezuela, the author concludes that Latin American reforms will not really serve their people or be secure until, like the Asian reforms, they stress competent and honest governance, shared growth, and basic education and health.

William Ratliff is a senior research fellow and curator of the Americas and international collections, Hoover Institution, Stanford University. His Ph.D. (in Chinese and Latin American histories) is from the University of Washington. He has taught in universities on four continents and lectured from West Point to the Chinese Academy of Social Sciences (Beijing). His most recent books are The Law and Economics of Development *(1997) and* The Law and Economics of Developing Countries, *with Edgardo Buscaglia (forthcoming).*

NOTE: Earlier versions of this article were presented in March 1998 at the Universidad de las Américas–Puebla, Mexico, and in June 1998 at the Institute of Latin American Studies of the Chinese Academy of Social Sciences in Beijing, China.

F IFTY years ago, Latin American and East Asian leaders had often similar challenges of economic and political underdevelopment before them, but they responded differently for many reasons: history, national conditions, culture, institutions, incentives, and objectives. The inspiration for breaking free from the past came mainly from the failures of the past in their own countries and abroad but also from varied success stories such as that of the United States, which had emerged as the First World superpower after World War II, and the Soviet Union, which seemed to offer a different and, in some respects, superior form of economic and social future. Newly victorious Communist leaders in the Soviet bloc, China, North Korea, and North Vietnam said it was historically destined that, under communism, the poor would prosper. History has proved that this is not true, but, in the mid-twentieth century, non-Communist leaders in Asia feared that that prophecy would get their people to support Communist upheavals in their own countries. Thus those leaders had strong incentives for calculating the real foundations for shared economic growth and for turning their political skills and powers toward bringing it about. In the process, they promoted those aspects of civil society that they thought would serve their economic needs.

The first Latin American country in the second half of the twentieth century to undertake sound macroeconomic development was Chile after the military coup of 1973, the only time a Latin American government made tough and correct economic and civil-society decisions as a direct response to the threat of communism. Few other political leaders in Latin America had comparable incentives, and thus, whether to protect their personal or group interests or because they were blinded by dependency thought and/or other ideologies, they failed to make and implement equally intelligent economic policies.[1]

Historically, some Latin American countries had more experience than Asian countries with several of the political and institutional factors that make up civil society, namely, (1) the accountability of the executive, (2) the quality of the bureaucracy, (3) the strength of civil liberties and political rights, (4) the rule of law, and (5) the transparency of the decision-making process (Campos and Nugent 1997, 87). By early 1999, however, Asia had surpassed Latin America in developing some but not all aspects of civil society.

This article will focus mainly on the practical problems of formulating, implementing, and maintaining free-market macroeconomic policies by individuals and institutions in a way that will tangibly benefit national populations. More specifically, it will examine the development and consolidation of civil society behind market reforms, with a focus on governance (Campos and Nugent 1997, 88, 92). This will be done by noting the similarities and differences between countries as well as basic trends in East Asia and Latin America and by drawing tentative conclusions as to what forms of governance offer the best prospects for permanent entry into the First World.

ECONOMICS AND CIVIL SOCIETY IN ASIA AND LATIN AMERICA

Though it is essential for leaders to make the right macroeconomic decisions, the main factors facilitating or preventing rational economic policies are often political, cultural, and institutional. Economic disasters have been perpetrated by Communist governments all over the world for largely political reasons, but the politics of bad or disastrous economics transcends any particular ideology. Domingo Cavallo, the economy minister who guided Argentina's reforms during the early and mid-1990s, has said that in his country implementing the right economic policies has been, above all, a political problem and that he was able to do so much during the 1990s only because he had the strong political support of a master politician, President Carlos Menem (Cavallo 1997b, 273; Corrales 1997, 64). Asian Development Bank economist Hilton Root has correctly noted that "good [economic] policies matter, but gaining a consensus to achieve growth is a political question. We know much more about the relationship of economic variables than about the interaction between economics and politics" (Root 1996, 158).

From the 1950s, many Asian leaders seriously calculated how they could bring about sustained national economic development in a way that would receive broadly based support for reforms—and for themselves. In general, they were successful in what

were long called the high-performing Asian economies of Japan, the Republic of Korea, Taiwan, Hong Kong, Singapore, Thailand, Malaysia, and Indonesia, and, beginning in the late 1970s, the People's Republic of China. In important ways, these countries offer lessons that other developing nations often seem—or should be—eager to learn, although, of course, Asia's image has been tarnished by the crisis that erupted in mid-1997.

Over the past 10-15 years, most Latin American leaders have finally turned to more productive macroeconomic policies because of economic crises and political pressures in their own countries. Since the late 1980s, possible answers to domestic problems have been seen increasingly in the context of the collapse of statist economies around the world and the equally obvious relatively greater success of economies in both the First World and those parts of the Third World—many countries in Asia, and Chile in Latin America—that opted for free-market-type economics (Ratliff 1996-97).

Now as we approach the twenty-first century, these two major regions of what used to be called the Third World are in the midst of profound changes that will shape the lives of their peoples for decades to come. Most serious reformers in these countries now recognize that the prerequisite to development is adopting some form of macroeconomic policies of the free market and at least some aspects of civil societies. Some countries have stepped forward only to fall back, but these reversals have usually been mainly matters of faulty economic adaptations and fine-tuning, rather than of mistaken macroeconomics, in the context of critically important politics, culture, and society. A long report on the Asian financial crisis in April 1998 by the International Labour Organization put it this way: "It was not only weaknesses in formal institutions that created the preconditions for the crisis, but also the contamination of market processes by politics. Unless the latter is contained no amount of tinkering with institutions and regulatory mechanisms will be to much avail" (chap. 4, p. 2).

HUMAN CAPITAL AND DEVELOPMENT

There are three essential aspects of the East Asian strategy to implement sound macroeconomic policies. The first is a focus on developing human capital through targeted social spending, with a strong emphasis on good basic health and basic education, objectives not so well identified and pursued in Latin America as Asia. Second is to develop a high-quality civil service through rigorous entrance requirements, giving it sufficient independence and incentives to make professional decisions in the national interest but keeping it accountable through independent oversight, a major concern of the present article. The third essential aspect is to incorporate the various sectors of society into a single program for growth by getting them involved in developing ideas and institutions that they believe will serve their own long-term interests with respect to opportunities and living standards. While Latin American countries have generally rated higher than Asian countries in political rights and civil liberties, the majority of Latin Americans historically have had little positive impact on the policies chosen and implemented by their governments, and they have not benefited equally from them (Campos and Root 1996; Stromquist 1997, 75-77; Campos and Nugent 1997, 88, 92).

Human capital is a critical factor for launching and sustaining shared economic growth. Economist Arnold Harberger, the primary University of Chicago mentor of many of Chile's reformers, has shown that "the state of underdevelopment for an economy stems from the low productivity of the great mass of the people." The best way to improve their productivity, he says, is public and private investment in human capital (Harberger 1995, 45). Gary Becker, who won the Nobel Prize in economics in 1992 for his work in applying economics to social problems, focuses on the basics of development that many East Asian leaders grasped decades ago. He and his coauthor write that "human capital is the foundation of a modern economy" (Becker and Becker 1997, 76), adding that East Asian countries have long paid much closer attention to basic education, training, work habits, and other aspects of developing basic human capital than the United States, let alone Latin America, has (74-76).

The real obstacle to greater government spending by Third World countries on basic education, combating crime and other important public activities is not their limited resources but the diversion of these governments from what should be their major priorities. They are too busy doing things that either should not be done at all—or that should be left to the private sector. Countries such as Brazil and Mexico have enormous human energy and economic potential. But they will further delay their entry into the First World if they continue to pay insufficient attention to the schooling and health of their poor. (Becker and Becker 1997, 68)

Successful East Asian governments got more of their priorities right and, much more impressively than Latin American governments, directed their funding to broadly based education and public health programs in rural and urban areas. Land reform, improved infrastructure, and development of human capital made life better and more productive in the countryside, thus reducing (but not ending) the temptation to migrate to already overcrowded cities. In the cities, education was important, as in some cases were other specific needs—such as public housing in Hong Kong and Singapore—to raise living conditions for the urban poor. These measures— and others such as promoting small and medium-sized enterprises—improved the lives and prospects of the people generally and played an important role in offering non-elites "opportunities for upward economic mobility" (Campos and Root 1996, 50, chap. 4).

CREATING OPPORTUNITIES VERSUS REDISTRIBUTION

Giving people a stake in the future of society "reduces the long-term danger that social movements will contest regime legitimacy and topple the government, which, in turn, induces longer time horizons in the investment calculations of the private sector, an important determinant of sustainable development" (Root, Ratliff, and Morgan 1999). A top Argentine economist points out that in Asia most people find new jobs in industry, agriculture, and the services, while in Latin America they most often find them in the government (López Murphy 1994, 15). Opportunities to prosper are often hard for non-elites to come by in Latin America.

When an effort to benefit the poor is made in the two regions, there is generally this major difference: "an implicit emphasis on opportunities for the poor in East Asia, versus an emphasis on redistributive transfers in Latin America" (Birdsall, Ross, and Sabot 1997, 113). In the past, populism has repeatedly undercut sustainable growth as political leaders looked for short-term solutions to long-term problems and turned from emphasizing production to redistribution. That is, Latin American governments have traditionally focused more on redistribution of income and wealth than on improving opportunities for productive labor. Although they have invested some in human resource and institutional development, they have usually done so less effectively than Asians. For example, while educational expenditures as a percentage of gross national product are about the same in the two areas, support for basic education is higher in Asia. Also, when primary school enrollments increase in Latin America, where the birth rate is higher, the quality of instruction often declines—which it does not in Asia— especially for the poor. Finally, substantially more of the Latin American educational budget goes into universities, which are used disproportionately by the elites, while universities in Asia are more often in the private sector (Birdsall, Ross, and Sabot 1997, 96, 122-25; Birdsall and Sabot 1997, 69; Stromquist 1997).

GOVERNANCE IN ASIA

In recent years, international financial organizations have become increasingly attentive to the need for effective public sectors like those found in the most successful East Asian countries. According to the World Bank, the public sector needs a (1) "strong central capacity for macroeconomic and strategic policy formulation," (2) "mechanisms to delegate, discipline, and debate policies among government agencies," and (3) "institutionalized links to stakeholders outside the government, providing transparency and accountability and encouraging feedback" (World Bank 1997, 81, chap. 5). To develop a civil service that will serve medium- and long-term national interests rather than the immediate interests of the bureaucrats themselves, political leaders have had to find a way to make the personal and

national interests coincide. They have done this by adjusting the "risk-reward calculation so that bureaucrats will use their knowledge of the economic consequences of policies to promote shared growth," an accomplishment two analysts of the phenomenon have called "one of the most original and successful of institutional innovations that distinguish the high-performing Asian economies from the patterns characteristic of Latin America and Africa" (Campos and Root 1996, 138-39).

If oversight bodies discover that a civil servant has used his knowledge to advance his personal interests, that bureaucrat risks exchanging his respected and generally well-remunerated employment for dismissal, disgrace, and punishment. The mixture and the effectiveness have varied even between developing Asian countries, however, for while the entire civil service of tiny Singapore is selected by means of a demanding competitive examination and given the full range of benefits, in Indonesia most of the enormous service is chosen through "largely perfunctory" exams and is poorly paid, with full benefits going only to a small core of experts. Thus Indonesia's civil service is one of the weakest in East Asia and, along with the Philippine bureaucracy (the most obviously Spanish-influenced in the region), is strikingly similar in some ways to the Latin American cases that will be discussed here. Not surprisingly, Indonesia also is the country that has suffered most dramatically in the end-of-century economic crisis (Campos and Root 1996, 138, 142).

In order to make and implement policy effectively, a capable and motivated civil service must be free of the kind of strictly self-serving policies that have been so common and counterproductive in Latin America. The best East Asian governments have better separated policy formation and implementation, established clear lines of responsibility and communication, and maximized opportunities to measure results and accountability. Government expenditures in the most successful countries are monitored by auditors with the authority to act and by independent, institutionalized anticorruption organizations that investigate and punish transgressors. Most effective East Asian leaders created strategy policy units within the executive branch that were responsible for a variety of tasks, ranging from strategic planning to coordinating and prioritizing development plans, overseeing the budget and its disbursement, and making sure that all public investments served national goals. Most leaders created business or deliberation councils involving private industry, labor, academia, the media, and consumer groups, in order to cultivate communication and confidence between the government and citizens. These councils have helped reduce waste and corruption, have encouraged informational ties between business and government, and have created an environment that has given business confidence in the direction of government policy. Thus Asian governments increased credibility by bringing a variety of voices into the planning of policy, not with the purpose of directing the markets but by using the markets as their guides (Campos and Root 1996, chap. 4).

CULTURE AND DEVELOPMENT IN LATIN AMERICA

Most Latin American governments have only recently responded more positively to the need for modernization programs with sound macroeconomics, and they have done so in their own ways. The study of these developments is complicated by the brevity of the reform experiments, in most cases less than 10 years; therefore few studies have been made of the problems, and evidence ranges from empirical to anecdotal. Nevertheless, though at this point conclusions must be tentative. Preliminary investigations suggest that, for a variety of reasons, the prospects for successful and lasting reforms are better in East Asia than in Latin America, the Asian financial crisis notwithstanding.

Among those planning, implementing, and analyzing reforms in Latin America, there is growing recognition of the cultural or institutional factor as it operates on leaders, bureaucracies, and populations in general. Countries with institutions of Spanish origin are characterized by personalistic relationships that often impede political stability and broadly based and shared economic growth. Nobel Prize–winning economist Douglass North correctly writes, "Although formal rules may change overnight as the result of political or judicial decisions, informal constraints embodied in customs, traditions, and codes of conduct are much more impervious to deliberate policies. These cultural constraints not only connect the past with the present and future, but provide us with a key to explaining the path of historical change." In considerable detail he traces Latin America's limited and unequal development to the deep-seated inheritance from Spain (North 1990, 6, 112-16; see also Waisman 1987, 39). Mexico's Nobel Prize–winning author Octavio Paz pointed out the problem as follows: "Though Spanish-American civilization is to be admired on many counts, it reminds one of a structure of great solidity—at once convent, fortress, and palace—built to last, not to change. In the long run, that construction became a confine, a prison" (Paz 1979, 78).

This problem of culture has been lamented by leaders and analysts of all periods, ranging from South America's "liberators" Simón Bolívar and Francisco de Miranda to the Spaniard José Ortega y Gasset and the Venezuelan Carlos Rangel. The Caracas-born Bolívar even fled to Europe to die, writing to a close colleague just before his death that Latin America is "ungovernable," that "whoever works for a revolution [there] is plowing the sea," and that the only recourse is to do what he did—emigrate (de Madariaga 1959, 527; Rangel 1987).

Although many Latin Americans have emigrated, moving abroad is obviously not a solution for most people in the region. The foremost current analyst of the cultural determinant, Lawrence Harrison, argues that in order to escape from the "prison" that Paz identifies,

better salaries, management, organization and methods must be accompanied by top-down anti-corruption campaigns, rewards on the basis of merit and the encouragement of honesty and dissent. Finally, there must be bottom-up inculcation of progressive values in the home, school, media and society. (Harrison 1998)

This message has been spread in Latin America in many forms, from the words and actions of reformers to think-tank studies and such organizations as the Institute of Human Development in Peru—founded in 1990 by businessman Octavio Mavila—whose Ten Commandments of Development have circulated throughout the hemisphere. The Ten Commandments are order, cleanliness, punctuality, responsibility, the will to succeed, honor, respect for the rights of others, respect for laws and regulations, love of work, and support for thrift and investment (Harrison 1998, 1985, 1997; Landes 1998, 310-28; Mendoza, Montaner, and Vargas Llosa 1996).

Others recognize the problems attributed previously to culture but, in the words of John Waterbury, argue that "culture modifies but does not determine." Culture, they say, "cannot be dissociated from institutions that themselves may be acultural or extra-cultural in origin" (Waterbury 1993, 9). Wherever one finds the source of the problem, bureaucracies or civil services in Latin America are not engines of change.

GOVERNANCE IN
LATIN AMERICA

The low quality of civil services and governance in Latin America has been noted in general terms by a number of analysts and reformers in the region. One of Mexico's leading market reformers, who has long experience in his country's bureaucracy, wrote in the mid-1970s that "perhaps no other group can be as detrimental to reform as the bureaucracy itself. Regardless of their functions . . . a bureaucracy owes its first loyalty to itself" (Waterbury 1993, 9). Peruvian political analyst and reformer Hernando de Soto (1998) says that "a developing country needs radical change and bureaucracies are not in the business of radical change," a fact that has some advantages as well. One of Argentina's foremost economists praised the capability, quality, and independence of civil services in East Asia as a preface to remarking on the "underdevelopment" and "low quality" of civil services in South America, especially in performance and incentives (López Murphy 1994, 12-17). A recent study by the Inter-American Development Bank reported that Latin America's most serious structural weaknesses have been "a bloated government bureaucracy and out-of-control public finances." While Latin American governments have been "largely successful" in dealing with the latter problem, they "have yet to take the final, most difficult step: to build strong public institutions capable of supporting an effective development policy" (Birdsall and Jaspersen 1997, 9).

The World Bank, an increasingly important actor in Latin America, has said that guidelines for developing a capable civil service include adequate compensation, merit-based recruitment and promotion, and esprit de corps. The problem is getting from current reality to that goal, a task that the Bank's analysts note has been accomplished in parts of East Asia but not Latin America (World Bank 1997, 91-98; Page 1997, 48-49). A leading Argentine reformer in the Menem government remarked that the World Bank formula is an ideal that had nothing whatever to do with realities in Argentina in 1989, when Menem took office, and not a great deal more almost a decade later (Ratliff 1998a).

A 1995 study by 12 Latin American economists for the Inter-American Development Bank pointed to a number of critical shortcomings in the region's governance, mostly the absence of those factors that made some Asian countries so successful. Among the problems were the widespread poor training of administrators at all levels of government, in skills ranging from record keeping to specific areas of expertise such as sanitation, building inspection, and urban planning; the lack of incentives for administrators to better serve the public; the absence of reliable data, guidelines, and personnel to plan and efficiently carry out programs or to evaluate current administrators, departments, and projects; the absence of means whereby central governments can monitor the use of funds in the provinces and municipalities; and the failure of governments to conduct programs that the vast majority of people believe give them a fair chance to succeed and serve their interests.

The Inter-American Development Bank study concluded that "the complexity of administering a centralized system, processing information, and issuing orders on time can not be resolved given the present capability of public administration in Latin America," adding that "overcoming the administrative flaws that Latin America has suffered demands that public administration be strengthened and that it function on different levels vis-à-vis the citizenry" (López Murphy 1995, 47, 17-18). A 1997 study by the World Bank found some indications of a "quiet revolution" in local governance in the region but is still largely negative (World Bank 1997, 166).

THE CHILEAN VANGUARD

Chile has accomplished more in governance—as in reforms generally—than any other country in Latin America. The Chilean government is highly centralized, with almost complete control over taxation and regulation of programs in the capital so as to maintain macroeconomic stability. Chile's capital markets measure favorably against Asia's, according to an Inter-American Development Bank official, because Chilean leaders (1) "learn from their mistakes," (2) "limit the government's direct role in financial markets," (3) "build upon their successes in the financial markets by creating politically independent, highly pro-

fessional regulatory institutions," (4) periodically update the policies and laws regulating financial markets, (5) "use market incentives when they decide to intervene to achieve a specific goal," and (6) have a long-term commitment to "the basic principles underlying the development of capital markets" (Howard 1997, 221). At the same time, considerable administrative authority in Chile is outside the capital, putting local bureaucrats in closer contact with the people they serve (López Murphy 1995, 30-32, 42, 48-49, 53-54; Yáñez and Letelier 1995, 168-72).

One critical issue that Chile has dealt with more successfully than any other Latin American country is shared growth. Since 1974, Chile has developed a relatively effective program for targeting the most marginalized sectors throughout the country and for significantly reducing levels of severe poverty[2] (Grosh 1994). Colombia's policies toward the poor have also been somewhat better than most others, though one analyst noted the critical problem that "it has not been easy to convince the poorer Colombians that they are truly getting their fair share" and that this has "lessened [the government's] legitimacy in the eyes of many" (Bushnell 1993, 276; see also Halperín Donghi 1993, 333, 380-82; Sánchez and Gutiérrez 1995, 204-6, chap. 4). In Argentina, income-transfer mechanisms serve some provinces at the expense of others so that "rich citizens in [some] poor provinces are being subsidized by poor ones in rich provinces" (López

Murphy and Moskovits 1997, 29; López Murphy 1995, 42, 53; Ratliff and Fontaine 1993).

Yet even Chile's bureaucracy has problems. Each year the top two levels are evaluated on the basis of dedication, capacity, and other characteristics, but the standards are sometimes unclear, not all of the processes are transparent, and some judgments are biased. The approximately 85 percent of the bureaucrats below these levels are career employees who are little checked and who have few incentives to do the best possible job for the nation as a whole. The Chilean government and independent scholars are currently examining the reforms undertaken in New Zealand—a World Bank model for Latin America—as a source of ideas for civil service reforms in Chile (Evaluation of Functionaries 1998; Beyer 1998; World Bank 1997).

REFORMING *CAUDILLOS* AND *EQUIPOS*

With such unreliable bureaucrats in most of the hemisphere, those Latin American leaders who have recognized what sorts of macroeconomic reforms are necessary—whether for personal political or long-term national reasons—have resorted to a typical Latin American approach to getting things done: strongmen, or *caudillos*. The *caudillo* in varying forms—military, presidential, and, more recently, ministerial—is endemic to Latin American history, and, under current conditions, a strongman or group of strongmen has been the logical and perhaps only way to undertake major reforms. José Piñera, one of Chile's most creative reformers, has argued that the key factor in the Chilean free-market revolution after 1973 was the power of the idea of liberty. But the idea, he says, was made a reality by a dedicated and coherent professional team, or *equipo*, made up mainly of economists, which was independent of the national establishment but nonetheless firmly supported by the government (Piñera 1993, 167, 170; 1997, 25). The first of these teams appeared in Chile after a military coup in 1973 and the sponsoring leader was General Augusto Pinochet.

A decade and more later, teams emerged under democratic presidents in most countries from Mexico to Argentina (Domínguez 1997). When reformers worked in more complex, somewhat freer societies than most in East Asia, they had to deal with such challenges of civil society as "the pervasive, persistent, and often 'invisible' influence of clientelist politicians, interest groups, and bureaucratic insiders" (Weyland 1997, 104). Under these more democratic circumstances, an elected president usually appointed a powerful economy minister, who brought with him a team of like-minded followers he had cultivated over the years. John Waterbury (1993) believes that "the crucial factor is the public backing of the team by the head of state" (27). With presidential backing, the best ministers, knowing that the task is as much political and cultural as economic, tried to generate public support through a variety of actions, ranging from close work with legislators—sometimes including bribing them to support reforms—to campaigns in the media.

LATIN AMERICAN CASE STUDIES

Latin American countries that have utilized teams to launch major reforms include Chile, Argentina, Mexico, and Peru. The following case studies show that Latin America's responses to the need for reform have not been nearly as institutionalized as those in Asia.

Chile

The first free-market reforming team went into action in Chile after the 1973 military coup that overthrew Socialist president Salvador Allende. In September 1973, Chile was on the brink of civil war, and some cities and areas of the countryside were in varying degrees of chaos. The new military overlords—who had been first brought into the government in 1972 by Allende himself—knew nothing about economics but, under the circumstances, were impressed by the proposals of the so-called Chicago Boys—most of whom had studied economics at the University of Chicago—and quickly gave them more freedom to act than any other group in Chile. By the time Pinochet relinquished power after the 1989 elections, Chile had the strongest economy in Latin America, with very broad popular support. Indeed, whereas public opinion polls in Chile in the early 1970s showed that an overwhelming majority favored an economy primarily under state control, by the late 1980s the vast majority had come to support just the opposite, Chile's new market economy. Popular support for the reforms was so strong that post-Pinochet presidents Patricio Aylwin and Eduardo Frei, Jr., both Christian Democrats who headed coalition governments including members of socialist parties, kept the economics basically unchanged while trying to expand social justice in the country.

Argentina

A century ago, Argentina was one of the fastest-developing countries in the world, seemingly destined to hold a place in what became the First World. But in the course of the twentieth century, Argentines decided to reverse direction and "opted to become a Third World nation" (Lewis 1990, 499). Indeed, state control was institutionalized and growth potential killed under Juan Perón during the very postwar years when Asian leaders got their sound macroeconomic reforms under way. Periodic post-Perón efforts to get macroeconomics right all failed until long-time Peronist populist Carlos Saúl Menem was elected president in 1989 amid soaring inflation and economic chaos. He immediately reversed all his populist campaign promises and began what he called "a complete structural, economic and social transformation of the country" (Menem 1990).

Argentina's economic reforms became the fastest on the continent after Menem appointed Domingo

Cavallo economy minister in January 1991. The president, his minister, and some hundreds of so-called Cavallo boys agreed to promote production and growth rather than redistribute goods on hand, with considerable success (Ratliff and Fontaine 1990). Cavallo later wrote that he and his team had the high responsibility of giving "a new organization to the economy based on rules of the game that were simple, transparent and automatically applied" (Cavallo 1997b, 60). He left office in 1996 with harsh criticism of corruption, the lack of transparency, and resurgent populism in the Menem government, pointing in particular to the need to reorganize the most intractable of the bureaucratic nightmares, education and social services (Cavallo 1997a, 1997b; López Murphy and Moskovits 1997).

Mexico

Miguel Centeno writes that during its decades of dominance in Mexico, the Institutional Revolutionary Party (PRI) "never functioned as a political party but rather as a 'political control' secretariat within the governing bureaucracy." In Latin America, only the Mexican PRI consistently built something like the Asian multiclass political alliance, but prior to the 1980s, when it held a monopoly on political power, the PRI adopted counterproductive macroeconomic policies. Carlos Salinas tightened the control of the presidency in the 1990s, while some Mexicans say he was an "effective president" even during much of Miguel de la Madrid's term, when the reforms

began under his leadership. The reforms of these years, Centeno continues, "would have been impossible without the centralization of power within a small nucleus inside the bureaucracy able to establish internal ideological homogeneity and to impose that vision on the rest of the regime" (Centeno 1997, 51, 75, 95, 141-42, 148; see also Camp 1995; Solís 1988).[3]

Camarillas, or political or professional networks that provided "the channels through which the new elite rose to power," have been central to the stability and cronyism, ideological and otherwise, of Mexican politics for decades. Like Argentine reformers, Mexican presidents de la Madrid and Salinas believed that social justice and reduced inequality would come from growth and greater employment rather than redistribution (Centeno 1997, 204), though this goal was not promoted nearly as effectively as in Asia. Some streamlining of governance went through fairly smoothly while in other cases—in customs and related areas, for example, where so many bureaucrats and others had so much to lose—change came gradually if at all (Ratliff 1998b; Cavallo 1997b). By the mid-1990s, many strong Mexican politicians inside the PRI had become openly critical of the power of the reform teams of the PRI president, saying that the teams had forgotten they were serving "the people." These generally old-style PRI politicians were branded "dinosaurs" but had considerable popular support (Ratliff 1997-98; Anderson 1998).

Peru

Over many decades, the Peruvian people came to openly distrust political parties and political promises even more than citizens in most other Latin American countries except perhaps Venezuela. By the end of his term in 1990, populist Aprista president Alán García had presided over the virtual collapse of the nation: inflation was 7000 percent, drug dealers were thriving, and the Sendero Luminoso guerrillas wrecked havoc almost at will around the country. The first round of the 1990 elections found free-marketer (and novelist) Mario Vargas Llosa and the virtually unknown middle-of-the-roader Alberto Fujimori thoroughly defeating the utterly discredited Left, which received only 10 percent of the vote. In the runoff election and afterward, Fujimori consistently presented himself as representing the anti-party, non-elite in a very elitist-led country, while Vargas Llosa discredited himself in the eyes of the voters by receiving the endorsement of some of the political elite. Fujimori took 70 percent of the votes in both shantytowns and highlands and became president.

As president, Fujimori immediately adopted a free-market program, and, after removing one legislature and getting its successor to change the Constitution, he was overwhelmingly reelected in 1995 (Fujimori 1996; Ratliff 1996). Peru's problem in the past was not that it lacked skilled and knowledgeable individuals and groups but that these groups did not want to tie themselves to discredited political parties. Fujimori, self-consciously operating as an outsider, could and did bring in the experts of the broader community (de Soto 1998).

Venezuela

With its rich petroleum reserves, good Caribbean location, and rich heritage, Venezuela might seem to have brighter prospects than most other Latin American countries, but this has not been the case. In recent decades, the country has had guerrilla wars and military coups, and, though it has had a significant period of democracy, its political parties have often been self-serving, corrupt, and dedicated to policies that are unresponsive to public needs. Frustrations and tensions rose for decades before the presidential election of December 1988 that sent a warning careening around Latin America. Hugo Chávez, a radical populist and former paratrooper, who had only years earlier led a bloody unsuccessful military coup, was overwhelmingly elected president. Chávez is a *caudillo* of the old sort but now in a democratic setting promising honesty, shared growth, jobs, and better health care and education.

Like Fujimori, Chávez pitted the rich against the poor, the "man of the people" against the self-serving elite and their traditional political parties. Even when, for the first time ever, all the traditional parties supported a single candidate, Chávez won by more than 15 percent. Typical comments by Venezuelan workers during the election campaign were: "If a dictatorship offers the kind of government where education, health care—all the public services—work, then I'm for it," and "Bring on the dictatorship, because this is no life" (Bajak 1998). Chávez's problems when he took office in early 1999 were not just a deeply divided and economically strapped country but a predictable challenge to live up to his campaign promises to the "masses." Having presented himself as the Messiah, people are likely to expect him to pass around the bread and fishes, but there are none. He will quickly find that populist promises may win elections, but they do not develop economies and meet the popular needs they raise. This election—like the Chiapas uprising in Mexico before it—was a shot across Latin America's bow, warning that populations will not wait forever for good leadership and may, in their frustration, opt for something even worse than they had (Ratliff 1998c).

RESULTS OF REFORMS
IN LATIN AMERICA

Although most Latin American countries were late in abandoning import-substitution industrialization and slow turning to market-oriented change, during the 1990s a number of countries made considerable progress in implementing first-generation economic reforms. As the World Bank points out, these reforms were largely drastic budget cuts, tax reform, price liberalization, trade and foreign-investment liberalization, deregulation, social funds, autonomous contracting agencies, and privatization. Second-generation reforms—in the areas of civil service, labor, social ministries, the judiciary, and central-local government relationships—that have usually been undertaken with some or much success in some Asian countries are just beginning, at best, in most of Latin America (World Bank 1997).

A study by the Cato and Fraser institutes ranked Chile and Costa Rica among the 15 nations that made the most progress in terms of market orientation between 1975 and 1990, while Argentina, the Dominican Republic, El Salvador, and Peru were among the 15 that made the most progress during the 1990-95 period. Latin America is still well behind Asia, and the Cato-Fraser study found that even Chile had a market orientation index significantly below the average of the industrialized and Asian nations. What is more, while Gini coefficients show that in East Asia the income gap decreased with rising overall productivity between 1965 and 1990, the same has not been true in Latin America. Concern that this gap will lead to social unrest—even when, as often happens, the overall standard of living has risen at least somewhat—has caused concern among those who know Latin American history (Root, Ratliff, and Morgan 1999). A similar set of indices from the International Country Risk Guide compares institutional foundations in Latin American and East Asian countries, specifically the quality of the judiciary, the level of corruption, and the quality of civil services. Latin American countries consistently have some of the greatest legal, political, and other problems in the developing world (Crossette 1995; Root, Ratliff, and Morgan 1999; Campos and Nugent 1997; Ratliff forthcoming; Buscaglia, Ratliff, and Cooter 1997).

South Korea encountered serious problems in 1998, but the following conclusions remain essentially correct on reforms and their results in Korea and Brazil, and as a generalization, the conclusions apply to much of Asia and Latin America generally:

In Korea, public policy—which contributed to high quality schooling, strong demand for labor and low income inequality—generated powerful incentives for the poor to invest in their children and to work more to finance that investment; in Brazil, public policy—which contributed to low quality schooling, weak demand for labor and high income inequality—created incentives for low levels of savings and investment among the poor and high levels of leisure. As a consequence, in Korea there was much more investment in human capital and much more "growth from below" than in Brazil. (Birdsall and Sabot 1997, 72)

CONCLUSION

East Asia's record shows that reforming nations must carry out sound macroeconomic policies with at least some effective aspects of civil society, prominent among them effective institutions and governance. Although inadequate transparency, cronyism, and other problems were central to the Asian crisis, leaders in the region often devised regulations, organizations, and institutions—in particular, higher-quality and more accountable civil services than in Latin America—to carry out economic policies focusing on the development of human capital and shared growth. In the past, at least, they effectively incorporated a broad cross section of the population in discussions and councils. Because of this, nationwide political support was deepened and government's actions were made more predictable and credible to all, from citizens to foreign investors.

Since the overlay of the past in Latin America has not been so shaken, much less shattered, by national and regional wars—or threats of communism—solutions were different from those in Asia. The emergence of political and economic *caudillos* and their teams recognized the reality that only thus could they undertake substantive free-market reforms by circumventing the embedded and largely intransigent existing bureaucratic institutions and some leadership elites. In some cases, the teams were largely independent of traditional political parties—as in Chile under Pinochet and Peru under Fujimori—while in others, a traditional party played a key role in placing and supporting the reforming team, as the Peronists did in Argentina and the PRI did in Mexico. In all cases, strong executive support was essential for such successes as were achieved. Without adequate presidential leadership, as in post-1989 Venezuela, reforms were much harder to launch, sell, and carry out, when they were tried at all (World Bank 1997, 156).

In the end, for a variety of reasons, Latin America's reforms seem to be on shakier long-term ground than many in Asia, though this became less so after mid-1997. Even the best Latin American reforms are mostly first generation and will hold and move ahead only with second-generation changes that are all the more difficult without long-term vision and good institutions. The prospects for moving from one stage to another are complicated when first-generation reforms were carried out via parallel structures, often creating distrust, resentment, and hostility between the teams of reformers and the bureaucrats who find their previously secure jobs or perks threatened. Historically, some reformers arrogantly excluded bureaucrats from participation in or even knowledge of the reforms. While in many respects understandable, this practice was also self-defeating because it left the latter not only hostile but ill trained to maintain the programs effectively—should they wish to do so—after the teams left. Also, as teams proliferate within as well as between administrations, rivalries or other failures of communication and cooperation may have serious consequences, a prime example being the Mexican peso crisis of 1994-95 (Ratliff 1998b; Golob 1997, 140).

There are often other serious problems with the team approach. Usually most attention is directed toward the critically important economy ministry, but reforms are essential in other ministries as well. In economic terms, most countries have high degrees of waste and corruption in social and education programs, for instance, which are extremely difficult to eliminate and can, over time, substantially weaken or undermine a national reform program. Also, while the primary focus of reformers is necessarily in and on central governments in capital cities, reforms must be implemented also in the provinces and municipalities or the effectiveness of even national-level change will be lessened or undercut. Although some beneficial changes have been made at lower levels, communication with the outlying areas has often been poor and enforcement of reforms and standards has often been difficult or impossible. Some of these problems exist as well in parts of East Asia.

There are other long-term dangers from dinosaurs, who would slow down or reverse reforms, and reform leaders themselves. Barbara Stallings has observed that Chilean reforms came under an authoritarian government—as did the earliest and most difficult Asian changes—and that this has made most other Latin Americans reluctant to hold Chile up as a model for development (Stallings 1997, 55). All the same, some Chilean reformers— for example, Hernán Buchi and José Piñera—have advised groups and governments all over the region and world since 1990. Most mainstream Latin American leaders and many citizens throughout the hemisphere today do shy away from dictators. But not all do, and this for several reasons. In line with its Hispanic history and culture, Latin Americans look to strong leaders to make changes or to stop them, some even suggesting that an authoritarian hand would be better than a democratic one. Over the past 20 years, I have heard many Latin Americans from Venezuela to Argentina say, "What we need is a Pinochet," meaning that they want an authoritarian government to impose market reforms as the Chilean government did without having to deal with the opposition that thrives in democracies.

But the call for a strongman may bring something very different in the future, perhaps beginning in earnest with Venezuela and Chávez. It could signal frustration with market reforms ineffectively or insincerely implemented, or simply the impatience that drives people to look for an easy way out through the redistributive policies that have so long been the bane of hopes for development in Latin America.

The other side of the same problem is reformers with limited power or dedication to carrying through. This has usually been rooted in either the difficulty of serious reform or the leader's private political interests, for not all politician reformers in democracies persist in changes when economic crises have passed, especially if doing so might threaten to undermine personal political power. There are reasons to suppose that, for many Latin American leaders, the turn toward sound macroeconomic policies was less deeply rooted—both theoretically and institutionally—than the turn in Asia. Hernando de Soto has written,

It is clear to me that the widespread support we see today for macroeconomic stabilization programs does not signal truly revolutionary changes in the thinking and objectives of Latin American leaders. These changes are prompted mainly by the need to respond somehow to hyperinflation and the chaos of the past. (de Soto 1997, xv)

Many of these leaders may be concerned that recent changes are, as

Timothy Brown says, "a confrontation between the emerging masses and entrenched oligarchies," which, if they continue, will in time "transform the region's political-economic systems away from highly stratified exclusionary patriarchies towards lowly stratified inclusionary societies" (Brown 1998, 43, 44). That is, the reforms today, if they are deepened and made to serve broader constituencies, could constitute the first true political, economic, and social revolutions in Latin American history, and it is far from certain that many Latin American elites support this level of change (Ratliff 1996-97). This may be true of many leaders, not just such obvious throwbacks to the past as Venezuelans Rafael Caldera and Hugo Chávez.

Despite first-generation progress, then, some analysts are skeptical about the longer-term prospects of many current reforms. To remedy this will require broadly based support for major civil-society and other second-generation changes. The challenge will be for leaders to persist in reforms or for the people to encourage or force them to do so. Víctor Bulmer-Thomas concludes his economic history of Latin America by noting that, "even if the goal is clear, the route forward is uncertain. Those countries that stumble through the incompetence, corruption, or greed of their elites can expect to be severely punished. That is the warning the privileged must heed" (Bulmer-Thomas 1994, 429). In addition, as Peruvian president Fujimori also warns, Latin Americans are not as patient as Asians (Fujimori 1996).

Finally, however, we must ask how patient—and how determined— are Asians themselves today? At the end of the twentieth century, both Latin Americans and East Asians face critical challenges across a broad spectrum. Without the life-or-death threat posed decades ago to East Asia and Chile by communism, one must wonder if current reforms will be deepened and consolidated, or will reformers in Latin America and even Asia be unable or unwilling to make the necessary hard decisions when critical situations arise? Will the significant economic and political shortcomings of what was indeed an Asian "miracle"— so mercilessly exposed since mid-1997—be dealt with as imaginatively as the (for many but not all countries) even greater challenges in the past? Japan's prolonged refusal to seriously face major banking and other problems that have been obvious for almost a decade is not at all encouraging. On the other hand, China's Zhu Rongji has shown a consistent willingness to deal creatively with major problems in his country, even though the challenges he faces are enormous and perhaps will prove to be overwhelming. Have Asian leaders—or which Asian leaders?—lost the insight and courage that enabled them to perform so brilliantly in decades past? The gauntlet has been thrown down for both them and Latin Americans, both of whom have accomplished much in the past. Their successes or failures in the future will deeply affect the lives of billions and not only in their countries but also the rest of the world.

Notes

1. For a review of the economic policies attempted during these decades, see Bulmer-Thomas 1994, 276-429. On the economics and politics of dependency, see Packenham 1992.

2. On the general problem of income distribution, see Bulmer-Thomas 1994, 308-22 and passim.

3. Leopoldo Solís, the mentor of many in the reform PRI, has long held up some aspects of the Asian experience for Latin America; see Solís 1988.

References

Anderson, John W. 1998. "Dinosaurs" Clash with Technocrats of Mexico's Soul. *Washington Post*, 6 Apr.

Bajak, Frank. 1998. Coup Plotter Leads Venezuela Polls. *Washington Post*, 5 Dec.

Becker, Gary and Guity Nashat Becker. 1997. *The Economics of Life*. New York: McGraw-Hill.

Beyer, Harald. 1998. Interview by author. Centro de Estudios Públicos, Santiago, Chile, 23 Apr.

Birdsall, Nancy and Frederick Jaspersen. 1997. Lessons from East Asia's Success. In *Pathways to Growth: Comparing East Asia and Latin America*, ed. Nancy Birdsall and Frederick Jaspersen. Washington, DC: Inter-American Development Bank.

Birdsall, Nancy, David Ross, and Richard Sabot. 1997. Growth and Inequality. In *Pathways to Growth: Comparing East Asia and Latin America*, ed. Nancy Birdsall and Frederick Jaspersen. Washington, DC: Inter-American Development Bank.

Birdsall, Nancy and Richard Sabot. 1997. Inequality, Savings and Growth in East Asia and Latin America. In *Rethinking Development in East Asia and Latin America*, ed. James W. McGuire. Los Angeles: Pacific Council on International Policy.

Brown, Timothy C. 1998. Realistic Revo-
lutions: Free Trade, Open Economies,
Participatory Democracy and Their
Impact on Latin American Politics.
Policy Studies Review 15(2-3):35-51.

Bulmer-Thomas, Víctor. 1994. *The Eco-
nomic History of Latin America Since
Independence*. New York: Cambridge
University Press.

Buscaglia, Edgardo, William Ratliff, and
Robert Cooter. 1997. *The Law and
Economics of Development*. Green-
wich, CT: JAI Press.

Bushnell, David. 1993. *The Making of
Modern Colombia*. Berkeley: University of California Press.

Camp, Roderic Ai. 1995. *Political Recruitment Across Two Centuries*. Austin: University of Texas Press.

Campos, José Eduardo and Hilton Root.
1996. *The Key to the Asian Miracle*.
Washington, DC: Brookings Institution.

Campos, Nauro F. and Jeffrey B. Nugent.
1997. Institutions and Capabilities. In
*Rethinking Development in East Asia
and Latin America*, ed. James W.
McGuire. Los Angeles: Pacific Council
on International Policy.

Cavallo, Domingo. 1997a. Interview by
author. Healdsburg, CA.

———. 1997b. *El peso de la verdad*. Buenos Aires: Planeta.

Centeno, Miguel Ángel. 1997. *Democracy
Within Reason*. University Park:
Pennsylvania State University Press.

Corrales, Javier. 1997. Why Argentines
Follow Cavallo. In *Technopols: Free-
ing Politics and Markets in Latin
America in the 1990s*, ed. Jorge
Domínguez. University Park: Penn-
sylvania State University Press.

Crossette, Barbara. 1995. A Global
Gauge of Greased Palms. *New York
Times*, 20 Aug.

de Madariaga, Salvador. 1959. *Bolívar*.
Vol. 2. Buenos Aires: Editorial Suda-
mericana.

de Soto, Hernando. 1997. Preface. In *The
Law and Economics of Development*,
ed. Edgardo Buscaglia, William Ratliff, and Robert Cooter. Greenwich,
CT: JAI Press.

———. 1998. Interview by author. Lima,
Peru, 13 Mar.

Domínguez, Jorge, ed. 1997. *Technopols:
Freeing Politics and Markets in Latin
America in the 1990s*. University
Park: Pennsylvania State University
Press.

Evaluation of Functionaries. 1998. *El
Mercurio* (Santiago, Chile), 11 Mar.

Fujimori, Alberto. 1996. Interview by
author. Lima, Peru, 28 June.

Golob, Stephanie R. 1997. Making Possi-
ble What Is Necessary. In *Technopols:
Freeing Politics and Markets in Latin
America in the 1990s*, ed. Jorge
Domínguez. University Park: Penn-
sylvania State University Press

Grosh, Margaret. 1994. *Administering
Targeted Social Programs in Latin
America*. New York: World Bank.

Halperín Donghi, Tulio. 1993. *The Contemporary History of Latin America*.
Durham, NC: Duke University Press.

Harberger, Arnold C. 1995. *Economic
Policy and Economic Growth*. San
Francisco: International Center for
Economic Growth.

Harrison, Lawrence E. 1985. *Underde-
velopment Is a State of Mind: The
Latin American Case*. Lanham, MD:
University Press of America.

———. 1997. *The Pan-American Dream:
Do Latin America's Cultural Values
Discourage True Partnership with the
United States and Canada?* New
York: Basic Books.

———. 1998. Interview by author. Washington, DC, 24 Feb.

Howard, Eleanor. 1997. Commentary. In
*Pathways to Growth: Comparing East
Asia and Latin America*, ed. Nancy
Birdsall and Frederick Jaspersen.
Washington, DC: Inter-American De-
velopment Bank.

International Labour Organization. Regional Office for Asia and the Pacific. 1998. *The Social Impact of the Asian Financial Crisis.*

Landes, David. 1998. *The Wealth and Poverty of Nations.* New York: Norton.

Lewis, Paul. 1990. *The Crisis of Argentine Capitalism.* Chapel Hill: University of North Carolina Press.

López Murphy, Ricardo. 1994. Commentary. In *La experiencia del Asia oriental.* Fundación de Investigaciones Económicas Latinoamericanas Documento de Trabajo, no. 40.

———, ed. 1995. *Fiscal Decentralization in Latin America.* Washington, DC: Inter-American Development Bank.

López Murphy, Ricardo and Cynthia Moskovits. 1997. *Decentralisation, Inter-Governmental Fiscal Relations and Macroeconomic Governance: The Case of Argentina.* Buenos Aires: Fundación de Investigaciones Económicas Latinoamericanas.

Mendoza, Plinio Apuleyo, Carlos Alberto Montaner, and Alvaro Vargas Llosa. 1996. *Manual del perfecto idiota latinoamericano.* Barcelona: Atlantida.

Menem, Carlos. 1990. Interview by author. Casa Rosada, Buenos Aires, Argentina, 7 May.

North, Douglass C. 1990. *Institutions, Institutional Change and Economic Performance.* New York: Cambridge University Press.

Packenham, Robert. 1992. *The Dependency Movement.* Cambridge, MA: Harvard University Press.

Page, John. 1997. The East Asian Miracle and the Latin American Consensus: Can the Twain Ever Meet? In *Pathways to Growth: Comparing East Asia and Latin America,* ed. Nancy Birdsall and Frederick Jaspersen. Washington, DC: Inter-American Development Bank.

Paz, Octavio. 1979. Reflections: Mexico and the United States. In *A New Moment in the Americas,* ed. Robert Leiken. New Brunswick, NJ: Transaction.

Piñera, José. 1993. *Camino nuevo.* Santiago, Chile: Economía y Sociedad.

———. 1997. *Libertad, libertad, mis amigos.* Santiago, Chile: Economía y Sociedad.

Rangel, Carlos. 1987. *The Latin Americans.* New Brunswick, NJ: Transaction Books.

Ratliff, William. 1996. Fujimori Speaks. *Wall Street Journal.* 23 Aug.

———. 1996-97. Will Latin America Finally Have a Real Revolution? *Journal of Interamerican Studies* 38(4):157-77.

———. 1997-98. Interviews of a probable Mexican presidential candidate by author. Mexico.

———. 1998a. Communication from a high-level Argentine reformer in Buenos Aires, 16 Mar.

———. 1998b. Interview of Mexican official by author. Stanford University, Stanford, CA.

———. 1998c. An Opportunity and a Warning for Latin America. *Los Angeles Times,* 11 Dec.

———. Forthcoming. Politics Bends the Law in Latin America: Three Case Studies. In forthcoming book, ed. Paul Rich and Guillermo De Los Reyes.

Ratliff, William and Roger Fontaine. 1990. *Changing Course: The Capitalist Revolution in Argentina.* Stanford, CA: Hoover Institution Press.

———. 1993. *Argentina's Capitalist Revolution Revisited: Confronting the Social Costs of Statist Mistakes.* Stanford, CA: Hoover Institution Press.

Root, Hilton. 1996. *Small Countries, Big Lessons: Governance and the Rise of East Asia.* New York: Oxford University Press.

Root, Hilton, William Ratliff, and Amanda Morgan. 1999. What Latin America Can Learn from Asia's Development Experience. In *Critical Issues for Mexico and the Developing World,* ed. Ken Judd. Stanford, CA: Hoover Institution Press.

Sánchez, Fabio and Catalina Gutiérrez. 1995. Colombia. In *Fiscal Decentralization in Latin America*, ed. Ricardo López Murphy. Washington, DC: Inter-American Development Bank.

Solís, Leopoldo. 1988. *Raúl Prebisch at ECLA*. San Francisco: International Center for Economic Growth.

Stallings, Barbara. 1997. Commentary. In *Pathways to Growth: Comparing East Asia and Latin America*, ed. Nancy Birdsall and Frederick Jaspersen. Washington, DC: Inter-American Development Bank.

Stromquist, Nelly P. 1997. Investment in Education and Women in Latin America and East Asia. In *Rethinking Development in East Asia and Latin America*, ed. James W. McGuire. Los Angeles: Pacific Council on International Policy.

Waisman, Carlos H. 1987. *Reversal of Development in Argentina*. Princeton, NJ: Princeton University Press.

Waterbury, John. 1993. *Exposed to Innumerable Delusions*. New York: Cambridge University Press.

Weyland, Kurt. 1997. Why So Little Bang for the Buck? In *Rethinking Development in East Asia and Latin America*, ed. James W. McGuire. Los Angeles: Pacific Council on International Policy.

World Bank. 1997. *World Development Report 1997: The State in a Changing World*. New York: Oxford University Press.

Yáñez, José and Leonardo Letelier. 1995. Chile. In *Fiscal Decentralization in Latin America*. ed. Ricardo López Murphy. Washington, DC: Inter-American Development Bank.

ANNALS, *AAPSS*, **565**, September 1999

Civil Society and NAFTA: Initial Results

By JOHN S. ROBEY

ABSTRACT: This article attempts to examine the initial results of the North American Free Trade Agreement (NAFTA). It is a preliminary review of examples of the successes and the failures of this historic agreement. The review leads to the conclusion that NAFTA has not been as successful as many had hoped. The usual economic reason given is the devaluation of the peso, but in this article, it is argued that the devaluation was the result of not only economic conditions but also cultural ones. The lack of intermediate groups between the state and the family as well as the lack of social capital has played a significant role in the economic development (or lack thereof) of Mexico. If NAFTA is to succeed, it may be that more attention must be given to creating the civil society.

John S. Robey is an associate professor of political science at the University of Texas–Brownsville. He has published social, political, and economic analyses of transportation, drug abuse, civil rights, and economic development policies in both the United States and Mexico.

NOTE: Support for the research reported in this article came from the University of Texas–Brownsville, which sent the author to the Puebla, Mexico, meeting of the Congress of the Americas.

F RANCIS Fukuyama contends in his book *Trust* (1995) that democratic capitalism appears to be the only alternative to which most countries may realistically aspire. Social engineering and even Keynesian countercyclical economics are seen to be self-defeating in the long term. The determining factor regarding the health of political and economic institutions is the civil society.

A civil society is a "complex welter of intermediate institutions, including business, voluntary associations, educational institutions, clubs, unions, media, charities and churches" (Fukuyama 1995, 4). These institutions are, in turn, the product of the institutional mainstay of society—the family. The family socializes the young and teaches them the values of society. It teaches them the skills needed to interact with and succeed in society. However, "strong and stable family structure . . . cannot be legislated into existence. . . . A thriving civil society depends on a people's habits, customs, and ethics—attributes that can be shaped only indirectly through conscious political action and must otherwise be nourished through an increased awareness and respect for culture" (Fukuyama 1995, 5).

Fukuyama maintains that the United States has been able to develop a strong cadre of intermediate groups between the family, on one end of the spectrum, and the state, on the other. But many Latin countries "exhibit a saddle-shaped distribution of organizations, with strong families, a strong state, and relatively little in between" (Fukuyama 1995, 5). The Latin countries are depicted as having great respect for the family but as lacking many of the intermediate organizations that make the civil society possible.

Robert Putnam's work on Italy draws attention to the importance of the civil society to economic development. "Civic community" is viewed as the degree to which people are organized in nonfamilial groups. In southern Italy, Putnam found a paucity of civic organizations (like labor unions, literary guilds, and music and sports groups). That was not the case in northern Italy, and he argues that the economic growth in northern Italy and the stagnation in southern Italy are related to "the degree of civic community or of spontaneous sociability that prevails in the respective regions" (Fukuyama 1995, 104).

Putnam contends that it is not economic development that leads to the civic society but civic society that leads to economic development. Fukuyama agrees and argues that the world's leading industrialized economies developed "because they had healthy endowments of social capital and spontaneous sociability, and not vice versa" (Fukuyama 1995, 110).

This poses something of a dilemma for those interested in the economic well-being of Mexico and in the success of the North American Free Trade Agreement (NAFTA). To the extent that Mexico conforms to the "saddle-shaped" civil society, the more difficult it may be for NAFTA to succeed. This article attempts to outline the evolution of NAFTA and examines some of its initial results. Are the successes and failures of the agreement due to cultural or economic causes or both?

The picture is very confusing because so many people and governmental agencies are issuing trade and job loss or gain figures that are contradictory. Few of the commentators do not have their own political agendas. Adding to the confusion is that an analysis of NAFTA must factor in the devaluation of the peso and the very severe recession that resulted in Mexico.

None of the economists, none of the sophisticated input-output models, and none of the politicians had foreseen such a swift collapse of the peso. It would appear that Mexico's economic collapse would have been even more severe without the U.S. guarantee of loans. It is also possible that the guarantees would not have been forthcoming without NAFTA.

NAFTA is a great experiment. For the first time, developed economies have said to a developing one, "Let us enter into an agreement that will closely intertwine our nations' economic destinies." Countries with well-developed systems of intermediate-level societal organizations are integrating their economies with a country that has not yet developed the civil society, at least not to the same degree.

No one knows what the long-term impact of this experiment will be. If the Clinton administration has its way, it is only the first step toward a hemisphere-wide free-trade zone extending throughout the Americas. The Americas Free Trade Agreement is to be the response of the Americas to the Asian tigers and the European Union.

There have been stumbling blocks with NAFTA. Examples include the peso's initial devaluation and its continuing deterioration into early 1999, Congress's reluctance to give the president fast-track authority to negotiate the admission of Chile to NAFTA, and the inability of the United States and Mexico to resolve disputes involving the weight and safety requirements of trucks. Little has been said about the devastation that has resulted in Mexico's lower classes, but that is a very significant problem as well.

There have also been some indications of substantial economic growth in all three countries that are a party to NAFTA. Mexico had to borrow funds during the economic crisis, but it paid back those funds early. Furthermore, it did so at a time when the price of oil was quite low. Institutions have been established where none existed before to monitor environmental and labor compliance with the terms of the treaty. A bank has been created to provide funding for environmental projects along the border, and additional infrastructure, in the form of roads and bridges, has been constructed to meet the growing trade between the three countries.

The creation of these institutions is not the same as the voluntary organizations promoted in the civil society literature. However, there is the hope that voluntary organizations could very well develop from their creation.

Some sectors of the U.S. economy may well be hurt by NAFTA (for example, tomato and citrus farmers, apparel and textile manufacturers, and border retail trade outlets). Others, however, will be helped (such as electronics, industrial equipment, and computers).

Has NAFTA helped Mexico, the United States, and Canada, or has it hurt them? In this article, I attempt to present a brief overview of the impact that NAFTA has had thus far. I concentrate on Mexico and the United States, with some emphasis on Texas. (Almost half of the United States's trade with Mexico goes through Texas.) If the agreement has not succeeded to the degree that many would have liked, would the nourishment of the civil society help, and is there still enough time to create such a society?

THE GENESIS OF NAFTA

In June 1990, Mexico and the United States issued a joint statement that supported the negotiation of a free-trade agreement, and President Bush notified Congress of his intent to negotiate such a treaty. In 1991, Canada agreed to join the negotiations, and the countries entered into trilateral discussions. Agreement was announced in August 1992. The goal of the agreement was to improve general living conditions by reducing the barriers to the free flow of goods, capital, and services.

The signatories announced that the objectives of the agreement were to

— eliminate barriers to trade in, and facilitate the cross-border movement of, goods and services between the territories of the parties;

— promote conditions of fair competition in the free-trade area;
— increase substantially investment opportunities in their territories;
— provide adequate and effective protection and enforcement of intellectual property rights in each party's territory;
— create effective procedures for the implementation and application of the agreement and for its joint administration and the resolution of disputes; and
— establish a framework for further trilateral, regional, and multilateral cooperation to expand and enhance the benefits of the agreement (U.S. Department of State 1992, 1-1).

Trade barriers and tariffs between Canada, Mexico, and the United States would be eliminated. The world's wealthiest and largest (over 360 million people) trading bloc would be created. Canada and the United States had negotiated a free-trade agreement in 1989. The trade between Canada and the United States was the largest amount of bilateral trade between any two nations in the world.

By bringing Mexico into the fold, the United States and Canada became the first countries with well-developed civil societies to extend free-trade status to a developing country that had not yet created the cultural infrastructure needed for a well-developed civil society. Because this was new and untested, many were worried about the impact of NAFTA.

During the debate over ratification, NAFTA enjoyed the support of the business community, but the loss of jobs was a concern of organized labor. In December 1991, President Salinas de Gortari of Mexico met with President Bush at Camp David. President Bush emphasized his support for the agreement but told him that because 1992 was an election year, NAFTA would not be submitted to Congress until after the election. Some political analysts believed that any legislation that could cost U.S. workers jobs posed a political risk that Congress would not wish to vote on in an election year (Huckshorn 1991).

Those opposed to the treaty included environmental activists, who were concerned that Mexico's lax environmental protection statutes would harm the rivers, air, and health of the peoples living in the Rio Grande Valley. The newly elected Clinton administration countered that $2 billion in the form of loan guarantees would be available to monitor pollution and to spend on cleanup projects (Lin 1993).

Opposition also came from independent presidential candidate Ross Perot, who claimed that NAFTA would put in jeopardy 5.9 million American jobs (Deans 1993). Little concern, however, was expressed for the *campesinos* in Mexico, who were suddenly confronted with the prospect of competing with large U.S. and Canadian agribusiness corporations.

The 2000-page treaty had been completed in August 1992, while President Bush was still in office. President Clinton announced that he would support the agreement, but he demanded three supplemental agreements on enforcement of environmental laws, guarantees of worker standards, and protection from sudden import surges.

RATIFICATION BY CONGRESS

In November 1993, Congress ratified NAFTA. One hundred fifty years of partisan divisions on international economics in Congress was reversed. The Democrats had traditionally supported lowering trade barriers, but the majority of them refused to support the treaty. The Republicans had traditionally been a protectionist party, but the majority of them voted for the agreement.

Change in Mexico was even more pronounced. For 50 years, Mexico had practiced economic nationalism. NAFTA meant a change not only in how Mexico would do business but even in how the country would look.

Harvard-educated President Salinas told his countrymen that free trade would deliver them from the Third World to the world of developed economies. He foresaw a rapid Americanization of Mexican consumer culture. Critics claim that he presented unrealistic expectations about what the agreement might accomplish. There was no debate about whether Mexico had the social capital or civil society that might be needed to make the agreement successful.

There were fears that Mexico would not be able to compete with the colossus to the North, but trade barriers had been falling since 1987, and Mexico was eager to attract foreign capital. President Salinas told his people, "I don't want Mexicans leaving the country anymore, only our products" (Golden 1992). Salinas believed that foreign capital would bring better wages, stronger industries, and cheaper services.

In one sense, NAFTA could be seen as a step toward the civil society with its emphasis on strong families. If NAFTA worked, maybe young men could stay home with their families and obtain work to support them. On the other hand, Mexico has never had a serious problem with weak familial institutions.

Offices were established to assist in the implementation of NAFTA. The office of the Labor Secretariat was established in Dallas, and San Antonio was picked to be the home of the North American Development Bank (NADBank). The Environmental Protection Agency (EPA) announced that it would open a regional office in El Paso, and the Border Environment Cooperation Commission established an office in Ciudad Juarez. It is not unreasonable to speculate that civic environmental organizations could develop as a by-product of the creation of these agencies.

The Labor Secretariat oversees the enforcement of labor laws and working conditions in the three countries. The NADBank is designed to work with the Inter-American Development Bank and was provided with $3 billion. Ninety percent of the $3 billion is to be used to finance environmental cleanup projects along the border, and the remaining 10 percent is earmarked for use by either Mexico or the United States for economic adjustment projects. El Paso's new EPA office opened in the fall of 1994 with a mandate to monitor border environmental projects.

In 1994, the World Bank announced that it had approved three loans. One of them, for $368 million, was authorized for the Northern Border Environment Project. The goal of this effort is to help cities enforce environmental protection laws. Twenty-three medium-sized cities were granted $200 million for the development of solid-waste services, and $350 million was loaned to Mexico to improve sanitation and water services (Campos Communications 1994, 3).

Not all the critics were satisfied, however. Ed Sills, communications director for the Texas AFL-CIO said, "Our reasons for opposing NAFTA remain valid. We see no evidence that the job flow is not going south as predicted. The environmental problems are not improving. The low wages along the border have not risen" (Kay 1994).

Three hundred economists, from conservatives like Milton Friedman to James Tobin, a noted liberal, sent a letter to President Clinton endorsing NAFTA. Citing a review of dozens of studies, Clinton said that "the effects on the U.S. economy—both good and bad—would be small for many years" (Nasar 1993).

NAFTA GOES
INTO EFFECT

The agreement went into effect on 1 January 1994. The impact on the U.S. economy was not dramatic. The tariffs in the United States on Mexican goods had already dropped to 4 percent, and the Mexican tariff was at a historical low of 10 percent. Texas's state comptroller, John Sharpe, released an analysis that maintained that "NAFTA [would] have a 'profound effect on Texas' future economy' and that without NAFTA, economic growth in Mexico would be 1.1 percent slower and job creation, 13 percent less" (Sharpe 1994, 1).

Sharpe's analysis projected that between 1992 and 2005, 17,400 jobs would be lost because of NAFTA but 139,600 jobs would be gained. Employment gains would be most pronounced in goods-producing industries such as electrical equipment and components, industrial machinery and computers, transportation equipment, and fabricated metal products. Those industries that were most vulnerable to free trade were retail border trade, the apparel industry, agricultural production (mostly tomatoes and citrus), and leather and leather products (Sharpe 1994, 3).

The initial results of NAFTA seemed encouraging. Charles Meissner, assistant U.S. secretary of commerce, came to the Rio Grande Valley and announced that, in the first six months of implementation, Mexican exports had increased 20 percent and U.S. exports to Mexico had jumped by 17 percent. In Laredo, 2500 18-wheelers were crossing the border every day. The San Antonio mayor announced that the city's unemployment rate was at a record low level, and the Big Three auto companies announced that they had shipped 23,275 cars to Mexico, compared to 3791 in the same period the previous year (Behr 1994, 74-75).

A survey of more than 1000 business executives by the KPMG Peat Marwick firm found that nearly half of U.S. companies planned, or already had launched, efforts to capitalize on the opportunities that NAFTA presented (Mexico Market 1994). At the end of the year, however, not all the news was so rosy. The Southwest Trade Adjustment Center, which assists companies that are hurt by trade, maintained that NAFTA "is really hurting our apparel industry. If it's labor intensive, it's on its way out, it's heading south" (Allen 1994).

In 1994, more than 200 U.S. firms moved their operations to Mexico, and more than 9200 workers qualified for a federal program aimed at assisting workers who are displaced because of NAFTA (Nusser 1994). In El Paso's apparel industry, 500 workers lost their jobs as the owners moved across the river to take advantage of cheaper labor (Valdez 1994).

On 20 December 1994, the Mexican government decided to let the peso float. By the end of January 1995, the peso had lost 50 percent of its value. Kimberly-Clark, PepsiCo, and Southwestern Bell all announced that they would take a fourth quarter charge because of currency exchange losses in Mexico. Wal-Mart curtailed its expansion plans, and Federal-Mogul Corporation announced that earnings would be hurt (Lamiell 1995).

Ford, Mercedes-Benz, and Volkswagen de México SA announced that they would suspend expansion operations. Gary Hufbauer, a trade expert with the Institute for

International Economics in Washington, D.C., surveyed the damage and announced that, regarding NAFTA, "without a doubt, the optimism in retrospect was way overblown" (Kalish 1995).

The Confederation of Mexican Workers announced that two businesses a day had been closing in Mexico since the inception of the crisis, and the nation's giant oil monopoly, Pemex, announced that 3000 of its employees would be laid off (DePalma 1995). Even plants in the United States were being forced to close. When the employees of RCA Thomson in Ciudad Juarez went on strike because their wages were not keeping up with the devaluation of the peso, 2400 workers were laid off in Indiana and North Carolina due to a lack of essential parts from the Juarez plant (Garcia 1995). Clearly, some type of economic intervention was necessary.

President Clinton proposed a $40 billion loan guarantee package. The president announced that his program was not a "bailout for big business" and that the United States had a lot at stake in Mexico. His proposal was not viewed favorably by the public; 70 percent of the public opposed the loan guarantee. But the governor of Texas, George W. Bush, announced his support. The governor said that the jobs of 260,000 Texans were linked to exports to Mexico (Kay 1994).

There were instances in which jobs were lost to Mexico, and some in Congress thought it best to withdraw from the agreement. Trade figures for 1995 showed that, during the first five months of that year, the United States ran a trade deficit of $6.9 billion. One year earlier, the United States had had a $1 billion trade surplus with Mexico. Opponents of NAFTA maintained that by running a deficit of $6.9 billion, the United States had lost more than 124,000 jobs. The big losers were the electronics and auto manufacturers, whose sales decreased by 50 percent (Nusser 1995).

When NAFTA was passed, President Clinton announced that that was "a defining moment for our nation," and supportive economists predicted that 170,000 jobs would be created during the first year. Because of the Mexican recession and the lack of social capital, that job creation did not occur. In fact, some jobs did go south. Professor Philip Martin, of the University of California–Davis, pointed out that it was cheaper to produce lettuce in the United States using Mexican labor than it was to produce it in Mexico. The unforeseen effect was an increase in the demand in the United States for Mexican workers. NAFTA was supposed to open up opportunities in Mexico that would reduce the immigration from Mexico (Sterngold 1995).

Another unforeseen consequence of NAFTA was the continued growth of border maquiladoras. The original theory was that, since tariffs would be eliminated, there would be little incentive to continue to build the maquiladoras along the border. Labor and land would be cheaper in the interior, and it would be the interior of Mexico that would see a growth in the maquiladora plants.

The devaluation of the peso, however, made border industries very profitable. They were paying less in wages (in dollar terms), and they were still close to the markets and transportation infrastructure of the United States. The result was that there was substantial growth in the number of maquiladoras even during the recession. Mexico approved the applications of over 300 new maquiladoras in 1995. This was an 80 percent increase over the previous year. However, only a minority of them were in Mexico's interior (Downie 1996).

Environmentalists were outraged when Mexico decided to relax environmental standards. Victor Escoto Zubiran, a Mexican attorney in Matamoros specializing in representing U.S. companies, responded that the Mexican recession had forced Mexico to set the attraction of industry as its first priority, and environmental protection would be second. This was exactly the opposite of what had been hoped that NAFTA would achieve. NAFTA was meant to encourage the border areas to stiffen environmental standards, not relax them (Nusser 1995, A5).

In December 1996, researchers at the University of California–Los Angeles published the results of research that claimed that NAFTA had a near-zero impact on the U.S. economy. The study found that NAFTA had cost the United States 38,000 jobs but that NAFTA had also created an additional 59,000 jobs (Vindell 1996).

At the end of 1996, many Mexicans found themselves wondering where all the new fortune that was to have come with NAFTA had gone. During 1996 in Mexico, a guerrilla war erupted in Chiapas, a presidential candidate was assassinated, the peso lost half of its value, and the purchasing power of most Mexicans was eroded. Some economic indices were showing that Mexico's economic collapse had bottomed out, and other indicators showed that the country was still mired in a guerrilla war and hampered by political instability.

Another problem that has not been successfully addressed is harmonization of truck weight and safety standards. Originally, NAFTA trucking rules were scheduled to go into effect on 18 December 1995. The Clinton administration blocked their implementation because of concern about the safety of Mexican trucks, which weigh up to 120,000 pounds. The U.S. interstate system was constructed to carry trucks that weigh 80,000 pounds. In 1996, Mexican trucks were to have access throughout the border states (that is, Texas, New Mexico, Arizona, and California), and by the year 2000 they were to have access throughout the United States and Canada. Mexican drivers are not screened for drugs, and their hours behind the wheel are not regulated.

Union leaders were concerned that Mexican drivers would put U.S. drivers out of business. Mexican drivers earned about $7 a day, and

U.S. drivers were averaging $19 an hour. Teamster International vice president John Riojas maintained that 50 percent of the trucks that are inspected when entering the United States from Mexico are turned back due to improper licenses, substandard tires, faulty brakes, unsecured loads, underage drivers, or the presence of toxic or hazardous cargo.

One interesting offshoot of the trucking controversy is found in the bus industry. NAFTA had given bus companies in the United States and in Mexico the right to carry passengers throughout each other's countries. Mexico has a very sophisticated bus industry. U.S. citizens make 25 million to 30 million long-distance bus trips per year. Mexicans make about 250 million such trips. Greyhound wanted to expand to offer bus service in Mexico and formed a partnership with the Crucero Mexican bus company. However, the partners never got all the applications approved.

Greyhound spokesman George Graveley announced that the approvals were denied as retaliation for the United States's denial of entrance to Mexico's trucks (Beachy 1997). It is more likely that the failure is due to cultural factors. Mexico has a tradition of protectionism. Most businesses are controlled within the family. There has been a reluctance to trust people who are not part of the family in business affairs. This impedes the development of the civil society, which requires intermediate groups working on behalf of a civic good.

CONCLUSION

Ronald Inglehart writes that "there is no question that economic factors are politically important, but they are only part of the story" (Inglehart 1988, 1203). What many failed to appreciate when NAFTA was inaugurated was the dearth of social capital in Mexico and the declining amount in the United States. Putnam found that, since 1972, there has been a decline of social capital defined as the number of visits by individuals to family and friends, the amount of trust expressed in other people, how involved people are in politics, and the number of organizations to which people belong (Putnam 1995, 134).

If it is the civil society that leads to economic development, and if the attributes of the civil society are sparse in one area and declining in another, it may not bode well for supporters of NAFTA. Paul Rich and Guillermo De Los Reyes (1998) write that "political culture has been underused in analysis of the current Mexican situation" (17). The emphasis on economic analysis, and the paucity of cultural research occurred at a very inopportune time.

What is one to make of the contradictory reports regarding the success of NAFTA thus far? It may well be that both the supporters and the opponents of NAFTA are overstating their cases. NAFTA may have accelerated some economic trends that were already in place, but it did not create them. It would appear that NAFTA will have a small impact on the U.S. economy, but, depending on where in the United States (for example, El Paso or other border areas), the impact could be significant. The impact on Mexico has been and will continue to be much more pronounced. Mexico's economy is smaller and more easily influenced by the course of economic events in the United States than the other way around.

This is not necessarily true for all parts of the United States. Border areas are particularly vulnerable to the vicissitudes of the Mexican economy. Certain sectors of the economy, such as border retail trade, and agricultural components, such as citrus, tomato, and other vegetable producers, may suffer as tariffs are phased out. Overall, it is too early to say how NAFTA will play itself out. NAFTA is to be phased in over a 15-year period. It would be premature to come to final conclusions after only four years, especially if during those four years economic anomalies—such as the 1994 devaluation and the 1995-96 recession—were present.

Added infrastructure on both sides of the border have been built to try to meet the projected demands created by increased trade due to NAFTA. Institutional arrangements are now in place to attempt to protect workers and the environment that did not exist prior to NAFTA.

Binational cooperation between Mexico and the United States is accelerating. Comprehensive regional planning is being done that attempts to address the problems of the frontier from the coordinated perspective of both sides of the river. The river has always been an artificial border in many respects. The typical Hispanic U.S. citizen that resides in Brownsville has much more in common with the culture of his neighbor in Matamoros than he does with his fellow countryman in Alaska. Likewise, the typical resident of Matamoros is much more comfortable with his compadre in Texas than he is with the indigenous peoples of the Yucatan.

There are, according to many people who live on the border, really three cultural entities. There is Mexico, there is the United States, and then there are people from the border areas where these two countries meet. These people have their own binational relationships, slang, customs, and so forth. It may be that the border states of Mexico and the United States will be more affected as NAFTA is implemented than will be the economies of the United States or Mexico in general.

It is the border areas of these two countries where the most pronounced differences in the development of the civil society may be observed. If NAFTA has done nothing else, it has brought these cultures closer together. As the two economies become more intertwined, the groundwork is being created for what may develop into a border civil society and perhaps a more stable and prosperous North America.

NAFTA has not been as successful as it might have been because of the glacial pace of change in culture. Politics in Mexico is still dominated by the Institutional Revolutionary Party (PRI), and the PRI still practices *personalismo*. It is not easy to accelerate cultural change, and, for many in Mexico, NAFTA has been a disaster. Rich and De Los Reyes (1998) write, "The NAFTA-sponsored lowering of trade barriers meant that the poor in Mexico, particularly the *campesinos* or peasants, faced competing with Canadian and U.S. industry and agribusiness" (18).

At the time of writing (early 1999), the peso continues in a slow downward spiral. What few social programs that did exist for the benefit of the poor are being dismantled, and the buying power of those lucky enough to be employed is diminishing. NAFTA's success, perhaps the success of all of North America, may rely not on economic policy but on devising policies that will induce the disenchanted to return and give the civil society another chance. That may not be an easy task to accomplish, given the skepticism that exists, yet there may be no other viable alternative.

References

Allen, Michael. 1994. When NAFTA Causes Pain, Not Everyone Will Suffer. *Wall Street Journal*, 24 Aug.

Beachy, Debra. 1997. Greyhound Hopes New Route Draws More Mexican Riders. *Houston Chronicle*, 9 Feb.

Behr, Peter. 1994. In the NAFTAmath, Some Texas-Sized Gains. *Washington Post Weekly Edition*, 29 Aug., 74-75.

Campos Communications. 1994. *NAFTA Works: An Update for Hispanics*, 19 July, 3.

Deans, Bob. 1993. Clinton Vows Fight to Pass Trade Pact. *Austin American Statesman*, 15 Sept.

DePalma, Anthony. 1995. Mexico's Big Companies Take Huge Exchange Losses. *Austin American Statesman*, 31 Jan.

Downie, Andrew. 1996. New Maquiladoras Not Border-Bound. *Houston Chronicle*, 9 May.

Fukuyama, Francis. 1995. *Trust: The Social Virtues and the Creation of Prosperity*. New York: Free Press.

Garcia, James. 1995. Mexican Workers on Border Strike. *Austin American Statesman*, 4 Feb.

Golden, Tim. 1992. In Free Trade, Mexico Sees an Economy in U.S. Image. *New York Times*, 23 July.

Huckshorn, Kristin. 1991. Bush May Postpone Free-Trade Treaty. *Austin American Statesman*, 12 Dec.

Inglehart, Ronald. 1988. The Renaissance of Political Culture. *American Political Science Review* 82(4):1203-30.

Kalish, David. 1995. U.S. Investors Bail out of Mexico. *Austin American Statesman*, 15 Jan.

Kay, Michele. 1994. Texas Becomes Center of NAFTA Activities. *Austin American Statesman*, 6 June.

Lamiell, Patricia. 1995. Peso's Problems Could Hinder U.S. Stocks, Analysts Warn. *Austin American Statesman*, 15 Jan.

Lin, Jennifer. 1993. Bentsen Says Tough Fight Ahead for NAFTA. *Austin American Statesman*, 4 Sept.

Mexico Market Draws Nearly Half of Firms Surveyed After NAFTA. 1994. *Wall Street Journal*, 12 May.

Nasar, Sylvia. 1993. Economists Predict Small Effect on U.S. from Free Trade. *Austin American Statesman*, 18 Sept.

Nusser, Nancy. 1994. NAFTA's Effect on Jobs Proving Perot's Predictions Wrong. *Austin American Statesman*, 21 Nov.

———. 1995. NAFTA's Effect So Far: Jobs, Trade Headed South. *Austin American Statesman*, 20 July.

Putnam, Robert. 1995. Bowling Alone: America's Declining Social Capital. *Journal of Democracy* 6:65-78.

Rich, Paul and Guillermo De Los Reyes. 1998. Community and Political Cultures in Post-NAFTA Mexico. Paper presented to the meeting of the American Political Science Association, Boston, MA.

Sharpe, John. 1994. The Year of NAFTA: Texas' New Trade Connection. *Fiscal Notes* Nov.:3-6.

Sterngold, James. 1995. Losses Mixed with Gains Give NAFTA a Dual Character. *Austin American Statesman,* 9 Oct.

U.S. Department of State. 1992. *The North American Free Trade Agreement.*

Valdez, Diana Washington. 1994. 500 Workers Eligible for Retraining. *El Paso Times,* 27 Sept.

Vindell, Tony. 1996. NAFTA Not to Blame for Job Slump. *Brownsville Herald,* 20 Dec.

Civil Society and Political Elections: A Culture of Distrust?

By ANDREAS SCHEDLER

ABSTRACT: After a long history of electoral fraud and especially after the fraudulent and conflictive presidential elections of 1988, Mexicans entered the 1990s with deep skepticism toward political elections. In the present decade, however, government and opposition parties have agreed to several profound electoral reforms that have succeeded in bringing fraud under control. How have Mexican citizens reacted to these institutional changes? Have they hibernated under the protective cover of an unchanging culture of distrust? Alternatively, have they adapted their expectations and perceptions of electoral fraud to the new democratic realities? The present article supports the hypothesis of change. Through analysis of data from various opinion polls, it arrives at an optimistic picture: trust in elections has steadily increased since 1988. Yet this optimism is diminished by a note of caution: more recent surveys indicate that distrust may be reemerging in the face of the critical presidential elections of the year 2000.

Andreas Schedler is professor of political science at the Facultad Latinoamericana de Ciencias Sociales in Mexico City. He also coordinates the SEA Network—Studies in Electoral Administration. Previously he was assistant professor of political science at the Austrian Institute for Advanced Studies. His current research focuses on Mexico's Federal Electoral Institute. His latest book (coedited with Larry Diamond and Marc F. Plattner) is The Self-Restraining State: Power and Accountability in New Democracies *(1999).*

NOTE: The author thanks Alduncin and Associates, the Centro de Investigación y Docencia Económicas, the Centro de Estudios de Opinión Pública, the Federal Electoral Institute, and Market and Opinion Research International Mexico for providing access to their data. He also thanks the Austrian Academy of Sciences for support of work on this article through the Austrian Program for Advanced Research and Technology.

L ESS than a decade ago, Mexico enjoyed a solid reputation as one of the world's leading manufacturers of electoral fraud. In its decades of authoritarian hegemony, the ruling Institutional Revolutionary Party (PRI), founded in 1929, was always willing (and known to be willing) to resort to electoral fraud—be it to embellish results, deter potential competitors, or keep opposition parties out of power. However, it was only in the mid-1980s—when opposition parties (especially the conservative Party of National Action in the North and later the left-wing Party of the Democratic Revolution in central and southern regions) gradually became able to challenge the PRI at the polls—that electoral fraud turned into a regular mechanism to decide electoral contests. Not surprisingly, postelectoral conflicts, often peaceful and sometimes violent, became a recurrent phenomenon as well.

The 1988 presidential elections fit perfectly into the logic of fraud escalating in response to the new competitiveness of the party system. It is probably no exaggeration to say that they represented "the most egregious violation of norms for free and fair elections in modern Mexico" (Eisenstadt 1999, 84). As a consequence, opposition parties' historical distrust in elections became monumental, and the wide credibility gap that had opened up looked unbridgeable.

Afterward, in several rounds of negotiated electoral reforms (in 1989-90, 1993, 1994, and 1995-96), parties struggled to render elections not only clean but also, and above all, credible. Electoral credibility was not just one goal among others that the reformers pursued. It was their genuine obsession. In fact, the distrust-driven reforms that they implemented overhauled Mexico's entire system of electoral administration and eventually pushed the country over the threshold of electoral democracy. Today, political elections in Mexico arguably fulfill democratic minimum standards; they are basically free, competitive, clean, and even fair (at least at the national level).

The control of electoral fraud has brought political party elites to accept the democratic game. Extrainstitutional postelectoral conflicts, which were so common until the mid-1990s, have become rare exceptions. But to what extent did this success story of institutional transformation change mass attitudes? To what extent did it affect citizen perceptions of electoral fraud? Did the endemic distrust that reigned before give way to more trusting attitudes, or are post-hegemonic systems such as Mexico's condemned to live with low levels of electoral credibility?[1]

BUILDING TRUST

In recent years, political science has rediscovered the importance of trust in politics. Seminal works such as Robert Putnam's *Making Democracy Work* (1993) and Francis Fukuyama's *Trust* (1995) have argued forcefully that trust matters— for the working of political as well as economic institutions, for democracy as well as for capitalism. These books have treated trust basically as an independent variable, which is either present in "civic communities" (Putnam) or "social virtue" (Fukuyama) or else is absent. Accordingly, they conceive eventual changes in levels of societal trust as cultural changes that are notoriously slow and take decades or even centuries to materialize.

The present focus on trust as a dependent variable inverts this perspective. Rather than as an exogenous and fixed parameter that determines institutional performance, it treats trust as an endogenous variable that may change in response to changing institutions. What is more, it also inverts the normative perspective on trust. In an authoritarian regime that stages fraudulent elections on a regular basis, institutional trust cannot be considered an attribute of civic virtue. In such a context, only the ignorant and the authoritarian trust in elections, while democrats do not. It is only in the course of democratization that rational democratic citizens may come to give the electoral process their seal of approval. But how long does it take them to abandon their well-founded caution acquired in decades of authoritarian electoral manipulation? Will they be able and willing to adapt their views to new realities, or will old habits of thinking prevail over new irritating experience by sheer force of mental inertia?

In the debate on political culture and democracy, many authors have long taken the view that there is no such thing as hard cultural prerequisites of democratic governance. Rather, culture and institutions interact, and, historically at least, some democracies have been able to create, after their foundation, the

cultural infrastructure they need to survive and to thrive. Norms may be hard to change, but, as the following reconstruction of trust in electoral institutions reveals, at least some cognitive aspects of political culture may be more malleable than we are usually inclined to assume.

METHODOLOGICAL PITFALLS

Public opinion research was close to nonexistent in Mexico until the late 1980s. In the 1990s, it took off quickly, but survey research on electoral issues has been uneven and dispersed. It is therefore difficult, first, to obtain the data and, then, to establish intelligible time series. Table 1 presents the results of a first, unprecedented effort to compile the existing data on public perceptions of electoral fraud since 1988. Summing up the results of 23 nationwide surveys, it contains 29 items that address the issue of electoral credibility in a direct way.[2]

I did my best to arrange the data in a clear, simple, and accessible way. The mere amount of data as well as their heterogeneous nature, however, creates an image of disorder, complex and impenetrable. A good table can be read and understood at a quick glance. This one cannot. The trust index reported in the extreme right-hand column, however, sums up a good deal of information.

The index shows the "correlation of forces" between trustful and skeptical respondents, with positive signs indicating that the former outnumber the latter, and negative signs

(text continues on p. 132)

TABLE 1

PERCEPTIONS OF ELECTORAL FRAUD IN MEXICO, NATIONWIDE OPINION POLLS, 1988-98 (Percentages)

Question Number	Survey Date	Question Wording	++	+	0	−	−−	Extreme Values (Positive/ Negative)	Trust Index
		1988 Federal Elections							
1	June 1988	In Mexican elections, there is no / some / widespread fraud.[1]	8		26		59	08/59	−51
2	1989	In the 1988 elections, the PRI won / who knows / did not win.[2]	23		32		36	23/68	−45
3	July 1991	In the 1988 elections, the vote was definitely respected / respected / regularly respected / not respected / definitely not respected.[3]	3	20	5	41	12	23/53	−30
4	Aug. 1991	The 1988 elections were very clean / clean / don't know / dirty / very dirty.[4]	4	30	33	23	8	34/31	3
		1991 Federal Elections							
5	July 1991	In the upcoming elections, the vote will be definitely respected / respected / regularly respected / not respected / definitely not respected.[5]	3	39	9	24	8	42/32	10
6	July 1991	The upcoming federal elections will be less than clean.[6]					61	—/61	—
7	July 1991	The upcoming federal elections will be clean / there will be some fraud but it will not affect the results / there will be more serious fraud affecting local and state elections but not national results / the final results at all levels will be corrupted.[7]	30	29	16		17	75/17	58
8	Aug. 1991	In the upcoming elections, there will be no fraud / don't know / fraud.[8]	39		24		36	39/36	3
9	Sep. 1991	In the past federal elections, there was no fraud / don't know / fraud.[9]	11		33		54	11/54	−43
10	Sep. 1991	The official results of the past federal elections are real / don't know / not real.[10]	56		22		19	56/19	37
11	Sep. 1991	The past federal elections were very clean / clean / don't know / dirty / very dirty.[11]	10	59	14	12	2	69/14	55
12	Sep. 1991	The past federal elections were very clean / somewhat clean / somewhat dirty / very dirty.[12]	14	41		19	11	55/30	25
		1994 Federal Elections							
13	Feb. 1993	The 1994 federal elections will be very clean / clean / neither clean nor fraudulent / fraudulent / very fraudulent.[13]	5	33	10	34	7	38/41	−3

(continued)

TABLE 1 Continued

Question Number	Survey Date	Question Wording	++	+	0	−	−−	Extreme Values (Positive/ Negative)	Trust Index
14	Oct. 1993	The 1994 presidential elections will be clean / neither clean nor fraudulent / fraudulent.[14]	45		8		37	45/37	8
15	May 1994	In the upcoming federal elections, the PRI or the government will not be able to alter results to its benefit / don't know / will be able.[15]	43		15		41	43/41	2
16	July 1994	The upcoming federal elections will be less than clean.[16]					47	—/47	—
17	July 1994	In the upcoming elections, the vote will be definitely respected / respected / regularly respected / not respected / definitely not respected.[17]	10	42	17	15	9	52/24	28
18	Sep. 1991	In the past federal elections, there was no fraud / don't know / fraud.[18]	55		14		29	55/29	26
19	Sep. 1994	The past federal elections were very clean / clean / don't know / dirty / very dirty.[19]	6	56	10	21	3	62/24	38
20	1995	Generally speaking, elections in Mexico are clean / fraudulent.[20]	12					12/—	—
21	Feb. 1996	I believe very much / little / not at all in the results the Federal Electoral Institute gives.[21]	51		34		7	51/7	44

1997 Federal Elections

Question Number	Survey Date	Question Wording	++	+	0	−	−−	Extreme Values (Positive/ Negative)	Trust Index
22	June 1997	In the upcoming elections, the vote will be definitely respected / respected / regularly respected / not respected / definitely not respected.[22]	13	47	19	18	3	60/21	39
23	July 1997	The past federal elections were clean / somewhat clean / not clean.[23]	54		18		22	54/22	32
24	July	The results of the past federal elections were very trustworthy / little trustworthy / not at all trustworthy.[24]	70		22		3	70/3	67

2000 Federal Elections

Question Number	Survey Date	Question Wording	++	+	0	−	−−	Extreme Values (Positive/ Negative)	Trust Index
25	1997	Generally speaking, elections in Mexico are clean / fraudulent.[25]	39				55	39/55	−16
26	Dec. 1997	Elections in Mexico are already clean / partially clean / not clean.[26]	30		23		47	30/47	−17
27	Aug. 1998	Elections in Mexico are already clean / partially clean / not clean.[27]	18		27		55	18/55	−37
28	1998	Generally speaking, elections in Mexico are clean / fraudulent.[28]	28				68	28/68	−40
29	Dec. 1998	Elections in Mexico are already clean / partially clean / not clean.[29]	19		27		55	19/55	−36

SOURCES:

1. Consultores 21, nationwide poll ($n = 1397$). Quoted in Domínguez and McCann 1996, 157.

2. Centro de Estudios de Opinión Pública (CEOP), "Encuesta nacional 1989 Los Angeles Times" ($n = 487$). Precise date not reported. Available at Market and Opinion Research International (MORI) Mexico, Concepción Beistegui 515, Col. del Valle, Del. Benito Juárez, CP 03100 Mexico City, telephone +525/687-9728.

3. CEOP, "Encuesta nacional Este País" ($n = 1606$). Available at MORI Mexico.

4. Asesoría Técnica de la Presidencia de la República, "Ambiente federal electoral: Encuesta nacional pre-electoral" ($n = 5000$). Available at the Centro de Investigación y Docencia Económicas (CIDE), Division of Political Studies, Carretera México-Toluca 3655, Col. Lomas de Santa Fé, Del. Alvaro Obregón, CP 01210, Mexico City, telephone +525/727-9800.

5. CEOP, "Encuesta nacional Este País" ($n = 1606$). Available at MORI Mexico.

6. Gallup México, 1991 preelection survey ($n = 3053$). Original wording and categories not reported. Quoted in McCann and Domínguez 1998, 488.

7. Gallup México, 1991 preelection survey ($n = 3053$). Quoted in Domínguez and McCann 1996, 157.

8. Asesoría Técnica de la Presidencia de la República, "Ambiente federal electoral: Encuesta nacional pre-electoral" ($n = 5000$). Available at CIDE.

9. Asesoría Técnica de la Presidencia de la República, "Ambiente federal electoral: Encuesta pos-electoral nacional" ($n = 5000$). Available at CIDE.

10. Asesoría Técnica de la Presidencia de la República, "Ambiente federal electoral: Encuesta pos-electoral nacional" ($n = 5000$). Available at CIDE.

11. Asesoría Técnica de la Presidencia de la República, "Ambiente federal electoral: Encuesta pos-electoral nacional" ($n = 5000$). Available at CIDE.

12. CEOP, "Encuesta nacional Los Angeles Times" ($n = 1534$). Available at MORI Mexico.

13. MORI Mexico, "Encuesta nacional Excélsior—Este país" ($n = 1451$). Available at MORI Mexico.

14. MORI Mexico, "Encuesta Bendixen" ($n = 1224$). Available at MORI Mexico.

15. Asesoría Técnica de la Presidencia de la República, "Ambiente federal electoral: Campaña, medios, IFE" ($n = 5000$). Available at CIDE.

16. Ciencia Aplicada, 1994 preelection poll ($n = 1526$). Original wording and categories not reported. Quoted in McCann and Domínguez 1998, 488.

17. MORI Mexico, "Encuesta nacional Excelsior—Este País" ($n = 2896$). Available at MORI Mexico.

18. Asesoría Técnica de la Presidencia de la República, "Ambiente federal electoral: Proceso electoral del 21 de agosto" ($n = 5000$). Available at CIDE.

19. Asesoría Técnica de la Presidencia de la República, "Ambiente federal electoral: Proceso electoral de 21 agosto" ($n = 5000$). Available at CIDE.

20. Latinobarómetro 1995 (sample size not reported). Precise date not reported. Quoted in Molina and Hernández 1998, 25.

21. Instituto Federal Electoral, "La reforma electoral y su contexto sociocultural" ($n = 3505$). Reported in Instituto Federal Electoral and Universidad Nacional Autónoma de México 1996, 140.

22. Alduncin and Associates, and El Universal, Department of Public Opinion Studies, "Encuesta elecciones federales 1997" ($n = 1260$). Street interviews, stratified random sample. Available at Alduncin y Asociados, Montaña de Auseva 40, Col. Jardines en la Montaña, Del. Tlalpan, CP 14210 Mexico City, telephone +525/630-1942.

23. CIDE and Asesoría Técnica de la Presidencia de la República, "Encuesta nacional sobre el votante mexicano" ($n = 2050$). Reported in Beltrán 1997, 424.

24. Instituto Federal Electoral, "Evaluación post-electoral del proceso electoral federal de 1997 y de la imagen del IFE" ($n = 1640$). Available at the Federal Electoral Institute, National Coordination of Social Communication, Viaducto Tlalpan 100, Col. Arenal Tepepan, CP 14610 Mexico City, telephone +525/655-3719.

25. Latinobarómetro 1997 (sample size not reported). Precise date not reported. Available at MORI Mexico.

26. Alduncin and Associates, and El Universal, Department of Public Opinion Studies, "Encuesta elecciones presidenciales 2000" ($n = 621$). Telephone interviews, stratified random sample. Available at Alduncin y Asociados.

(continued)

TABLE 1 Continued

27. Alduncin and Associates, and El Universal, Department of Public Opinion Studies, "Encuesta elecciones presidenciales 2000" (*n* = 802). Telephone interviews, stratified random sample. Available at Alduncin y Asociados.

28. Latinobarómetro 1998 (sample size not reported). Precise date not reported. Available at MORI Mexico.

29. Alduncin and Associates, and El Universal, Department of Public Opinion Studies, "Encuesta elecciones presidenciales del año 2000" (*n* = 803). Telephone interviews, stratified random sample. Available at Alduncin y Asociados.

NOTES: Italicized question numbers indicate preelection surveys; roman numbers, postelection surveys. Most percentages do not add up to 100, since the table usually does not report "no" answers or "don't know" answers. Extreme values: Figures usually sum up the positive (clean election) answers and the negative (fraudulent election) answers, leaving aside the intermediate category. Only in one case (question 2) did question wording justify computing the middle category on the negative side, and in another one (question 7) on the positive side. Trust index: Positive values minus negative values (based on the previous column). The index gives a "correlation of forces" between trusting and incredulous citizens.

showing the opposite. A quick review of these figures reveals that the abyss of distrust that opened in 1988 had already closed by 1991. Afterward, popular trust in elections made slow albeit solid progress but apparently plunged again after 1997. Yet, before revising the results in more detail, we have to pause a bit and take a look at some crucial methodological issues that do some partial damage to the validity of these data.

Simple dichotomies

In many transitional democracies, political elections are neither clinically clean (democratic) nor thoroughly fraudulent (authoritarian) but something in between. Still, democratic actors will strive to trace a dividing line between clean and fraudulent elections.[3] In such fuzzy cases (as in Mexico), however, drawing this distinction is not a matter of establishing the presence or absence of vote rigging but of assessing its relevance. If we expect such ambiguous transitional elections to be immaculate, we set an unrealistic standard. We will always see some fraud. The question is how much fraud and the extent to which it alters actual outcomes.

Some surveys nevertheless dichotomize their questions by asking whether respondents qualify elections as either clean or fraudulent. They thereby do violence both to reality and to the real judgments citizens have to make in the electoral world. We can expect that their binary simplifications produce a distorted picture of popular attitudes. In any electoral process in contemporary Mexico, at least some irregularities are bound to occur, even if they are localized, isolated, and unsystematic. Respondents are therefore unlikely to certify elections as straightforwardly clean. Rather they will classify them as dirty or else take refuge in "don't know" answers.

Most of the binary statements reported in Table 1 bear out this expectation. Questions 8 and 9 as well as the Latinobarometer items 20, 25, and 28 show extraordinarily high percentages of distrustful respondents as well as (where reported) of "don't know" answers. Items 10 and 18, by contrast, report high levels of confidence, quite in line with the findings of other, temporarily contiguous polls.[4] I am nevertheless inclined to conclude that binary categories, in addition to poor information, indeed tend to produce biased information. Their broad brush swiftly erases the all-important fine distinctions.

Invalid intermediate categories

Given the limited informational value as well as the doubtful validity of binary response schemes, most surveys actually do offer some intermediate categories between the extremes of clean and dirty elections. Unfortunately, a good number of these middle categories are middle categories only in appearance. Instead of occupying an approximate intermediate position in the semantic space between the poles, they are close to or even overlap one of the extremes.

For instance, elections that are "little trustworthy" (see item 24) do not lie on neutral ground between trustworthy and suspicious elections. They are basically untrustworthy, even if some partial results may come close to reality. In the same way, electoral contests that are "somewhat clean" (see item 23) are not equidistant to cleanness and fraud. They are fundamentally fraudulent, even if they may display some laudable spots of purity. Or else (as in item 21), if I believe "little" in

the results the Federal Electoral Institutes disseminates, I am very close to those skeptics who do not believe at all in these results.

Thus, taken literally, these presumptive intermediate categories do not measure mixed feelings but unambiguous distrust. Nonetheless, the surveys present them as middle categories that are supposed to offer a quasi-neutral choice, something in between the extreme statements. How will respondents perceive such biased intermediate options? What are they trying to say when choosing these categories? Do they understand and support the semantic closeness to skeptical attitudes, or will they treat them as genuine middle categories that express some moderate judgment about the quality of elections? It is hard to say, although it is evident that polling results look very different depending on which of these interpretations is adopted.

In several surveys, about one-fifth of the respondents supported such intermediate categories. It makes a big difference whether we count their answers as ambivalent statements or as expressions of distrust. In fact, it alters our basic diagnosis about prevalent perceptions of fraud. For example, if we read the middle category of question 23—18 percent saying the 1997 elections were "somewhat clean"—as a cautious note of optimism, we may celebrate that only a small minority of 22 percent disbelieved the official results. Yet if we take it as an indicator of distrust, the radiant 54 percent majority held by the trustful suddenly looks narrow and fragile. Both interpretations can be suspected of being arbitrary and tendentious. Sad to say, but given the ambiguity of the data, reading them one way or the other comes down to a matter of interpretative discretion.[5]

Ambiguous cleanness

Problematic response categories are one impediment to establishing valid time series on public perceptions of electoral fraud. The problematic wording of questions is another. Most questions are framed in terms of electoral cleanness. They ask respondents whether they think some election X was or will be "clean" or its opposite ("dirty" or "fraudulent") or something in between. But does this way of putting things really uncover (only) what it is supposed to, namely, perceptions of electoral fraud?

The concept of electoral cleanness seems unproblematic at first sight. But a closer look reveals the potential breadth of the term, breadth that is troubling for the validity of our data. In political discourse, the idea of clean elections often includes more than the absence of fraud. It embraces two additional dimensions: structural fairness and the rhetorical style of electoral campaigns. In this sense, to qualify as clean, an election must be free of vote rigging; offer equitable conditions of political competition; and unfold in an inoffensive climate where candidates abstain from mudslinging.

Mexico's opposition parties have routinely relied on similar wide conceptualizations of electoral cleanness. They have often used the vocabulary of fraud to denounce not fraud but inequitable conditions of interparty competition. For instance, the Party of the Democratic Revolution, the main left-wing opposition party, still tends to cry fraud anytime it loses at the polls; and when pressed to be precise, its leaders come forward with allusions to unfair practices and the inequitable resource endowments of political parties.

Two July 1997 surveys permit estimates of the impact that wording may have on results. According to item 23 (see Table 1), only a bare majority of 54 percent approved the midterm elections as "clean." By contrast, according to statement 24, framed not in terms of cleanness but of credibility, close to no one thought the results were "not at all trustworthy," while a supermajority of 70 percent gave an unambiguously positive evaluation. We may conclude that even trustworthy elections may fall short of the hygienic standard of cleanness.

The relevance of fraud

If not all questions about clean versus fraudulent elections are clearly about vote rigging, even those that are sometimes miss the crucial point: the relevance of fraud. They tell us how many people observe or expect the presence of fraud in a given election (see, for example, items 1, 8, 9, and 18). But they do not tell us how many people think the presence of fraud alters the outcome of the election. They do not tell us whether fraud matters or not, whether people think it is systematic and decisive or not.

As before, wording matters. Compare, for example, items 9 and 10 from the same 1991 postelectoral survey. Only 11 percent of voters think there was "no fraud" in these elections. But 56 percent think that the results were real. It seems that the occurrence of fraud, when perceived to be irrelevant, does not hamper electoral credibility.

Apparently, the concrete relevance of fraud seems to be of little relevance to public opinion pollsters. Yet respondents are perfectly capable of forming sophisticated judgments about the incidence of fraud, when only given the opportunity to do so. According to item 7, only 30 percent of respondents thought the upcoming 1991 midterm elections would be "clean." However, another 29 percent thought that fraud would not affect the results and another 16 percent that it would affect results only in the concurrent local and state elections. Only 17 percent thought that the irregularities they expected would alter national results.

Diffuse objects

All of the data reported in Table 1 stem from nationwide polls, and most of them refer explicitly to federal elections. Usually they ask respondents to assess one concrete election between 1988 and 1997: the 1988 legislative and presidential elections (where Carlos Salinas was elected president), the 1991 midterm elections (where the PRI recovered), the 1994 legislative and presidential elections (where Ernesto Zedillo was elected president), or the 1997 midterm elections (where the PRI lost its majority in the Chamber of Deputies). By contrast, a handful of questions asks respondents to pass judgment on the country's political elections in general (items 1, 20, and 25-29).

Given the fact that today, at least in certain areas, local and state elections are much more vulnerable to manipulation than federal contests, we may expect that broad questions about elections in Mexico in general evoke more skeptical responses than those more specific questions that focus on federal contests. In accordance with this hypothesis, all general questions included in Table 1 report high degrees of distrust, which commonly stand in stark contrast to the levels of confidence found by other, more specific studies carried out at roughly the same period.

Selective reporting

Finally, a methodological problem traceable not to the design but to the use of surveys is selective reporting. Where authors provide just one part of the data (such as in statement 20, where we are given the positive answers only but neither the negatives nor the "don't know" responses), we are unable to assess them properly. Alternatively, where authors collapse response categories and relabel the resulting aggregate values in their own words, without providing the original sources (in terms of wording, categories, and results), we cannot be sure about their meaning. For example, according to the 1991 preelection survey reported by McCann and Domínguez (1998, 488), 61 percent of respondents said the elections would be "less than clean" (see also item 6 in Table 1). But this was not the original question posed to the interviewees. The authors report the full data in their earlier work (Domínguez and McCann 1996, 157), which led to a radically different picture, with only 17 percent saying that fraud will alter outcomes (see also item 7 in Table 1).[6]

THE DECLINE OF DISTRUST

Having explored all these methodological caveats, we can now take a look at the substance of the data and see what they tell us about the evolution of trust in elections since 1988. Did the distrust-driven electoral reforms of the 1990s achieve their objective of building trust in the electoral process? For all the ambiguities that some of our survey data contain, the overall picture is quite unambiguously positive. At least from 1988 to 1997, we observe a sustained reduction in perceptions of fraud in federal elections—even if the presidential elections of the year 2000 may well be resuscitating old fears of fraud. Let us now analyze the data year by year in some more detail (adding, in each case, a few explanatory conjectures).

1988: The climax of distrust

Before and after the conflictive 1988 presidential contest, distrust ran at dizzying heights. In the month preceding these watershed elections, close to no one thought political elections in Mexico were fraud free (see item 1 in Table 1).[7] After the fact, only about one-fifth of the electorate was sure the official winner, Carlos Salinas de Gortari, had actually won the race (see item 2). Still in 1991, more than half of the respondents

declared that the popular verdict had not been respected (see item 3). The trust index that measures the balance of power between trusting and skeptical citizens was consistently in the negative, and clearly so, with the latter vastly outnumbering the former (by 30 to 50 percent).

Most observers would agree that, in 1988, the public perception of widespread fraud was not the result of some inherent cultural or psychological proclivity to distrust public institutions. Rather, it reflected a realistic assessment of how electoral administration in Mexico worked at that time—as a well-lubricated machinery of fraud subservient to the hegemonic state party, the PRI.

1991: The surprising recovery

The August 1991 midterm elections not only brought a surprising recovery of the official party; they also brought a surprising recovery of trust in elections. In preelection as well as in postelection surveys, the credibility of federal elections took a big leap forward. While in 1988 up to two-thirds of respondents thought electoral fraud would possibly determine electoral outcomes, in 1991 this percentage was down to less than one-third, according to most polls. Accordingly, the distrustful lost their former overwhelming majority, turning into a minority group. Our trust indices start showing positive figures, and, what is more, they report astounding majorities of the trusting vis-à-vis the skeptical population. According to some surveys, those respondents who expected the elections to be basically clean as well as those who perceived them as such in retrospect outnumbered those who either expected or perceived them to be fraudulent by well over 50 percent (see items 7 and 11).

Items 6, 8, and 9 are outliers that seemingly contradict this trend. However, the unclear origins of the first (see the section Selective Reporting in the present article) and the infelicitous wording of the latter two (see Simple Dichotomies and The Relevance of Fraud) suggest that the deviant figures they give may well be methodological artifacts.

Curiously, the positive perception of the 1991 elections also had, it seems, an embellishing effect on the memory of the 1988 elections. As Table 1 shows, with respect to the 1988 contest, the majority distance between the skeptics and the trusting had already fallen from 50 to 30 percent from the preelectoral survey of June 1988 to the preelectoral survey of August 1991. Yet, only weeks afterward, in the September 1991 postelectoral survey, the retrospective evaluation of the 1988 electoral process had improved further and dramatically so. Up to this point, only one-third of the electorate maintained its skepticism with regard to the 1988 elections. Another third had turned agnostic. It seems that the favorable impression that the 1991 elections made on citizens obliterated their remembrance of the prior electoral process.

How can we explain citizens' reevaluation of the electoral process between 1988 and 1991? It is counterintuitive if we recall that in the same period the country experienced a constant stream of dramatic, often violent, postelectoral conflicts at local and state levels. At the national level, however, it is likely that two crucial factors boosted the credibility of the electoral process: (1) President Salinas's personal popularity and (2) the 1990 electoral reform whose (insufficient but nevertheless significant) innovations included a new law, a new election management body (the Federal Electoral Institute), a new voter registry, and new voter identification cards.

1994: Sustained progress

Surveys during 1993 and through the spring of 1994 show an electorate that is evenly divided between the trustful and the incredulous. With the trust index hovering around zero, skeptics seemed to have won some ground when compared with the prior period. While in the immediate aftermath of the 1991 elections, 55 percent of respondents had described those elections as "clean" or "very clean" (see item 12), in early 1993 only 38 percent expected the 1994 presidential elections to meet that standard (see item 13). Since stakes are higher at presidential elections when compared to midterm legislative elections, more cautious expectations about their democratic quality seem to be justified.

However, in the weeks immediately before and after the 1994 elections, electoral credibility rose again, to levels superior to the ones achieved in 1991. According to one preelection survey, for example, 52 percent of respondents expected that the citizens' verdict would be respected, while only 42 percent did so in 1991 (see items 17 and 5). In another poll, taken after the elections, 55 percent stated that the election had been fraud free, while only 11 percent had expressed the same view in 1991 (see items 18 and 9). As in similar cases before, I consider items 16 and 20 to be somewhat dubious and artificial outliers, since we are not given full information on wording or results.

The year 1994 was Mexico's *annus horribilis*. Yet, its most disturbing events, the Zapatista rebellion in Chiapas and the assassination of PRI presidential candidate Luis Donaldo Colosio, had at least one beneficial side effect: political elites converged around the need to ensure political stability and, to that end, the legitimacy of the upcoming presidential elections that year. The ensuing round of negotiations led to a set of electoral reforms that pushed Mexico over the threshold of electoral democracy. According to many political as well as academic observers (including the author), the 1994 electoral contest could be considered a fundamentally clean election; although irregularities still occurred, they did not affect basic results. In any case, they brought very significant advances and it should not surprise us to see them translated into higher levels of popular confidence.

1997: The credible election

In 1995 and 1996, under President Ernesto Zedillo (1994-2000), political parties negotiated yet another round of electoral reforms, which this time was thought to be definitive. The 1997 midterm elections represented the first test case of the new institutional framework. In those elections, the ruling PRI lost its majority in the

Chamber of Deputies for the first time in its close to 70 years of existence, and the "general consensus is that the electoral process was basically fair and transparent" (Blum 1997, 28). One might expect that both the clean organization of the contest and legislative alternation in power injected a good dose of further credibility into the electoral process.

The data, however, bear out this expectation only to a certain extent. Surveys do indeed measure a decrease of expected fraud before the 6 July 1997 elections as well as a relatively favorable evaluation of the process afterward. But the changes are far from spectacular. For instance, item 22 shows an increase in the percentage of trusting citizens of only 8 points (when compared to the 1994 item 17), while item 23 indicates a decrease in the percentage of incredulous citizens of only 2 points (when compared to the 1994 item 19). Only the postelectoral survey conducted by the Federal Electoral Institute (see item 24) reflects something of a qualitative change. Following this survey (whose focus on electoral credibility I consider to be of high validity), close to nobody thought the official results were not trustworthy at all. The corresponding trust index of 67 percentage points, breaking all previous records recorded in Table 1, justifies qualifying these elections as overall credible.

2000: The resurgence of distrust?

If the (uneven) time series of public opinion data presented in this article would stop shortly after the

1997 elections, the story to tell would be a clear success story—a romance in which a lucky combination of institutional engineering and institutional performance succeeded in melting down an iron reputation of fraud. But, unfortunately (for the elegance of my argument as well as for political life), the polls included in Table 1, which all look forward already to the next presidential elections in the year 2000,[8] throw some doubt on the neat story line of linear progress.

According to all five nationwide polls taken between the autumn of 1997 and December 1998, the skeptics have gained the upper hand again and now are enjoying majorities nearly as wide as in 1988, the golden year of electoral distrust. Items 27 and 29, for example, indicate that the percentage of trustful citizens is lower today than anytime since 1988 (excepting the questionable items 9 and 20), while the share of skeptical respondents is larger than anytime since 1988 (excepting the questionable item 6). It goes without saying that according to all five polls, the trust index changes its sign and shows large to overwhelming majorities of incredulous citizens.[9]

How solid are these results? It seems quite evident that the surveys have their weak points. Three of the five polls had small sample sizes (with relatively high margins of error) and are based on telephone interviews (which tend to introduce certain distortions into the sample). More important, all pose general questions that do not address federal elections specifically, and the

Latinobarometer questions are dichotomous in structure. Both of the latter features—generality and dichotomy—clearly tend to bias results toward the distrustful end.[10]

Even if we concede that the results may be pure methodological artifacts, we have to consider the possibility that on the eve of the next presidential elections, old fears of fraud may be reemerging not only at the elite level but also at the level of ordinary citizens. Given the high stakes of a presidential contest as well as the heightened uncertainty that the new competitiveness of Mexico's party system produces, a more cautious attitude may well be a rational response to the upcoming critical juncture at hand. Until more survey research puts us on firmer empirical ground, we are left with the warning that the advances in electoral credibility from 1988 to 1997 represent a significant achievement—but, nevertheless, a possibly fragile, conditional, and reversible one.

CONCLUSION

As the preceding analysis reveals, Mexican citizens have not been immersed in some self-sustaining culture of distrust impenetrable to outside developments. Quite to the contrary, their expectations and perceptions of electoral fraud have improved at a rhythm roughly parallel to real improvements in the administration of elections. This relative malleability of institutional evaluations gives credence to the idea that institutional trust is not so much a self-reinforcing path-dependent phenomenon as one that depends on the empirical structure and performance of institutions. In addition, it supports the idea that political culture is not entirely external to democratic institutions, which, to the contrary, possess a certain capacity to foster democratic norms and beliefs themselves.

In academic terms, our effort to reconstruct empirical trends in the perception of fraud revealed, above all, how much there is still do be done in this field. Future research could go in three directions: (1) the analysis of electoral trust and distrust at the level of individuals (rather than at the aggregate level analyzed in this article); (2) the comparative analysis of national and subnational data sets; and (3) the comparative analysis of international data on perception of electoral fraud. All three are virtually virgin territories that offer marvelous employment opportunities to the cartographer of fraud and perceptions of fraud.

In practical terms, the present analysis suggests that opinion polls on the credibility of elections could proceed with much more methodological care. Under survey, civil society does not reveal its secrets spontaneously. Above all, questionnaires should be designed in a way that takes citizens seriously. If the questions posed are not reasonable, relevant, realistic, precise, and sophisticated, the answers will not be either.

Notes

1. For example, according to Molina and Hernández (1998), in "hegemonic party systems in transition" such as Mexico's, trust in elections is quasi-naturally low. In such con-texts, they write, "the credibility of elections is low . . . independently of the type of electoral organism or the effective number of parties" (which are the two institutional variables they study) (10).

2. Domínguez and McCann 1996 and McCann and Domínguez 1998 discuss Mexicans' perceptions of fraud quite extensively. But they barely rely on direct questions about the cleanness of elections. Rather, they use indirect questions, such as listings of the country's main problems; the reasons respondents give for why others abstain from voting; or respondents' answers to questions about the relevance of voting in general.

3. For an enlightening discussion of the difficulties of assessing whether elections are (reasonably) "free and fair," see Elklit and Svensson 1997.

4. Throughout the present text, all references to numbered "questions," "items," or "statements" refer to data reported in Table 1.

5. Note that the extreme values reported in Table 1 usually treat intermediate categories as such, which introduces a certain optimistic bias into their interpretation.

6. I should mention, though, that in this case, selective reporting came about for defensively pragmatic reasons. In McCann and Domínguez 1998, the authors wanted to compare earlier findings with later data, which, however, did not involve the original finely graded wording anymore (McCann 1999).

7. The question, asked in June 1988, refers to elections in general. But given the intense interparty competition and the corresponding climate of expectation that characterized the 1988 presidential campaign, it seems reasonable to interpret the responses as judgments on the imminent 6 July federal elections.

8. Three of the surveys are primarily interested in present voting intentions for the year 2000 (within the universe of known presidential precandidates). In the other two (Latinobarometer) studies, the frame of reference remains more implicit. But given the pivotal importance the 2000 elections have acquired in Mexican politics at least three years ahead of that date, it seems quite clear that any general question asked after July 1997 about the cleanness of elections tends to have the "mother of all elections" in the year 2000 as one of its primary reference points.

9. By the way of a weak consolation, we may add that the 1997 Latinobarometer data reported in item 25 sound bad—but look much less gloomy when put into comparative perspective. In that year, Mexican voters were less distrustful than the citizens of Bolivia, Brazil, Colombia, Ecuador, Paraguay, Peru, and Venezuela (the latter being the most distrustful, with 83 percent of respondents describing elections as fraudulent).

10. The surveys have some distinctive strengths as well. Items 26, 27, and 29 (which ask respondents to rate how "clean" they consider elections to be) are less ambiguous than comparable polling questions. In all three cases, the surveys explicitly introduce the distinction between electoral cleanness and electoral fairness, by inquiring into the degree of equity, competitiveness, and legitimacy of elections at the same time that they inquire into their degree of cleanness.

References

Beltrán, Ulises. 1997. Encuesta nacional sobre el votante méxicano: Primeros resultados. *Política y gobierno* 4(2):407-67.

Blum, Roberto E. 1997. Mexico's New Politics: The Weight of the Past. *Journal of Democracy* 8(4):28-42.

Domínguez, Jorge and James A. McCann. 1996. *Democratizing Mexico: Public Opinion and Electoral Choices*. Baltimore: Johns Hopkins University Press.

Eisenstadt, Todd A. 1999. Off the Streets and into the Courtrooms: Resolving Postelectoral Conflicts in Mexico. In *The Self-Restraining State: Power and Accountability in New Democracies*, ed. Andreas Schedler, Larry Diamond, and Marc F. Plattner. Boulder, CO: Lynne Rienner.

Elklit, Jørgen and Palle Svensson. 1997. What Makes Elections Free and Fair? *Journal of Democracy* 8(3):32-46.

Fukuyama, Francis. 1995. *Trust: The Social Virtues and the Creation of Prosperity*. New York: Free Press.

Instituto Federal Electoral and Universidad Nacional Autónoma de México, Instituto de Investigaciones Sociales, eds. 1996. *La reforma electoral y su contexto sociocultural*. Mexico City: Instituto Federal Electoral and Universidad Nacional Autónoma de México, Instituto de Investigaciones Sociales.

McCann, James A. 1999. Personal communication with the author, 23 Feb.

McCann, James A. and Jorge Domínguez. 1998. Mexicans React to Electoral Fraud and Political Corruption: An Assessment of Public Opinion and Voting Behavior. *Electoral Studies* 17(4):483-503.

Molina, José and Janeth Hernández. 1998. La credibilidad de las elecciones latinoamericanas y sus factores. Paper prepared for presentation at the Twenty-first International Congress of the Latin American Studies Association, 24-26 Sept., Chicago.

Putnam, Robert D. 1993. *Making Democracy Work: Civic Traditions in Modern Italy*. Princeton, NJ: Princeton University Press.

ANNALS, *AAPSS*, **565**, September 1999

Civil Society and Attitudes: The Virtues of Character

By ARMANDO CÍNTORA

ABSTRACT: It is argued that the new globalized economy increasingly requires more specialized and better-trained individuals. Without adequate qualifications, it is extremely difficult to have a quality job, or even any job, in the new world market. Some cultures give a high value to formal education and the virtues of character that a long process of education require. On the other hand, traditional mainstream Mexican culture seems to be dysfunctional in terms of economic competition, because it does not put enough value on education and the virtues of character such as self-discipline and responsibility that a long process of schooling requires. The author concludes that if Mexicans desire to compete successfully in the new globalized economy, they require a cultural revolution.

Armando Cíntora teaches philosophy of science at Metropolitan University in Mexico City. He has published several articles on philosophy of science in Mexican journals. He expects to sit for his Ph.D. examination in philosophy of science this year at the London School of Economics.

I N our contemporary world, increasing economic globalization is a fact. Not all cultures are well adapted to this new situation, however. With respect to becoming successful competitors in the new globalized world, some cultural values and attitudes are dysfunctional. The idea that attitudes and values have an impact on economic success is found both in popular fables such as the Ant and the Grasshopper and, famously, in Max Weber (1976). It is frequently said that Confucian values or the Protestant work ethic makes good economic competitors of the individuals—and the communities—that hold them. "Economic life is deeply embedded in social life, and it cannot be understood apart from the customs, morals, and habits of the society in which it occurs. In short, it cannot be divorced from culture" (Fukuyama 1995, 13).

The globalized world is being transformed, at least in part, by a new scientific-technological revolution—that of information technologies—and a consequent increased automatization. In such an environment, to be economically successful, individuals require high qualifications, that is, many years of sophisticated training and education. The contemporary job market needs and values highly trained specialists. Thus

in 1979, a 30-year-old man with a high school diploma earned a yearly average of $27,700 in 1993 dollars. By 1993 a high school graduate was only earning $20,000. Fifteen years ago, the typical worker with a college degree made 38 percent more than a worker with a high school diploma. Today, the typical

college-educated worker makes 73 percent more. (Applebome 1997)

Without an adequate education, in the contemporary job market, it is extremely difficult to earn a decent salary or to have a job at all because when automatization is introduced in some industry, jobs with low qualifications are the first to go.

Specialized training, in turn, needs individuals that value education as a way of social mobility. Such training requires individuals to have self-discipline, courage, and a sense of responsibility. These last virtues are necessary for a person to be able to undergo many years of specialization and education successfully. There are cultures, or traditional idiosyncrasies, that put little value on formal education and little value on the virtues needed by a lengthy process of education.

An example of such a culture is that of Eastern European Gypsies. These Gypsies are usually uneducated, even though Eastern European Gypsies are mostly sedentary nowadays (Fraser 1992, 309). Because of their comparative lack of schooling, these Gypsies have very high rates of unemployment or, if they are employed, they do mostly menial or poorly paid jobs. For instance, in the Czech Republic, 95 percent of the Gypsy children do not go beyond grade school (Los gitanos a España 1996), so these Gypsies mostly lack the skills and specialization that a globalized economy requires more and more. Gypsies are not effective economic competitors in the contemporary world with its high division of labor. If Gypsy culture does not adapt and become economically competitive, it could well disappear in the coming decades. The cultures that have a higher probability of survival are those that are more adaptable; in particular, they are those that are more adaptable to the new globalized economy.

In contrast with Gypsies are the Eastern European Jews. Traditionally, these Jews do much better economically, even though both groups have a history of discrimination. The main difference seems to reside in their different attitudes toward education. Jewish culture, possibly because of ancient religious prescriptions favoring study of the Torah (Tamari 1987, 269-73), has valued schooling and the virtues that a prolonged education process requires. For example, poor Russian Jews at the end of the nineteenth century were significantly better educated than their non-Jewish Russian counterparts (Perlmann 1988, 124).

VALUES OF MAINSTREAM MEXICANS

What are the genuine values and attitudes toward education held by mainstream Mexicans and Mexican Americans? I emphasize genuinely held values and attitudes as opposed to explicit ones. Even if the subject does not intend to lie, explicit values can be different from genuine ones because genuine values can be held only tacitly or unconsciously.

Assuming genuine values and attitudes can be inferred from behavior, it seems that most Mexicans do not put much value on prolonged

education as a strategy for social promotion. This conclusion is suggested[1]—though it is far from proved—by the following data:

1. During 1997, only 3 of 10 Mexico City residents bought a book (*Reforma* 1997a).

2. A Mexican student reads an average of half a book per year, while in other countries a student reads an average of one book per month (*Reforma* 1997c).

3. Mexico City residents, probably the best educated in the country, dedicate on average only three minutes per day to reading books. The books that are read tend to be very lightweight ones, such as those by Carlos Cuauhtémoc Sánchez (Zaid 1997).

4. Nonetheless, 87 percent of Mexican urban households are rich enough to own a color television, and 64 percent can afford also to own a videocassette recorder (*La Jornada* 1996).

5. Meanwhile in the United States, between 1970 and 1988, only 5.5 percent of Mexican Americans aged 25 years or older had completed four or more years of college studies. For white Americans, this percentage was almost four times as high, and the percentage of black American college students was more than twice that of Mexican Americans (Schick and Schick 1991, D2-4).

6. In 1988, in the United States, the percentage of Mexican Americans between 25 and 34 years of age who completed less than 12 years of schooling was three times the percentage for white Americans (Schick and Schick 1991, D2-4).

7. Mexican Americans are severely underrepresented among university faculty (Schick and Schick 1991, 79).

8. In June of 1998, President Clinton said that Hispanics are the minority that has shown the least economic improvement, and explained this as a consequence of a high rate of school dropout among Hispanics (*Reforma* 1997b).

That these data cannot be explained only in terms of economic disadvantages is suggested by a study in the spring of 1986 of the highest level of education attained by 1980 high school seniors. The subjects were of various race and ethnic backgrounds, and all of them were of high socioeconomic status. The economically privileged Hispanic high school seniors in the sample had, after six years, only an eighth of the percentage of graduate and professional degrees that equally privileged Asians had and only a third of the percentage of graduate and professional degrees that privileged non-Hispanic whites had (Schick and Schick 1991, D2-11). Since all these students were economically privileged, their differences in educational attainment appear to be due to their various cultural attitudes and values.

And as a result of their educational disadvantages, Mexican Americans are rare in jobs with high educational requirements.

Mexican-Americans, among others, are not as upwardly mobile as rapidly as members of some other ethnic groups with similar class situations because their culture does not see higher education and rising status as the normal or appropriate lot of ordinary people, but as the prerogative of the higher classes. . . . They wanted to raise their status and make more money but they did not see education as a likely means. Formal higher education and the style of life that went with it seemed stuck-up and alien. They expected a lot of disappointment to follow the pursuit of higher education. (Sewell 1989, 38)

Mexican Americans contrast with Korean Americans, who also arrive poor to the United States but who use education as their preferred avenue for social mobility. Thus Koreans "are twice as likely to get a college degree as Whites, and their academic performance is improving daily" (*Economist* 1997, 65).

Another glimpse into the tacit values of Mexicans is provided by some Mexican popular sayings and expressions. Three examples follow:

—*Ahí se va*, which is translated approximately as "Who cares? That is good enough." This expression is frequently used when concluding a task or project, and it shows a lack of pride in one's job and a lack of responsibility.

—*Mañana se lo tengo*, which is translated as "Tomorrow it will be ready," a statement that will be iterated day after day. It shows the Mexican tendency to procrastinate and a lack of self-discipline.

—*El vale madrismo*, an expression that describes a nihilist attitude common among Mexicans, one that says that nothing is really worthwhile and that therefore it is not worthwhile to exert oneself. The result is bad workmanship and a lack of will to succeed.

If mainstream Mexicans are to compete successfully in the new globalized economy, it seems that they need to undergo a change in values and attitudes, that they require a cultural or axiological revolution. A cultural revolution is not sufficient to secure economic success, but it seems to be a necessary requirement for the economic well-being of average Mexicans.

PROMOTING
AXIOLOGICAL CHANGE

The problem now arises of how to promote the axiological change required by Mexicans. If this axiological change is going to be the result of a rational process, one would need first to make Mexicans (businesspeople, government, and the population in general) aware of the conditional that, to be a successful economic agent or competitor in the new globalized economy, education and virtues such as responsibility and self-discipline should be valued. In addition, one must hope that, once Mexicans become aware that their values and attitudes are dysfunctional with respect to economic improvement, they would make an effort to gradually change their set of values and hierarchies.[2] This process of self-awareness and value change could be promoted by a network of adequate voluntary associations.

That nongovernmental organizations can modulate attitudes and valuations is demonstrated by the impact of rural environmental voluntary associations. These associations have helped modify the attitudes of many rural communities toward the environment and toward development as a whole by promoting in these communities feelings of collective self-esteem, solidarity, and empowerment (Natal 1998, 55-57). Two difficulties arise, however, for any program with the aim of reform via voluntary associations. One is in harmonizing the possible cacophony of the goals of the various voluntary associations so that all the associations pull in the same direction. The other is in the creation of adequate reformist associations. Mexican NGOs may themselves share the ethos of their milieu, which they must overcome if they are to be aware of the need to change Mexican attitudes toward work and education.

There are, furthermore, limits to what can be rationally achieved concerning value change. For example, if somebody were not to care enough about his economic well-being, because he had other priorities, and if he were ready to fully accept the consequences of his value priorities, such as a high probability of unemployment or a high likelihood of an onerous, insecure, and poorly paid job, then there would be little that one could do to rationally argue against this hypothetical agent's values. This agent would be rational, at least prima facie, if he had a consistent and fully considered set of values; that is, this agent would be rational if he did not deceive himself about the consequences of his value hierarchy.

If one were to try, *malgré tout*, to rationally argue such a consistent subject out of his values, out of his value hierarchies, one would likely end up arguing circularly (A is valuable because A is valuable, or A is more valuable than B because A is more valuable than B); when the argumentative circles have wide diameters, they can be very difficult to discover. Alternatively, one would end up with an infinite regress when trying to justify some value hierarchy. Due to this limitation of rationality when arguing about values, values have through history often been changed by nonrational strategies. Such strategies include force (the conquest of Mexico provides an instance) and propaganda, indoctrination, and brainwashing, as in many arational or irrational religious conversions and ideological gestalt switches. Thus religiously inspired movements have often produced dramatic social transformations.

Notes

1. To discover the genuine values and attitudes of average Mexicans would require a serious empirical study. It is hoped that the present article will encourage the implementation of such a study.

2. One would also hope that once Mexicans had changed their values and aims, they would not then suffer from acratia, or weakness of will, which would be a deterrent to achieving what they would then consider their appropriate aims. Acratia seems to be a form of irrational behavior since the agent's behavior is contrary to what the agent considers that reason requires. Acratia has been excluded from the discussion because I have been assuming fully rational agents.

References

Applebome, Peter. 1997. Better Schools, Uncertain Returns. *New York Times*, 16 Mar.

Economist, The. 1997, 26 Apr.

Fraser, A. 1992. *The Gypsies*. Cambridge, MA: Basil Blackwell.

Fukuyama, Francis. 1995. *Trust: The Social Virtues and the Creation of Prosperity*. New York: Free Press.

Gitanos a España, los. 1996. *El país* (Madrid), 12 June.

Jornada, la (Mexico City). 1996, 16 Apr.

Natal, Alejandro. 1998. How State Funds Impact NGOs' Capacity to Foster People's Participation. Research done for the World Bank.

Perlmann, J. 1988. *Ethnic Differences: Schooling and Social Structure Among the Irish, Italians, Jews and Blacks in an American City, 1880-1935*. New York: Cambridge University Press.

Reforma (Mexico City). 1997a, 10 Feb.

———. 1997b, 15 June.

———. 1997c, 7 Dec.

Schick, L. F. and R. Schick, eds. 1991. *Statistical Handbook on U.S. Hispanics*. Phoenix, AZ: Oryx Press.

Sewell, D. 1989. *Knowing People: A Mexican-American Community's Concept of a Person*. New York: AMS Press.

Tamari, Meir. 1987. *"With All Your Possessions": Jewish Ethics and Economic Life*. New York: Free Press.

Weber, Max. 1976. *The Protestant Ethic and the Spirit of Capitalism*. 2d ed. London: Allen & Unwin.

Zaid, Gabriel. 1997. Note. *Reforma* (Mexico City), 3 Feb.

Entrepreneurs in Emerging Economies: Creating Trust, Social Capital, and Civil Society

By M. B. NEACE

ABSTRACT: This article reports on findings from interviews with fledgling entrepreneurs in four former Soviet republics (Belarus, Kazakhstan, Russia, and Ukraine). Analysis of the interviews was conducted against a backdrop of concepts from the literature of civil society, social capital, and entrepreneurship as applied to small business development. The main finding of the study was the unanimous claim by the entrepreneurs that trust was one of two prime requisites for success, and this in societies that had been culturally depraved for many years. From this finding, two models were developed incorporating civil society, social capital, and trust to more fully depict the entrepreneurial environment.

M. B. Neace is professor of international business and environmental management, Mercer University, Macon, Georgia. During the past 12 years, he has written and published numerous papers focusing on small business development in emerging economies and the business–natural environment interface. Presentation of these works is most often in an international setting. Dr. Neace is also active professionally; for example, he serves as the vice chair of the Governor's (Georgia) Environmental Advisory Committee and is a member of the U.S. Committee to ISO 14000.

NOTE: Support for the research reported by this article was provided by the Center for East European Studies, University of Pittsburgh; Provost's Office, Mercer University; and the Stetson School of Business and Economics, Mercer University.

L ONG-TERM success in economic development, particularly in developing economies, depends to a significant degree on a growing network of small entrepreneurial enterprises. This requires a dynamic interaction of culture; social capital in the form of trust, among a host of economic entities; and human capital in the person of an entrepreneur. Entrepreneurial efforts in the absence of cultural values or a civil society that supports and generates social capital and trust will, in most cases, fail. A major finding of the research is that social capital and trust among entrepreneurs, employees, suppliers, and customers are a vital underpinning resource necessary for creating business networks that lead to sustainable economic growth. For many developing economies, particularly those that are relatively small and those with few developed factor endowments, this is a conundrum. Without well-developed human and social capital and a supporting civil society, how can economic development take place? The present analysis will be through the eyes of entrepreneurs and will focus on their attempts to create sustaining economic linkages when, for the most part, there was an absence of trust, social capital, and civil society due to years of cultural depravation.

This study specifically examines the role of entrepreneurs as agents for creating social capital in emerging economies, thereby creating a seedbed of civil society, a crucial element in sustainable economic development. Thirty-two interviews were conducted in four major capital cities of Central Asia (see Table 1). Nine of the subjects were entrepreneurs, and the remainder comprised supporting cast members such as employees, government officials, and nongovernmental counselors. I conducted the interviews with the assistance of a colleague from Mercer University and an interpreter. From the analysis of the interview data and literature search, two models emerged. Both models incorporate trust, social capital, and civil society into the established models of small business development that conventionally include human capital and resource capital. Adding trust, social capital, and civil society to these models presents a fuller, more vibrant, holistic perspective of the entrepreneur milieu. This holistic perspective has important policy implications for economic development in emerging economies.

DEFINITIONS AND MODELS

I will provide concept definitions and discuss the two models derived from interview analyses and the literature review to provide a context for understanding and appreciating the findings and their implications.

Figures 1 and 2 depict paradigms of small business development. Depending upon the context, some writers would describe these models as representative of entrepreneurism— the milieu and the process of small business development. Some writers— for example, Drucker (1985)—make a distinction between entrepreneurship and small business development, as do Say (1827) and Schumpeter (1942). This distinction will be

TABLE 1

PROFILE OF INTERVIEW SAMPLE, BY COUNTRY AND PROFESSION

Country (city)	Profession							
	Small business entrepreneur	U.S. business executive	Other foreign business executive	University professor or administrator	Non-governmental organization	U.S. government	Local government	Total
Belarus (Minsk)	4			5	1		1	11
Kazakhstan (Almaty)		1	1	1	6	3		12
Russia (Moscow)	2			1		1		4
Ukraine (Kiev)	3			1	1			5
Total	9	1	1	8	8	4	1	32

recognized in the research reported in this article.

As the reader probably appreciates, the terms "civil society," "social capital," and "trust" do not have generally accepted interpretations. Quite to the contrary, they are dynamic and the source of stimulating research and lively discourse. The definitions used for the present analysis blend several sources, with recognition given to the major contributors. The models are a blend as well, including literature review sources and field research data, particularly from entrepreneurs. To provide the reader a context for understanding and appreciating the findings and their implications, the two models derived by induction from the analysis are presented prior to a discussion of the data.

Definitions

The terms that will be defined here are "civil society," "social capital," "trust," and "entrepreneur." "Civil society" refers to the kind of character and life of a society that occur in the social space between the individual family and the state. It is made up of autonomous, freely chosen, intermediary organizations (for example, issue-oriented nongovernmental organizations, churches, fraternal groups, private universities, and businesses), supported by a system of behavioral norms that include refined and civil manners (Rau 1991; Shils 1997; Walzer 1991). The concept has its origins in eighteenth-century England and Scotland (Landes 1998).

"Social capital" is the ability of a people to work together for common purposes in groups, organizations, and communities and is a harmonious comingling of trust, viable channels of communications, and norms and sanctions (for example, Coleman 1989; Putnam 1993). In addition to knowledge and skills (human capital), sufficient levelS of social capital are essential for social and economic development.

"Trust" is the expectation of or within two or more entities (persons, organizations) that regular day-to-day behavior will be honest, cooperative, and predictable based on shared norms (for example, Fukuyama 1995b).

An "entrepreneur" is a person or entity that searches for opportunities to change the status quo and exploit them through innovation and the creative use of resources, often transmuting values in the process (for example, Drucker 1985).

Models

Inputs for the construction of these models came from two sources: (1) information gleaned from the interviews that are part of this study; and (2) a historical amalgamation of literature representing a wide spectrum of disciplines, including business management, cultural anthropology, economics, history, political science, sociology, and religion. The origins of these models have their roots in Say's revelation (1827) of the concept of the entrepreneur and what he or she does. Entrepreneurs are change agents, disavowing the status quo, moving and reordering resources, striving for sustainable better results. Schumpeter (1942) described such behavior as "creative destruction." The present article focuses on specific elements of Figure 1—social capital, trust, and entrepreneurial qualities—and the process of small business development—entrepreneurship—as presented in Figure 2 because these were the major findings emanating from this research.

Trust, social capital, and civil society only recently have become areas

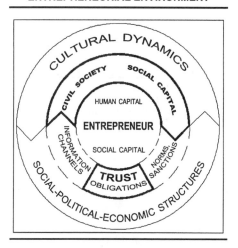

FIGURE 1
**OVERVIEW OF THE
ENTREPRENEURIAL ENVIRONMENT**

of serious study of the importance of social relationships in commercial and small business development. Scholars have long discoursed their meaning, development, and impact in the larger context of human behavior (for example, Cox 1995; Ferguson [1767] 1966; Hayek 1960; Hume [1738] 1967; Smith [1759] 1817). Human capital has a long history of research as applied to entrepreneurs (for example, Becker 1975) and the qualities necessary for success (Drucker 1985). As Fukuyama (1995b) recounts in his seminal work on the role of trust in business success, Aristotle and, more recently, Weber (1930) both argued that a moral, open community—a civil society—was crucial for the creation of social and economic wealth.

A major finding gleaned from the interviews and incorporated into the models is that trust is a major resource for small business success and crucial for starting and sustaining

FIGURE 2
ENTREPRENEUR PROFILE AND THE PROCESS OF SMALL BUSINESS DEVELOPMENT

ENTREPRENEUR PROFILE

HUMAN CAPITAL (INTERNAL)   +   SOCIAL CAPITAL (EXTERNAL)
  VISIONARY   ASSOCIATIONAL
  SELF-CONFIDENCE   INTERPERSONAL, ORGANIZATIONAL
  KNOWLEDGEABLE, LEARNER   TRUST
  AMBITIOUS   INTERMEDIARY NETWORKS
  CHARISMATIC   GATHERER, DISSEMINATOR
  SKILLS, EXPERIENCE   OF INFORMATION

ENTREPRENEURIAL PROCESS

PERCEIVED OPPORTUNITY   →   VALUE CREATION   →   PERCEIVED REWARDS
                              THROUGH INNOVATION

MARKET DEMAND: APPLICATION OF   PERSONAL:
  MORE EFFECTIVE,   HUMAN AND SOCIAL   FINANCIAL REWARD
    EFFICIENT USE OF   CAPITAL TO RESOURCE   RECOGNITION
    RESOURCES   CAPITAL: POWER
                              FINANCIAL
                              TECHNOLOGICAL   SOCIAL:
                              MATERIAL   CONSUMER
                              LABOR   SATISFACTION
                              PHYSICAL, MATERIALS COMMUNITY
                                                     WELL-BEING

new enterprises (Newton 1997). Yes, generous quantities of human capital are very important, but they are not sufficient for success. Relatively high levels of trust, or the creation of trust by the entrepreneur, were viewed as essential for sustainable success. That this was discovered in Central Asia is all the more remarkable because individuals there were trying to create successful small businesses in a social climate where trust and other elements of social capital and civil society were largely nonexistent. Many decades of Communist rule had devalued civil society (Mishler and Rose 1997; Taylor, Kazakov, and Thompson 1997) and had decimated many traditional cultural and social structures, leaving these societies bereft of social capital and trust, the very glue of sustainable relationships and a civil society. How does an entrepreneur establish a successful small business in the absence of social capital? The following sections discuss how these individuals tackled these issues in efforts to establish viable, sustaining small businesses. The results have implications for entrepreneurial and social research, professional education, and social and economic policy.

THE SETTING: SMALL BUSINESS DEVELOPMENT IN TURBULENT TIMES

The Soviet Union was no more. As a result of the disintegration during the latter days of 1991, 15 republics were in the throes of revolutionary social change, redefining themselves culturally, socially, politically, and, most urgently, economically. Political and economic infrastructures were chaotic. Inflation was rampant. Uncertainty was the order of the day. This was the climate I found in four major cities of Central Asia in the summer of 1994.

Thirty-two interviews were conducted in the capitals of four republics of the former Soviet Union: Minsk, Belarus; Almaty, Kazakhstan; Moscow, Russia; and Kiev, Ukraine. Of the 32 subjects, 9 were owners of a new business in the start-up phase; the remainder were employees or experts providing support activities. (See Table 1 for a profile of the persons interviewed.) Initial analysis revealed an interesting characteristic of the interview data: all of the owners were of one voice in their response to the questions. Their responses were exactly the same, even to the point of using the same words and phrases, despite coming from four widely separated locations. Additionally, what they said was a surprise and at the outset confounding. A search of the literature by people like Drucker (1985), Say (1827),

and Schumpeter (1942) provided a good background for analyzing the data but was less than adequate for understanding some of the responses. This bafflement plus the small number of small business owners in the study led me to set the study aside and ponder the results. Two years later, I discovered the concepts of civil society, social capital, and trust in ethics research. This body of literature opened a new perspective on my data on small business development and reenergized my interest. Adding the concepts of civil society, social capital, and their core element, trust, to the analysis gave the study new life and meaning.

Even though the sample is quite small, the results of the analysis, particularly the models that resulted, do make an interesting addition to the literature of entrepreneurship and small business development and both agree and disagree with other research concerned with similar issues in this troubled area of the world.

ANALYSIS OF INTERVIEWS

The nine entrepreneurs were engaged in six distinct business activities (manufacturing; wholesaling; transportation; financial services; research and consulting; construction) and operated, in some cases, several small businesses. For all of these entrepreneurs and small business owners, this was their first business venture and they were confronted with typical start-up small business problems: pricing of products and services, cost of supplies, cash flow, and external support (government and nongovernment; wanted and unwanted). All of this was taking place in an environment of hyperinflation and an infrastructure in disarray, with the potential of criminal activity lurking in the background. Delayed salaries, wages, and so-called unpaid holidays were not uncommon. Several employees expressed their faith and trust in the owners to make the venture work, and owners were looked to for not only leadership but also inspiration (Coleman 1989; Drucker 1985).

Private universities were some of the very first small businesses to rise from the collapse of the Soviet Union and were very similar to what existed prior to the breakup. With the dissolution of the Soviet Union, state financial support for state universities was drastically reduced, and, in some cases, it totally ceased. The necessity of earning a living and the opportunity for providing business education in the new environment were the stimuli for starting a private university focusing on business management. The owners of these new businesses came from similar positions prior to the breakup (for example, from dean to owner). These new enterprises were not innovation, were not "creative destruction," in the classic sense of the term (Drucker 1985; Say 1827; Schumpeter 1942). Education programs in business management and student customers were essentially the same as before. The major difference was in program focus: it was now market oriented, as student consumers were aspiring to own their own business or to be employed in the private sector rather than by the state.

Unlike entrepreneurs, owners of these small business educational ventures had established relationships with their employees (faculty) prior to the establishment of their new enterprises. Additionally, there was no need to develop external networks, or relationships outside of their educational enterprises, to produce a product. This was not the case with entrepreneurs interviewed who were faced with creating value-chain networks. Although nonexistent in the larger environment, social capital was at work in the new private universities in the form of intra-organizational subcultural professorial communities. Observable levels of trust and faith were remarkably high under the circumstances. Prior to the breakup, Soviet bureaucracy squelched most activities that would lead to the creation of social capital and the development and maintenance of a civil society. Depravation of social and cultural activities was experienced by all sectors of these societies.

Entrepreneurs engaged in manufacturing, wholesaling, transportation, financial services, consulting and research, and construction faced a much different scenario. Theirs was not one of reconstituting what was already a traditional, acceptable activity, such as an educational program; they were engaged in what Drucker (1985), Say (1827), and Schumpeter (1942) described as entrepreneurship: they created new products or services; they developed new organizational structures and networks; they engaged in "creative destruction." They went outside the usual boundaries of economic activity to satisfy perceived market needs, and this in an environment where years of cultural depravation had left their communities bereft of a cultural heritage and with very low levels of social capital. When asked to "show us your city," the entrepreneurs most often, very proudly, showed us their old churches and cathedrals, many of which were still not operating or were used for other purposes, such as government offices. Some scholars have noted that religion and church communities are important as seeds of a civil society and in spawning the growth of trust in relationships and that they are necessary for a successful economy (for example, Dionne 1996; Fukuyama 1995a). A few of the churches had recently been reactivated, and a few were being renovated. These churches served as one of the last major vestiges of once proud cultures and some housed major collections of art from earlier periods.

With social capital so necessary to the formation of interpersonal and interorganizational economic networks (as shown in Figure 2), where would the source of social capital be found in the absence of a civil society? The answer lies within each of the entrepreneurs. Even though the entrepreneurs were striving to run successful, profitable enterprises, their social behavior also served as a forum whereby they had the potential to fulfill a natural longing for recognition, belongingness, and community creation (Fukuyama 1995b; Durkheim 1933; Putnam 1995). They were exemplifying the saying that no man is an island. Durkheim

(1933) observed that the workplace serves as a community in which individuals can satisfy their natural longing for recognition and belongingness. In other words, social capital and trust are essential not only for economic activity (a form of social behavior) but also for human well-being.

In this sense, as the entrepreneurs strove for personal and social well-being, they were also progenitors of social capital, creating the trust crucial for the development of economic networks. Assuredly, all the participants—be they employees, suppliers, or customers—were necessary for sustaining the networks, as they simultaneously enhanced their self-worth, but it was the entrepreneurs, through their entrepreneurial qualities, that were the provenance of the process (see Figures 1 and 2). They, too, needed to be a part of community. In addition to the creation of a business as their major focus, these entrepreneurs were also, probably unknowingly, creating the fabric of social capital necessary for the functioning of a civil society (Henton and Walesh 1997).

SOCIAL CAPITAL AT WORK: THE MILIEU OF ENTREPRENEURSHIP

All of the entrepreneurs were asked three basic questions: (1) What encouraged you to start your business or businesses? (2) What difficulties did you encounter? (3) What must you do to remain successful?

The responses were remarkable for their similarities; the respondents often used the same words.

Their answers provided the input for Figures 1 and 2. Without exception, the entrepreneurs responded to the questions in a single voice. They all spoke English, some better than others, but an interpreter was always available to clarify uncertainties. Their answers were candid and simple and often exhibited a passion about what they had undertaken. They were curious about the investigator and were pleased to have been singled out to participate in the study (and thereby recognized). A search of the literature reveals these personality traits are quite common, maybe even necessary (Collins 1964).

Reasons to start a business

What encouraged these entrepreneurs to start their businesses? Perceived market opportunity was the unanimous reply. The perception was largely based on observation; some experience, although, in most cases (except for the education ventures), limited experience; deduction; and adventure. All were able to articulate the market opportunity based on commonsense consumer needs. Shortages of consumer goods and services (cosmetics and hair care products; consumer nondurables, such as candy, cigarettes, soft drinks, packaged snacks; currency exchange) were obvious. The decision to try to fill the need for commercial products and services was based on a combination of perception, some knowledge and experience, and being in the right place at the right time. For example, one entrepreneur had been a construction supervisor for the state, specializing in the construction of large facilities. The state had neither the resources nor the desire to construct smaller buildings, such as small warehouses and schools. He started a construction company specializing in schools and small commercial industrial buildings. His major customers were local government agencies. Another entrepreneur, who had worked in a telecommunications bureau for the state, recognized the need for communications technology information and demand forecasting for state governments. After a very slow start (state communications agencies, after the breakup, had few funds available for market studies, nor did they appreciate their significance), the entrepreneur targeted those who did appreciate the forecasts and feasibility studies, namely, Western firms interested in establishing joint-venture operations.

Some of the businesses were born of necessity. One entrepreneur, a manufacturer of shampoo, found it difficult to get supplies and services. Realizing that other manufacturers had similar problems, he started a trucking firm to deliver raw materials and finished goods not only for himself but for others as well. Because his first year of operation proved successful financially, his Western joint-venture partner invested additional funds so that the entrepreneur could build a facility for manufacturing plastic containers for shampoo and other liquid consumables, which were difficult to purchase and receive in a timely manner to match production schedules.

In addition to foresightedness, these entrepreneurs possessed a venturesome spirit. They knew they were creating something different, making something happen that had never happened before in their sphere of operation.

Difficulties encountered

The difficulties experienced by the entrepreneurs were very similar: cash flow; developing stable and sustainable networks; and exposure of physical assets, which made them targets for taxation, theft, and corruption (such as "protection"). The first two were not surprising and were normal for most startup businesses (Collins 1964). Their life's savings, as well as what they could borrow from family, friends, and investors, were on the line. As Schumpeter (1942) noted, very few people in the general population have the personality capable of handling this kind of constant pressure. To do so requires charisma, confidence, and determination.

The third difficulty is unique to this part of the world at this time and explains why, generally, much of the entrepreneurial activity in this part of the world is focused on service and trade, minimizing exposure of assets. In the long run, this will have to change for economic development to thrive. Much of the effort for increased economic well-being can and will be driven by entrepreneurial endeavors, but such efforts will surely be dampened and may even fail if the state does not support some democratization of the social and economic process (Evans 1996; Fox 1996) and if movements toward a civil society are thwarted (Becker 1994; Cox 1995; Pehe 1996).

Responses to the first two questions were not terribly surprising and are readily confirmed by the literature on entrepreneurial activity. Even though the setting for entrepreneurial activity and economic development was unique because of the vacuum created by the collapse of the Soviet system, entrepreneurs, regardless of the socioeconomic climate, perceived opportunities in similar ways and were confronted with similar problems. The shocking finding in this research was their response to the third question, regarding what was needed to stay successful.

Maintaining success

Responses to the question, "What must you do to remain successful?" were exactly alike. Each entrepreneur said the same thing, even using the same terminology, and often with passion: that one never, ever gives up, and that one needs the trust of one's employees, suppliers, and customers.

Never giving up was a somewhat surprising but not totally unexpected response. Never giving up is an expression of both ambition and determination and was usually expressed passionately. A strong desire to achieve and firmness of purpose were evident throughout the interviews. As the entrepreneurs saw it, not giving up was the most important controllable behavioral trait necessary for success. They were revealing their own inner qualities of ambition and determination. Research by Becker (1975), Collins (1964), and Vesper (1980) support these findings. The in-depth interviews also revealed the presence of the other human capital qualities shown in Figure 2, such as being knowledgeable, being a good learner, and being a visionary.

The response of "trust" was a complete surprise. Every entrepreneur explicitly used the term "trust" (a few used a synonym, such as faith or confidence, sometimes using the words interchangeably). They did so with a sense of its underpinning necessity for success (Arrow 1974; Coleman 1989; Fukuyama 1995b). These entrepreneurs recognized the social dimensions of their economic behavior, and trust served as an adhesive factor essential for developing sustainable value-creation networks. In another study of small entrepreneurs in Russia after the breakup, Taylor, Kazakov, and Thompson (1997) found that half of their respondents ($n = 25$) claimed that success (profits) was dependent on trust between partners. Networks of social interactions (social capital) created by entrepreneurs feed on their own successes. Reciprocity and learning among network members increase as success increases, as do effectiveness and efficiency in achieving network goals, leading to greater rewards for members (Chung and Gibbons 1997; Minkoff 1997; Putnam 1995). In building their own value-creation networks out of self-interest, these entrepreneurs were also planting the seeds of a civil society.

CONCLUSION

Three major findings come from the study. One is that human capital, in the form of an entrepreneurial personality, is crucial and at the core of entrepreneurship and small business development. The entrepreneurs interviewed were well endowed with the qualities listed in Figure 2. They unanimously said that ambition and determination were the most important factors necessary for success. The in-depth interviews revealed that they had an abundance of these and the other necessary qualities. As noted by Schumpeter (1942), very few individuals in a society have this complex of traits in the quantities necessary to be successful entrepreneurs. These entrepreneurs did. Others in the study, support professionals and employees, did not. Skill and experience, which many of the support professionals and employees possessed, are not sufficient. They recognized these traits in their entrepreneur-employer, looking to him for leadership, with a strong desire to be parti- cipants in making the visions a reality.

The second major finding had to do with trust. Social capital in the form of trust was, in the view of these entrepreneurs, the second factor essential to establishing viable, sustainable small businesses. They explicitly stated that, without the trust of their employees, suppliers, and customers, their businesses would not survive. They also saw trust as facilitating learning, reducing uncertainty, and therefore increasing efficiency and effectiveness. They saw themselves as responsible for creating this trust. This is a remarkable perception on their part as it comes in a social climate that has experienced several decades of government suppression of social and cultural capital generation activities.

Supporting the research of Coleman (1989), Fukuyama (1995b), and Putnam (1995), the research being reported here found that trust was a vital element for human well-being as well as for sustainable economic activity. The need for associations and connections was seen not only as the means to an end but also as an end in itself (Durkheim 1933). Successful small business development is a blending of human and social capital toward a specific economic goal. Successful entrepreneurship requires input of both. It is a known fact that businesses function best when there are high levels of commitment and trust (Hutton 1997). Coleman (1989), Fukuyama (1995b), and Putnam (1995) also noted that communities and societies with high levels of social capital and trust, compared to those with low levels of social capital, are much more likely to be open, fluid, creative, effective, and efficient in economic and community endeavors.

Entrepreneurs in the present study fully appreciated the role of trust in their efforts to create sustainable enterprises. Trust can be created even in the absence of social capital when given the opportunity because of its innate ability to foster inner human well-being. These are important findings and extend our knowledge of the milieu of small business development.

Therefore, trust creation has a twofold impact. First, it is crucial for the establishment of sustainable economic (and social) relationships.

This was particularly true for these entrepreneurs because of the climate of distrust that overlaid their societies, certainly between the state and individuals. There was no base or heritage of social capital in the form of interpersonal or interorganizational trust to underpin their efforts. They had to create the trust. Second, as Durkheim (1933) noted, trust creation, leading to meaningful associations with fellow human beings, is a natural phenomenon and necessary for total individual fulfillment. It was the synergy of the two dimensions that contributed to these entrepreneurs' early successes.

The third major finding is that entrepreneurship, to be successful in the long run, will require participation by society—a civil society—and the state. It cannot succeed in the long run in a vacuum. Similar observations were made by Taylor, Kazakov, and Thompson (1997) in their study of the milieu of Russian entrepreneurship. As Landes (1998) has so well noted, culture drives economic development, and as John Locke (1690), Adam Smith ([1776] 1796), and David Hume ([1738] 1967) observed over 200 years ago, for the energies and innovativeness of human (and financial) capital to be set loose, the dynamics of entrepreneurship require the context of a moral civil society. Modern-day scholars echo these same ideas (see, for example, Evans 1996; Fox 1996; Kentworthy 1997).

In a climate of interdependence, social capital, civil society, and contemporary democracy interact with each other in a variety of forms, providing the fabric for a social order (see, for example, Hayden 1997). Entrepreneurs in the present study were vital elements in the interplay between the stakeholders (customers, suppliers, employees, and community), creating economic value; trust and social capital; and a sense of stability in turbulent times. In emerging economies bereft of civil infrastructure, entrepreneurs have the potential to make significant contributions toward creating civil societies. Other writers have also concluded that businesses, as social institutions, are crucial for the sustenance of civil society (for example, Novak 1995).

The great similarity of the responses of these nine entrepreneurs and their cohorts, coming from different societies, is what triggered the analysis leading to the development of the two models discussed in this study. Surely, more studies of a like nature are needed, from a variety of economic settings, to confirm or modify these models. Recent interest in the concepts of civil society, social capital, and trust in commerce strongly encourages the inclusion of these social elements in economic development and entrepreneurial paradigms.

References

Arrow, Kenneth J. 1974. *The Limits of Organization*. New York: W. W. Norton.

Becker, Gary S. 1975. *Human Capital: A Theoretical and Empirical Analysis*. 2d ed. New York: National Bureau of Economic Research.

Becker, Marvin B. 1994. *The Emergence of Civil Society in the Eighteenth Century*. Bloomington: Indiana University Press.

Chung, Lai Hong and Patrick T. Gibbons. 1997. Corporate Entrepreneurship: The Roles of Ideology and Social Capital. *Group and Organization Management* 22(1):10-30.

Coleman, James S. 1989. Social Capital in the Creation of Human Capital. *American Journal of Sociology* 94:S95-120.

Collins, Orvis. 1964. *The Enterprising Man*. East Lansing: Michigan State University, Graduate School of Business Administration, Bureau of Business and Economic Research.

Cox, Eva. 1995. *A Truly Civil Society*. Sydney, Australia: ABC Books.

Dionne, E. J., Jr. 1996. Can Government Nurture Civic Life? *Brookings Review* 14(4):3.

Drucker, Peter F. 1985. *Innovation and Entrepreneurship*. New York: Harper & Row.

Durkheim, Emile. 1933. *The Division of Labor in Society*. New York: Macmillan.

Evans, Peter. 1996. Introduction: Development Strategies Across the Public-Private Divide. *World Development* 24(June):1033-37.

Ferguson, Adam. [1767] 1966. *An Essay on the History of Civil Society*. Reprint, Edinburgh: Edinburgh University Press.

Fox, Jonathan. 1996. How Does Civil Society Thicken? The Political Construction of Social Capital in Rural Mexico. *World Development* 24(June):1089-1103.

Fukuyama, Francis. 1995a. Social Capital and the Global Economy. *Foreign Affairs* 24(Sept.-Oct.):89-103.

———. 1995b. *Trust: The Social Virtues and the Creation of Prosperity*. New York: Free Press.

Hayden, Goran. 1997. Civil Society, Social Capital and Development: Dissection of a Complex Discourse. *Studies in Comparative International Development* 32(1):3-30.

Hayek, Friedrich A. 1960. *The Construction of Liberty*. Chicago: University of Chicago Press.

Henton, Douglas and Kimberly Walesh. 1997. The Age of the Civic Entrepreneur: Restoring Civil Society and Building Economic Community. *National Civic Review* 86(Summer):149-56.

Hume, David. [1738] 1967. *A Treatise of Human Nature*. Reprint, London: Clarendon Press.

Hutton, Will. 1997. Six Stakeholding Propositions. *Business Strategy Review* 8(2):7-9.

Kentworthy, Jane. 1997. Civic Engagement, Social Capital and Economic Cooperation. *American Behavioral Scientist* 40(Mar.-Apr.):645-56.

Landes, David S. 1998. *The Wealth and Poverty of Nations*. New York: W. W. Norton.

Locke, John. 1690. *An Essay Concerning Human Understanding*. London: Eliz. Holt for Thomas Bassett.

Minkoff, Debra C. 1997. Producing Social Capital: National Social Movements and Civil Society. *American Behavioral Scientist* 40(5):606-19.

Mishler, William and Richard Rose. 1997. Trust, Distrust and Skepticism: Popular Evaluations of Civil and Political Institutions in Post-Communist Societies. *Journal of Politics* 59(May):418-51.

Newton, Kenneth. 1997. Social Capital and Democracy. *American Behavioral Scientist* 40(5):575-86.

Novak, Michael. 1995. The Business Corporation: A Distinctive Social Institution. *Business Korea* 12(7):44-49.

Pehe, Jiri. 1996. After the Soviet Empire: Civil Society in Democratizing States. *Current* Mar.:27-30.

Putnam, Robert D. 1993. *Making Democracy Work*. Princeton, NJ: Princeton University Press.

———. 1995. Bowling Alone: America's Declining Social Capital. *Journal of Democracy* 6:65-78.

Rau, Zbigniew, ed. 1991. *The Reemergence of Civil Society in Eastern Europe and the Soviet Union*. Boulder, CO: Westview Press.

Say, Jean Baptiste. 1827. *A Treatise on Political Economy*. Trans. C. R. Prinsep. Philadelphia: J. Grigg.

Schumpeter, Joseph A. 1942. *Capitalism, Socialism and Democracy*. New York: Harper & Brothers.

Shils, Edward. 1997. *The Virtue of Civility: Selected Essays on Liberalism, Tradition and Civil Society*. Ed. Stenen Groshy. Indianapolis, IN: Liberty Fund Index.

Smith, Adam. [1776] 1796. *An Inquiry into the Nature and Causes of the Wealth of Nations*. Reprint, Philadelphia: Thomas Dodson.

———. [1759] 1817. *The Theory of Moral Sentiments*. Reprint, Boston: Wells & Lilly.

Taylor, Thomas C., Alexander Y. Kazakov, and C. Michael Thompson. 1997. Business Ethics and Civil Society in Russia. *International Studies of Management and Organization* 27(1):5-18.

Vesper, Karl H. 1980. *The New Venture Strategy*. Englewood Cliffs, NJ: Prentice Hall.

Walzer, Michael. 1991. The Idea of Civil Society. *Dissent* 38(Spring):293-304.

Weber, Max. 1930. *The Protestant Ethic and the Spirit of Capitalism*. London: Allen & Unwin.

ANNALS, *AAPSS*, **565**, September 1999

The Aztec States-Society: Roots of Civil Society and Social Capital

By MARCO A. ALMAZÁN

ABSTRACT: This article argues in favor of a new image of pre-Hispanic politics in Mesoamerica by positing the existence of an Aztec states-society during the fifteenth and early sixteenth centuries. This society was based on a series of common assumptions, interests, and institutions that fostered a close degree of cooperation between member states.

Marco A. Almazán is an associate professor at the Universidad de las Américas–Puebla, where he lectures on the history and theory of international politics. His current research interests are the comparative study of states systems, the history of international political thought, and the undergraduate teaching of international relations.

I NDIGENOUS communities are an important part of contemporary civil society in Mexico. In recent years, many of them have become more vocal so as to ensure their cultural survival and increase their economic prosperity and political autonomy. In order to succeed, it is surely important for them to possess a positive self-image, one serving to strengthen their determination to struggle against the odds they face.

The indigenous communities' self-image is ill served by prevailing historical interpretations of the politics of pre-Hispanic Mesoamerica. A different and more accurate view, however, one that highlights the political sophistication of past Mesoamerican societies, is possible. This article seeks to contribute to such a view by presenting an alternative account of how Aztec city-states dealt with each other during the fifteenth and early sixteenth centuries. My contention is that, during this period, a fully fledged Aztec states-society existed in that Aztec city-states had common assumptions and interests and participated jointly in a series of institutions in order to achieve common goals. This society was characterized by a high level of interstate cooperation.

COMMON ASSUMPTIONS

There was a marked degree of cultural unity within the Aztec states-society. This is reflected in the assumptions that its members shared with regard to nature of the universe, humankind, and the state.

Aztec cosmology

Detailed descriptions of what we know about Aztec cosmology can be found in Brundage (1985), León-Portilla (1992), and López Austin (1988). Only a very basic sketch of this cosmic theory will be presented here.

For the Aztecs, the source of all creation was a deity, Ometeotl, who was in fact a combination of Ometecuhtli ("Two Lord") and Omecihuatl ("Two Lady"). The latter produced four sons, or cosmic forces: the elements of air, earth, fire, and water. These, in turn, created other phenomena, including the rest of the gods of the Aztec pantheon and human beings. Each of the forces was eager for supremacy, and this led to a great cosmic struggle. According to the Aztecs, a series of four ages, called Suns, had existed, in each of which one of the cosmic forces had been paramount and a certain type of human being had existed. Each Sun had been ended by a cataclysmic event. At the beginning of the fifth age, two deities, Tezcatlipoca and Quetzalcoatl, re-created the earth. Quetzalcoatl then proceeded to form the present type of human being, that is, the one that subsists on maize. Afterward, the gods assembled at Teotihuacan in order to create the Fifth Sun, as well as the moon. In order to set them in motion, the gods offered themselves as sacrifices.

The Aztecs believed that the current age of the Fifth Sun would eventually end in destruction via a cataclysm (in this case, a series of earthquakes). However, it would not be followed by a Sixth Sun. According to López Austin (1988),

The number 5 corresponds to the central point, the most important position in a stable world, since each of the former suns had belonged to one of the four extremes of the earth's surface. . . . The Nahuatl man thought, in fact, that the true human species occupied the center of the world and that it had been formed in the fifth creation and that another stage, a generation that would surpass his own in time and quality, was inconceivable. In the Fifth Sun, in the last of the positions possible to the terrestrial plane, the possibilities for creation were exhausted. (67, 240)

After the end of the present age, "the world would simply fall into deep darkness" (Berdan 1982, 121).

The Aztecs worshiped a large number of gods, who sent their divine forces, both favorable and unfavorable, to the earth. These forces influenced everything in existence and could be manipulated on the basis of proper communication with the gods through ritual and precise knowledge of calendrical cycles. The deities required adequate nourishment, and this was to be provided through human blood. H. B. Nicholson (1971, cited in Berdan 1982, 129) has classified the Aztec gods into three basic types, each related to a particular theme. One type was mainly concerned with celestial creativity; a second, with rain, moisture, and agricultural fertility; and a third, with war and sacrifice. The latter type of god was especially in need of human nourishment.

Although the Aztecs worshiped the whole pantheon of deities, it was customary for each state to have its own patron god. Each patron god, represented by an idol, was housed in a special temple and served by its own priesthood.

Humankind

One of the basic premises of Aztec religious thought was the human being's responsibility for the maintenance of the equilibrium of forces that enabled the age of the Fifth Sun to exist. Humankind's principal task was to serve the gods and contribute to their preservation. This entailed the provision of *chalchihuatl* ("precious liquid") for the gods through human sacrifice. According to Berdan (1982),

The Aztec perception of the world stressed uncertainty: the present was tenuous, the future was fragile. In this forbidding precarious situation, the people's only recourse was to maintain proper moral conduct and strictly observe religious duties. In the abstract, the most critical activity was to guarantee the human blood required for cosmic preservation. . . .

The most commonly practiced form of human sacrifice was autosacrifice. The priests, in particular, often drew blood from the fleshy parts of their own bodies. . . . Virtually everyone, at some ceremonial event, was required to draw blood to demonstrate religious devotion. Even very young children were not exempt, although adults performed the rite for them, most typically piercing the child's earlobes. (112, 114)

It was also held that human sacrificial death was necessary in order for there to be life. For twentieth-century people, this notion is repellent. For the Aztecs, however, it embodied a positive value. Sacrificial death always took place within a religious context and was performed by priests. Davies (1973) comments that "one factor entirely absent from such slaughter was any feeling of hate or cruelty" (173). It was considered a great honor to have been predestined to provide nourishment to the gods, and it was believed that the victim died not for the god but as the god to whom he or she was being sacrificed. Hence he or she was guaranteed a wonderful afterlife. It is claimed that few sacrificial victims resisted, as this conduct would have been inappropriate: "If a man was to be sacrificed . . . the gods would be pleased if he bore his fate willingly" (Berdan 1982, 120).

The state

The fundamental political entity of the Aztecs was called the *altepetl*. It was based on several principles that were universally accepted, including what might be called the boundary and monarchical principles. The boundary principle established that each *altepetl* possessed a precisely demarcated territory (cf. Gibson 1964, 23-24). The monarchical principle held that the *tlatocayotl* ("rulership") of the *altepetl* was to be in the hands of individuals who belonged to certain dynasties. These rulers, or *tlatoque* (singular: *tlatoani*), were considered to be representatives of the gods and therefore governed by divine right. They were regarded as belonging to the same category and hence met as equals on formal occasions. Two corollaries followed from all this: (1) the principle that no dynasty could be dissolved

without doing violence to the cosmic order (thus "it was assumed that . . . dynasties would remain in power even if conquered in war" [Calnek 1982, 59]) and (2) the principle that to kill a *tlatoani* was to commit a form of sacrilege. The latter did occur on occasion, however. For example, Ahuitzotl, *tlatoani* of Tenochtitlan from 1486 to 1502, had Tzutzumatzin, the ruler of Coyohuacan, killed after a disagreement over the building of an aqueduct. Davies (1973) informs us,

This assassination, for such it was, caused consternation among Ahuitzotl's advisers . . . it might be one thing occasionally to slay a remote provincial prince after a bitter war; it was quite another to kill the sovereign of a neighboring city in cold blood. It virtually amounted to an offense against the gods, whom this ruler, in his own sphere, represented. And in the end even Ahuitzotl himself felt remorse, and did his best to compensate the sons of the deceased. (193)

On the relatively few occasions when a ruler was deposed or executed, he was replaced by someone with the proper dynastic credentials. Writing in relation to the so-called Aztec Empire, Calnek (1982) observes,

In cases when a military governor [*cuauhtlatoani*] was imposed, he was likely, as in the case of Tlatelolco after that city's conquest in 1473, to be a lower ranking member of the local nobility. If a royal prince was sent out from the capital to govern . . . he was usually a kinsman of his new subjects through a maternal connection formed by an earlier marriage. (5)

While the *tlatoque* were regarded as formally equal in the sense that all of them were representatives of the gods, the city-states that they ruled did not all possess the same status. Indeed, the role of hegemon was considered to be completely legitimate. An example of this can be seen in the struggle between Azcapotzalco and Texcoco for the right of their rulers to hold the title of *chichimeca tecuhtli* ("lord of the Chichimecs"). According to the annals of Texcoco, Xolotl, the leader of the Acolhua tribe, arrived in the Valley of Mexico and proceeded to establish a "powerful empire" with Tenayuca as its capital. He then assumed the aforementioned title. In later years, the title was claimed by the ruler of Azcapotzalco after having defeated Tenayuca in the late fourteenth century. Shortly afterward, however, Quinatzin (a great-great-grandson of Xolotl who had left Tenayuca to reside in Texcoco) defeated Azcapotzalco and the latter acknowledged the former's right to be lord of the Chichimecs. In 1418, Tezozomoc of Azcapotzalco defeated Texcoco and had himself formally invested with the title in a ceremony that was reportedly attended by representatives of a great number of Aztec states. Shortly after Tezozomoc's death, Azcapotzalco was defeated in the Tepanec War, and in 1431 Nezahualcoyotl was crowned *tlatoani* of Texcoco and declared to be *chichimeca tecuhtli*.

By then, however, this particular title had become purely honorary. Much more important was the claim to be the successor of Tollan, who had reputedly controlled all of central Mexico in its heyday. The Toltec "empire" had at one point existed in the form of a coalition of three major states, Tollan, Otompan, and Culhuacan. The Aztecs thus tended to conceive of two categories of rulership: the common *tlatocayotl* and the *hueitlatocayotl* ("great rulerships"), the latter being coalitions of three members that claimed to be the legitimate successors of Tollan and, as such, the protectors and benefactors of all men. In return for offering such social goods, they demanded recognition of their divinely begotten power in the form of alliance and tribute on the part of other states.

The assumptions that the Aztecs shared about the nature of the universe, humankind, and the state determined what was considered acceptable in their interstate relations. It is important to note that some of these assumptions provided a raison d'être for warfare as a normal state of affairs. At the same time, however, other assumptions limited what could be legitimately accomplished through war and promoted the ideal of a system of formally autonomous (though not necessarily equal) states.

COMMON INTERESTS

Bull (1977) reminds us that "to say that x is in someone's interest is merely to say that it serves as a means to some end that he is pursuing" (66). In order to speak of the common interests of states, it is necessary to know what purposes they share. In the case of the members of the Aztec states-society, there was a sense of common interest in achieving the following goals:

— the preservation of the cosmic order. As was mentioned earlier, this entailed the aversion of cosmic cataclysm by ensuring that the gods received adequate nourishment in the form of human blood. This in turn implied the need for sacrificial victims.

— the preservation of the *altepetl* and its various attributes, including its territory and the institution of divine rulership. The latter entailed the preservation of the ruling dynasties, these being the only legitimate providers of rulers for the different city-states.

— the preservation of the states-society's institutions. The institutions were an important means of achieving the other two goals.

INSTITUTIONS

The institutions of the Aztec states-society contributed to the realization of common goals. Some of these institutions involved the use of formal intergovernmental organizations. Others were simply standardized modes of coactivity involving two or more states. The principal Aztec interstate institutions will be dealt with under the following headings: warfare and diplomacy; economic exchange; dynastic interaction; and alliances.

Warfare and diplomacy

The Aztecs shared two different conceptions of the nature of war. One word for war was *yaoyotl*, which meant "that for which the enemy stands, his business" (Brundage 1972, 96). In this sense, war was understood to be a confrontation between two or more states for purposes of obtaining (or preventing others from obtaining) material gain or prestige. War was an instrument to obtain tribute from or hegemonic control over other states.

A different conception of war is inherent in the phrase *teoatl tlachinolli*, which means "divine liquid and burnt things." Brundage (1972) informs us that

the first element signifies "blood," and the second is a shorthand statement for the practice of cremating dead warriors on the battlefield, a Toltec custom that released the fortunate soul like a sunburst to ascend into the heavens. War means the spilling of human blood, which was by definition a liquid destined for the support of the gods. (97)

From this perspective, what was being sought through war was sacrificial victims in order to contribute to the preservation of life on earth. However, there were positive side effects as well. If a warrior died in battle, he faced a glorious afterlife as part of the Sun God's entourage. If he was captured by the enemy, his destiny was the same, for he would be sacrificed. If a warrior succeeded in taking a captive, he won prestige and the opportunity for social advancement. For example, when a Tenochca nobleman had taken his fourth captive,

he became a *tequihua*, "one with a commitment." ... As a tequihua he could now sit in the war council and could begin a move up the line of appointments to high office. Yet much of his remaining rise had still to be justified by his continuing performance on the field of battle. (Brundage 1985, 138)

Two types of war existed in the Aztec world—conquest wars and flower wars. The former embodied both of the aforementioned conceptions of war. The latter were justified solely in terms of the second conception.

Conquest wars between Aztec states were based on a series of conventions. They could be justified on several grounds, such as the closing of roads to commerce (blocking a road constituted a clear signal that a state was adopting a hostile attitude, for the expectation was that there would be free passage of peoples), the killing of merchants or ambassadors, and the refusal to honor commitments to pay tribute. A refusal to tacitly acknowledge the superiority of a hegemon could also prove a motive for war. For example, we are told that, in 1410, Azcapotzalco sent cotton to Texcoco as if in a gesture of friendship, requesting that fine mantles be made. Davies (1973) comments that "although the request was phrased in the diplomatic language of the times, and so presented as if a mere favor were expected, in fact it was intended, and understood, as a token of submission" (56). Texcoco refused the request and this was interpreted as a hostile gesture by Azcapotzalco. The two states were soon involved in a major war.

When a conflict occurred, envoys were usually sent in order to negotiate. In the case of the Triple Alliance of Tenochtitlan, Texcoco, and Tlacopan, Hassig (1988) writes,

After the Aztecs decided to go to war, ambassadors were sent to the city in question to announce that it had wronged the Aztecs and to ask for satisfaction. Three different embassies were sent; the first to the rulers, the second to the nobles, and the third to the people. If the enemy city still failed to provide redress, war followed. (8)

Davies (1973) comments that "it was usual to let pass three periods of twenty days, involving a further series of visits and ceremonies, before the start of actual warfare" (65).

During the course of battle, certain conventions also prevailed. For one thing, there were certain dress codes:

Voluminous quantities of fancy devices and insignia [were] required, and considered quite as indispensable as arms and ammunition. . . . To us, such adornments might appear as an absurd encumbrance; however, in Mexico war was conceived within a magico-religious framework. The gods decided, and men merely executed their will. To secure victory, one first had to make sure that the former would be favorable to the outcome. Any failure, therefore, to comply with tradition, or any attempt to discard the customary paraphernalia, would be fatal to one's chances. (Davies 1973, 185-86)

Both sides fought to capture enemies rather than to kill them on the battlefield, for it was only by such means that sacrificial victims would be obtained from the enemy and that status could be gained.

Conventions also existed as to what constituted a victory. Taking prisoner the opponent's commander was one such convention. Another was the burning of the enemy *alte-petl*'s central temple: "When the torch was successfully put to this, all resistance on the part of the losing side ceased, for the identity of the city in the person of its divine talisman had been obliterated" (Brundage 1972, 218). Once victory had been achieved, a peace process took place in which ambassadors of the victorious state were sent to the enemy, usually with a demand for the latter to become a tributary.

Once a nobleman warrior had been captured, he was treated with great consideration by his captor, who now considered him to be his son. The captive was expected to accept his fate with calm dignity. If he escaped and returned to his *alte-petl*, he was normally strangled for engaging in such disgraceful behavior. However, commoners who escaped were rewarded by their state.

Flower wars, or *xochiyaotl*, existed for the express purpose of obtaining sacrificial victims; in addition, they served as a means of training warriors and keeping them fit and of preserving the social status system within the state. They were called "flower wars" because the warriors, with their colorful dress and armor, were likened to exotic flowers that waved and surged in the wind. Often they were scheduled on a regular basis between enemy states who nevertheless "recognized a close kinship in the service of the gods" (Brundage 1985, 132).

Flower wars took place on special fields called *teoatempan* ("on the shores of sacrificial blood"). Only noblemen fought in them, and

participation was voluntary. Numbers did not matter, for "such gatherings were in no sense armies with national objectives. They were spontaneous esquadrilles of individual knights whose only objective was personal glory" (132). Priests from both sides signaled the commencement by burning a pyre of paper and incense, and they determined when the encounter should end. Dead warriors were ceremoniously cremated once the battle was over.

The flower war was a long-standing Toltec tradition. However, the most famous of them are the ones that took place between the members of a triple alliance (that of Tenochtitlan, Texcoco, and Tlacopan) and Tlaxcallan and Huexotzinco as of the mid-fifteenth century.

Economic exchange

Berdan (1982) writes that in Aztec times, "intense specialization in the production of goods, coupled with large surpluses, generated a need for intricate webs of economic exchange" (35). She distinguishes between three institutions of economic exchange: the local market, long-distance trade, and tribute.

The local market played a major role in that all commercial activities took place in the marketplaces, or *tianquiztli*. These served as a network for the distribution of a great variety of specialized products. They were an important source of goods for the commoners and of products required for payment of tribute in kind.

Although daily markets existed in the largest city-states, the majority of markets were held once every five days. Some markets specialized in particular products; for example, Tepeyacac, Otompan, and Tepepulco were famous for birds; Azcapotzalco and Itzocan, for slaves; Acolman, for dogs; Cholollan, for precious stones and feathers; and Texcoco, for clothes and pottery vessels (Hassig 1985, 111).

Rules regarding prices, merchandise quality, and theft existed, and marketplace officials were usually present to enforce them. There were also generally accepted norms regarding commercial transactions. The most common means of exchange was barter, but certain universally accepted currencies were also used, namely, cacao beans, copper bells, cotton cloaks, and quills filled with gold dust.

Long-distance trade differed from the local marketing system in terms of participants, types of goods traded, and form of transaction. Long-distance trade was in the hands of professional merchant guilds rather than individual traders. These associations of *pochteca* had their own residential quarters, internal hierarchy, and laws. *Pochteca* living within states allied to the Triple Alliance of Tenochtitlan, Texcoco, and Tlacopan were exempt from tribute in labor and often received gifts from their rulers. They maintained close ties with their states and sometimes served as both official representatives (*teucnenenque* ["travelers of the lord"]) and spies.

The commodities of long-distance trade consisted mainly of luxury products such as quetzal feathers, jade, obsidian, turquoise, gold products, and various kinds of elaborately designed articles of clothing. Davies describes these goods as "necessary luxuries" in the sense that they were indispensable symbols of social status. They also played an important part in Aztec warfare. Davies (1987) comments as follows:

The warriors' costumes, laboriously confected out of precious feathers and other costly items, were not exactly a "luxury" . . . these costumes served the practical purpose of striking terror into the enemy. Established convention and respect for the gods demanded that leading warriors should enter the fray thus gorgeously attired. Had they denied themselves this indispensable finery, the outraged gods would have granted not victory but defeat. (135)

Long-distance trade transactions often took place in what are known as ports of trade. These were neutral city-states where *pochteca* from different regions could trade directly with each other in a secure environment. Examples of these ports of trade are Ayotlan, which stood along the frontier between Xoconochco and Cuauhtemallan on the Pacific coast, and Xicallanco, situated on the Gulf of Mexico coast near the Yucatan peninsula. The merchants who arrived at these centers engaged in two different types of transaction. On the one hand, they brought gifts from their *tlatoque* for the rulers of these city-states as a symbol of friendship and in order to have continued access to these states. On the other hand, they traded with other merchants—who purchased their goods either to resell them at other locales or in order to obtain products for the payment of tribute—and sought to make a profit from these exchanges.

Tribute was considered to be an important and completely legitimate symbol of power relationships as well as a source of material wealth for the ruling elites. Together with state control over long-distance trade, it could also provide an effective means of exercising economic control over different regions.

Several conventions existed pertaining to this form of exchange. For example, a state might be both a recipient and a provider of tribute. Tribute might be paid to one or several states. It could be in kind or in the form of labor service. Berdan (1982) writes that "goods of all kinds were demanded in tribute: luxury and subsistence items, manufactured and raw materials. Typically, the people of a province surrendered goods which were locally available to them" (36). As Smith (1986) has pointed out, tribute was paid solely by the commoners of a subordinate state (and usually only by those residing in a specific calpulli), the nobility often being considered as allies under the nominal protection of the hegemon.

Tribute was collected on a periodic basis. The members of the Triple Alliance of Tenochtitlan, Texcoco, and Tlacopan gathered tribute every 80 days, 6 months, or 12 months, depending on the type of good and the distance involved. They had a system of official tribute collectors, or *calpixque*, who were stationed in the various tribute provinces in order to ensure prompt delivery. However, each tribute-owing state determined how the tribute was to be obtained.

In addition, it should be noted that the amount of tribute to be paid was usually fairly moderate (Davies 1987, 158), although it was sometimes drastically increased if a state reneged on its promises. Weak states may have considered the payment of tribute a small price for security.

Dynastic interaction

Aztec ruling dynasties interacted with certain frequency. This interaction took two principal forms: royal marriages and participation in ceremonies.

Royal marriages were used to acquire status and legitimacy by establishing kinship ties with the leading dynasties. They were also used to seal new alliances or for purposes of hegemonic control. Often, the ruler of a would-be hegemon would attempt to co-opt less powerful states by giving his sisters or daughters in marriage to their rulers. From the latter's perspective, these marriages were a means of gaining political standing and influence.

Joint participation in ceremonies on the part of rulers and nobles from different states was widespread in the Aztec world. These ceremonies included religious festivals such as that celebrating the eighteenth Aztec month, Izcalli, and another known as *Tlacaxipehualiztli* ("the flaying of men"), celebrated at the beginning of spring and dedicated to Xipe Totec, the Flayed God. State funerals and coronations were also often attended by foreign rulers, including those of enemy states.

Indeed, attendance by enemy rulers was a barometer of a state's power. Thus, the fact that several powerful rulers declined to attend Ahuitzotl's coronation in 1486 was a sure sign that recent military setbacks had diminished Tenochtitlan's standing. One year later, and after several spectacular military victories on the part of the Tenochca, most of these rulers were quick to accept Ahuitzotl's invitation to attend a ceremony celebrating the rebuilding of the Great Temple of Tenochtitlan.

During state ceremonies, rulers exchanged expensive gifts and took part in lavish feasts, in the course of which numerous victims (often prisoners of war) were sacrificed. These festivities have been viewed as an instrument of propaganda and terror used by hegemons. Davies (1973) quotes Diego de Durán, a sixteenth-century Spanish chronicler, to this effect:

The intentions of these Mexicans, in preparing a festival . . . was to make known their king, and to ensure that their enemies . . . should be conscious of the greatness of Mexico and should be terrorized and filled with fear; and that they should know, by the prodigality and wealth of jewels and other presents given away at the ceremonies, how great was the abundance of Mexico, its valor and its excellence. (162)

Others are skeptical about this interpretation and offer an alternative that stresses the role of ceremonies in promoting interdynastic solidarity. Thus Smith (1986) writes that

the descriptions of Mexica state ceremonies emphasize grandeur, sumptuous feasting, gift giving, and royal redistribution to the gathered nobility. The impression is given that the nobles were enjoying themselves, and that to them the human sacrifices were not an instrument of terror but rather a form of religious entertainment along with the dances, speeches, processions, and other theatrical ceremonies. (75)

Smith goes on to quote Tlacaelel, a statesman from Tenochtitlan, as an example of a contemporary who "explicitly articulates this notion of elite solidarity":

It seems to me that it would not be unreasonable to ask them [the nobles and rulers of the enemy states of Tlaxcallan and Metztitlan] again to this solemn occasion because, even though we are enemies in the wars that we wage, in our festivities we should rejoice together. There is no reason why they should be excluded since we are all one. It is reasonable that there be truces and greetings among the nobles. (76)

It might also be argued, of course, that there was no contradiction involved in attempting to use ceremonies as a means of simultaneously fostering brotherhood and fear.

Alliances

According to Hodge (1984), "it was a long-established practice for [Aztec] polities to join together for mutual defense and to go to war together" (18). She identifies eight "leagues," or "confederations," in the Valley of Mexico in the early sixteenth century: those of the Tenochca, Tepaneca, Acolhuaque, Chalca, Xochimilca, Culhuaque, Cuitlahuaca, and Mixquica. Other confederations existed elsewhere, examples of these being Tlaxcallan and Cuauhtinchan in the Valley of Puebla. Hodge (1984) describes these leagues or confederations "as territorial blocs of city-states with shared interests" and adds that they were often chartered on geographical proximity and a mythology about common origins (18).

In addition to these coalitions, there was also a tradition of triple alliances between great powers, or *hueitlatocayotl*. The oldest triple alliance of which we have knowledge in central Mexico is that between Tollan, Culhuacan, and Otompan, which existed before the fall of Tollan in the second half of the twelfth century. Subsequent coalitions of major powers within the Valley of Mexico included one between Culhuacan, Tenayuca, and Xaltocan, and another between Azcapotzalco, Coatlinchan, and Culhuacan. However, the most famous and best documented of them all is the one between Tenochtitlan, Texcoco, and Tlacopan. This triple alliance was formed in the aftermath of the Tepanec War of 1428, in which Azcapotzalco was defeated by a grand coalition that included forces from Tenochtitlan, Texcoco, and Tlacopan. The triple alliance was proclaimed to be permanent in 1441, and, indeed, it lasted until the Spanish Conquest. According to Brundage (1972), it did not formally end until 1525, "when Hernando Cortez hanged the kings of all three cities from the same tree" (121).

In this article, I have posited the existence of an Aztec states-society during the fifteenth and early sixteenth centuries. Aztec states had common assumptions and interests and participated jointly in a series of institutions designed to preserve each state's political identity and socioeconomic well-being, as well as to promote interstate cooperation, by regulating issues related to diplomacy, warfare, and economic interaction.

In my view, there is one major objection that might be made to the notion of an Aztec states-society. This has to do with the question of interstate violence. It is generally held that a states-society exists for the purpose of promoting interstate order and that interstate order includes as one of its major ingredients the limitation of interstate violence. Thus, when Bull (1977) adds war to his list of the modern European international society's institutions, he is at great pains to point out that

war has a dual aspect. On the one hand, war is a manifestation of disorder in international society, bringing with it the threat of breakdown of international society itself into a state of pure enmity of war of all against all. The society of states, accordingly, is concerned to limit and contain war, to keep it within the bounds of rules laid down by international society itself. On the other hand, war—as an instrument of state policy and a basic determinant of the shape of the international system—is a means which international society itself feels a need to exploit so as to achieve its own purposes. Specifically, in the perspective of international society, war is a means of enforcing international law, of preserving the balance of power, and, arguably, of promoting changes in the law generally regarded as just. (187-88)

By "enforcing international law," "preserving the balance of power," and "promoting changes in the law," war contributed to the maintenance of that particular international society, which in turn served not only to preserve the independence of its member states (or, at any rate, of most of them) but also to guarantee order, by which is meant the limitation of violence, the keeping of promises, and stability of possession.

At first sight, it would seem that Aztec states, far from wishing to limit interstate violence, were keen on promoting it. However, these states were by no means interested in violence for its own sake. From the perspective of the Aztec states-society, war was in part a means of obtaining necessary sacrificial victims. In theory, this created order in the universe (thanks to which life on earth could continue) and also within each state. It was thus important that war continue in existence as an institution, but measures were taken to control it and thereby contribute to the maintenance of interstate order as well—for example, the establishment of flower wars and norms related to the proper conduct of hostilities and the treatment of defeated states.

It is interesting to compare the Aztec states-society with the modern European one and its contemporary offshoot, the contemporary global international society. A number of similarities can readily be detected.

Like the modern European one (but unlike the contemporary global one), the Aztec states-society was based on a strong degree of cultural unity between its members, a unity that was based on common assumptions of a religious kind; and there was a strong awareness among these states of their common interests. Many of the purposes for which the Aztec states-society existed are essentially the same as those of the other two societies: for example, the preservation of the state as a politically autonomous entity, the preservation of interstate order, and the preservation of the states-society's institutions. In all three states-societies, the main purposes of interstate order have been, as Bull (1977) leads us to expect, the limitation of violence, the honoring of commitments, and the stability of possession (the latter implying, in all three cases, the preservation of the state as an independent entity).

In addition, certain institutions have been shared by all three societies, namely, warfare, diplomacy, commerce, great power management, and interstate rules vis-à-vis the other four. Formal intergovernmental organizations are to be found in all three, as well as interstate regimes (in the case of the Aztec states-society, these included tribute, marketing, long-distance trade, and security regimes).

Finally, both the Aztec states-society and its modern European counterpart were long-term enterprises, each having lasted for several centuries—thanks in no small part to the presence of certain institutions aimed at promoting interstate cooperation. Perhaps there are lessons to be learned from both of these societies for the adequate management of contemporary global politics.

References

Berdan, Frances F. 1982. *The Aztecs of Central Mexico: An Imperial Society*. New York: Holt, Rinehart & Winston.

Brundage, Burr C. 1972. *A Rain of Darts: The Mexica Aztecs*. Austin: University of Texas Press.

———. 1985. *The Jade Steps: A Ritual Life of the Aztecs*. Salt Lake City: University of Utah Press.

Bull, Hedley. 1977. *The Anarchical Society: A Study of Order in World Politics*. New York: Columbia University Press.

Calnek, Edward E. 1982. Patterns of Empire Formation in the Valley of Mexico, Late Postclassic Period, 1200-1521. In *The Inca and Aztec States 1400-1800: Anthropology and History*, ed. G. A. Collier, R. I. Rosaldo, and J. D. Wirth. New York: Academic Press.

Davies, Nigel. 1973. *The Aztecs: A History*. Norman: University of Oklahoma Press.

———. 1987. *The Aztec Empire: The Toltec Resurgence*. Norman: University of Oklahoma Press.

Gibson, Charles. 1964. *The Aztecs Under Spanish Rule: A History of the Indians of the Valley of Mexico, 1519-1810*.

Stanford, CA: Stanford University Press.

Hassig, Ross. 1985. *Trade, Tribute, and Transportation: The Sixteenth-Century Political Economy of the Valley of Mexico*. Norman: University of Oklahoma Press.

———. 1988. *Aztec Warfare: Imperial Expansion and Political Control*. Norman: University of Oklahoma Press.

Hodge, Mary G. 1984. *Aztec City-States*. Memoirs of the Museum of Anthropology, no. 18. Ann Arbor: University of Michigan.

León-Portilla, Miguel. 1992. *The Aztec Image of Self and Society: An Introduction to Nahua Culture*. Salt Lake City: University of Utah Press.

López Austin, Alfredo. 1988. *The Human Body and Ideology: Concepts of the Ancient Nahuas*. Salt Lake City: University of Utah Press.

Nicholson, Henry B. 1971. Religion in Pre-Hispanic Central Mexico. In *Handbook of Middle American Indians*. Vol. 10. Austin: University of Texas Press.

Smith, Michael E. 1986. The Role of Social Stratification in the Aztec Empire: A View from the Provinces. *American Anthropologist* 88:70-91.

ANNALS, *AAPSS*, **565**, September 1999

Religion and Civic Engagement: A Comparative Analysis

By CORWIN SMIDT

ABSTRACT: This study examines the relationship between religious involvement and civic engagement in a comparative, cross-cultural perspective. Using data from a 1996 survey of 3000 Canadians and 3000 Americans, the study assesses religion's relative contribution to civic engagement in the two settings. The study reveals that both religious tradition and, more important, church attendance play an important role in fostering involvement in civil society in both countries, even after controlling for the effects of other factors generally associated with fostering civic activity among members of society.

Corwin Smidt is professor of political science and holds the Paul Henry Chair in Christianity and Politics at Calvin College, where he serves as director of the Paul Henry Institute for the Study of Christianity and Politics. He is a coauthor of The Bully Pulpit: The Politics of Protestant Clergy *(1997) and coeditor of* Sojourners in the Wilderness: The Christian Right in Comparative Perspective *(1997).*

DEMOCRACY, as Tocqueville (1969) insisted, requires civic associations that are not specifically political in nature yet that still function as sources of meaning and social engagement. For Tocqueville, associational life was essential for the protection of individual liberty and the overall well-being of democracy, and he argued that democracy could not survive unless citizens continued to participate actively, joining with others of similar mind and interest to address matters of common concern.

While most civic associations do fall directly within the public realm and while much of associational life may not be explicitly political in nature, nonpolitical civic associations have important political consequences, for example, with regard to the role that civic associations may play in promoting civic education, fostering civic skills, and bridging social cleavages. Moreover, associational life may serve to help undergird the public realm in that such civic activity may serve to keep the power of governmental coercion at bay. Thus, while much of associational life may not be explicitly political in nature, it is inherently political given its possible ramifications for fostering democratic life.

Religious life, in particular, frequently serves as an important contributor to civil society. In fact, given the vibrancy of religious life among those Americans he observed at the time, Tocqueville (1969, vol. 1, chap. 17) argued that religion in America should be regarded as the first of its political institutions. Certainly, congregational life has traditionally been a major component of associational life in many cultural settings (and particularly so in the United States). Congregations are often regarded as important components of civil society in local communities, as they frequently provide physical care, spiritual guidance, and social networks to their members and others in the community. Likewise, religious beliefs can help to shape associational life by affecting the ways in which people view human nature, the extent to which members in one religious community may relate to those located outside their community, and the priorities given to political life. Finally, religious behavior may contribute to a vital civic society, as volunteering, charitable contributions, and other distinct acts of mercy can, at least in the short run, help to provide a safety net for members of society who are at risk.

The present article examines the relationship between religion and civic life in the United States and Canada, and it does so largely through what might be called a "most similar" strategy of comparative analysis (Lipset 1990, xiii). A comparative, cross-national study provides a stronger test of the posited relationship between religion and associational life than does an analysis within one cultural context. By engaging in a comparative, cross-national study of the relationship between religion and civic life, relationships that may exist between the two should be clarified in terms of what may, or may not, be unique to one particular setting, and, as a result, the analyst should be better able to identify those particular religious factors that may, or may not, serve to undergird associational life cross-nationally.

RELIGION AND CIVIL SOCIETY

Many analysts have contended that religious life contributes to a vital civic society. Historically, many analysts have contended that religious associations and structures are an important component of civil society. Certainly, as noted earlier, Tocqueville (1969, vol. 1, chap. 17) saw religious life and institutions as constituting central components of American civil society possessing crucial importance for American political life. But Tocqueville was not alone. Other social analysts, for example, have contended that rational self-interest alone is not a sufficient basis for social order and that religion serves as the basis of social order; accordingly, it is religious life, located within the sphere of civil society, that enables public moral choices to be made and makes basic forms of civility and social restraint possible.

Moreover, a variety of contemporary research findings suggest that the religious associations and structures of civil society help to generate what has been called "social capital" (Coleman 1988; Putnam 1993). Social capital can be viewed as a set of moral resources that lead to increased cooperation between individuals, "making possible the achievement of certain ends that would not be attainable in its absence" (Coleman 1990, 302).

How does religious life help to generate a vital civil society? First of all, religious life fosters social connectedness, as church life is an important mechanism drawing individuals together and forging associational ties. Such networks of civic engagement are an essential form of social capital; moreover, the denser the networks, the more likely that community members will work together to achieve something of mutual benefit (Putnam 1993, 173). Church life, in particular, can contribute to relatively dense social networks, as members of congregations not only worship together but also develop friendship networks based upon such church involvement.

Second, religious life can foster social and political participation. Some social analysts have contended that participation in associations of any kind, including church associational life, provides "the social contacts and organizational skills necessary to understand political action and to exert effective influence" (Houghland and Christenson 1983, 406). In fact, religious life has been found to foster certain civic skills, as church involvement can provide opportunities to practice civic skills (for example, organizing and leading a committee, taking and defending a particular position, bargaining between committee members and negotiating compromises, organizing and administering fund-raisers) that can be applied to political life. Several recent studies have found, for example, that greater levels of involvement in decision making within the church correlate positively with political interest, information, and participation—lending support to a notion of a "spillover" effect from religious to political activism (Peterson 1992; Verba, Schlozman, and Brady 1995).

Finally, religious life has been found to promote civic behavior outside the institutional life of the church as well. The various activities associated with church life tend to spill over into other facets of civic life. Those who engage in volunteer work within the church (for example, teaching Sunday school, working in church food pantries, serving on committees) also tend to engage in other kinds of voluntary efforts (Wuthnow 1991, 199-200). Thus it appears that "the social capital generated by religious structures supports not only formal religious volunteering but 'secular' volunteering as well" (Greeley 1997, 592).

DATA AND METHODS

In order to assess the relative contribution of religious life to the vitality of civic engagement across different national contexts, data were analyzed from a telephone survey of 3000 Americans and 3000 Canadians conducted by the Angus Reid Corporation in the fall of 1996 (19 September to 10 October). This survey was designed, in part, to address the issue of involvement in civil society and contained a variety of questions used to tap various components of social capital and civic engagement. As a result, the survey is ideally suited for the analysis proposed. Statistical weighting was applied to the survey data to adjust the sample of each country in terms of its gender

and age composition so as to mirror the distribution within the Canadian and U.S. populations, and, in the case of the U.S. sample, in terms of the representation of African Americans as well. The U.S. sample also included a targeted sample booster of 200 Hispanic Americans (Spanish-language interviews were part of the U.S. survey).

Several variables, embodying both attitudes and behavior, are examined in this study—specifically, attitudes of social trust are examined along with the respondents' reported behavior related to membership in social organizations and volunteer work within those organizations. Two items within the survey tapped social trust. Respondents were asked in a Likert format (a five-point scale of responses ranging from "strongly agree" to "strongly disagree") to indicate their positions with regard to the following statements: (1) "When I put my trust in other people, they usually disappoint me," and (2) "People can generally be trusted to do what is right."

Respondents were also asked whether they were a member of any voluntary organizations or associations. If they answered "yes," respondents were then asked whether they were a member of an organization or association that might be included within a battery of 14 different categories of associations and organizations: professional or job-related groups; social service groups for the elderly, poor, or disabled; religious or church-related groups; environmental groups; youth groups (Scouts, youth clubs); community-based or neighborhood associations; health-related groups; recreational groups; senior citizen groups; veterans' groups; women's groups; political groups; educational, arts, music, or cultural organizations; and/or a small group that "meets regularly and provides support or caring for those who participate in it." If the respondents indicated that they were a member of some voluntary organization or association associated within the particular category of groups listed, then they were further asked whether they did volunteer work of any kind for that group. Thus, with regard to both social membership and volunteering, one can compose a composite index ranging from 0 to 14 in terms of the kinds of social organizations with which the respondent reported being affiliated as well as the number of different kinds of organizations with which the respondent reported having engaged in some voluntary activity.

The analysis presented here consists largely of an examination of the lay of the land. The initial task of the analysis is simply to examine whether or not religious life in Canada differs from that in the United States. If religious life does contribute to patterns of engagement in civil society (and to formation of social capital), then variation in the religious life across two different countries should lead to differences in civic engagement within those countries as well. Second, the relative level of civic engagement in the United States is compared to that evident in Canada. Once these cross-national patterns are examined, the

TABLE 1

RELIGIOUS TRADITION AND CHURCH ATTENDANCE, BY COUNTRY (Percentages)

	Canada	United States
Religious tradition		
Evangelical Protestant	11	25
Mainline Protestant	21	19
Black Protestant	1	9
Roman Catholic	33	20
Other	34	27
Church attendance		
Rarely	33	17
Occasionally	30	23
Periodically	17	20
Regularly	14	21
Frequently	7	18

focus shifts to an examination of those factors that account for any differential levels of civic engagement that may be evident across the two countries.

ANALYSIS

Tables 1 and 2 present the patterns of religious affiliation, church attendance, and religious beliefs evident among Americans and Canadians. Table 1 presents the distribution of religious affiliation by country in terms of the particular religious tradition[1] with which the respondent is associated and the pattern of church attendance evident across the two countries. The pattern of religious affiliation differs between the United States and Canada. First, there is a higher percentage of Americans (25 percent) than Canadians (11 percent) who are affiliated with an evangelical Protestant denomination. There is a much

TABLE 2
RELIGIOUS BELIEFS, BY COUNTRY

	Percentage Agreeing		Mean		
	Canada	United States	Canada	United States	Eta
The concept of God is an old superstition	23%	10%	2.08	1.51	.22***
Human beings are not special creation	40%	21%	2.68	1.94	.24***
Salvation is through the life, death, and resurrection of Jesus Christ	63%	84%	3.50	4.32	.28***
Jesus Christ was not the divine Son of God	19%	12%	2.08	1.62	.18***
Bible is the inspired Word of God	65%	83%	3.54	4.24	.25***

***Statistically significant at .001 level.

higher percentage of Americans than Canadians affiliated with a black Protestant denomination (9 percent versus 1 percent, respectively), while there is a much higher percentage of Roman Catholics in Canada than the United States (33 percent versus 20 percent, respectively). The percentage of mainline Protestants is fairly comparable in magnitude, with about 20 percent of both Americans and Canadians tied to mainline Protestantism.

Americans are much more likely than Canadians to report relatively high levels of church attendance. Nearly one-third of all Canadians (33 percent) report that they rarely attend church, while only about one-sixth of all Americans (17 percent) do so. Conversely, about 40 percent of all Americans report that they attend church either regularly or frequently,[2] while only about 20 percent of all Canadians report doing so. Thus Canadians differ from Americans both in terms of their patterns of

religious affiliation and in terms of their patterns of church attendance.

Table 2 examines whether such differences in affiliation and attendance are also reflected in differences in religious beliefs. It takes only a very quick examination of the table to recognize that Americans are much more likely than Canadians to report a religious answer to the various questions posed. Regardless of whether one examines belief in God, specific beliefs related to the Christian faith, or the significance of a particular faith tradition, Americans are significantly more likely than Canadians to provide what might be called religious responses.[3] Thus, the first criterion, namely that there be important cross-national religious differences, has been met.

Differences in social trust

Now that it has been demonstrated that Americans are more religious than Canadians, we can

TABLE 3
MEASURES OF SOCIAL TRUST, BY COUNTRY

	Canada	United States	r
When I put my trust in other people, they usually disappoint me			
Strongly agree	13%	17%	
Agree	20%	20%	
Not sure	1%	1%	−.04***
Disagree	40%	35%	
Strongly disagree	26%	27%	
People can generally be trusted to do what is right			
Strongly agree	18%	18%	
Agree	45%	39%	
Not sure	1%	1%	−.06***
Disagree	22%	22%	
Strongly disagree	14%	20%	

***Statistically significant at .001 level.

turn our attention to whether Americans also tend to exhibit higher levels of social capital than do Canadians. Table 3 begins to address this question in terms of respondents' attitudes toward social trust, as trust in others is seen by many as a core component of social capital (Putnam 1995, 665). Specifically, responses to two statements are examined: (1) "When I put my trust in other people, they usually disappoint me," and (2) "People can generally be trusted to do what is right." An affirmative answer to the first statement is interpreted to reflect an absence of social capital, while an affirmative answer to the second statement is interpreted to reflect the presence of social capital. Hence, the lower the percentage of affirmative responses to the first statement, the higher the level of social capital evident; the converse is true with regard to responses to the second statement.

A majority of both Americans and Canadians responded to the state-ments tapping social trust in a manner that suggested that they believed that their neighbors could be trusted. For example, most Americans and Canadians disagreed with the assertion that one is likely to experience disappointment when one places trust in other people. Similarly, most Americans and Canadians agreed with the assertion that people can generally be trusted to do what is right.

However, Americans tended to exhibit slightly lower levels of social capital than Canadians. Americans were slightly more likely than Canadians to agree with the statement that when they, as individuals, placed their trust in other people, they usually experienced disappoint-ment, and Americans were less likely to assert that people can generally be trusted to do what is right. These differences are relatively small, however, as the percentage distributions of the two countries largely mirror each other.

TABLE 4
MEAN SCORES OF SOCIAL TRUST AND CIVIC ENGAGEMENT, BY COUNTRY

	Canada	United States	Eta
When I trust people, they usually disappoint me	3.46	3.35	.04**
People can generally be trusted to do what is right	3.31	3.13	.06***
Social trust index (range 1 to 5)	3.44	3.28	.06***
Mean number of organizational categories with which respondent reported membership	1.75	2.31	.10***
Mean number of organizational categories with which respondent reported having volunteered	1.29	1.66	.09***
Mean score on civic engagement: index combining membership with volunteer activities	3.03	3.97	.10***

**Statistically significant at .01 level.
***Statistically significant at .001 level.

Differences in civic engagement

What about behavior with regard to membership in social organizations and volunteer activity? Given the relatively lower levels of social trust evident among Americans, do Americans exhibit lower levels of social engagement than Canadians?

Table 4 addresses this question. It first presents responses to the two statements in Table 3 as mean scores. Responses to these two statements have been recorded, however, so that higher values reflect more trusting or higher social capital scores. In addition, Table 4 presents (1) the mean number of organizational categories with which the respondent reported having some kind of affiliation or organizational membership and (2) the mean number of organizational categories with which the respondent reported having engaged in some volunteer work. Finally, Table 4 presents the mean scores associated with a composite measure tapping social trust as well as a composite measure tapping social membership and volunteer activity.

The data related to organizational affiliation or membership and to voluntary activity suggest that Canadians rank lower in terms of such memberships and activities than do Americans. Such differences are consistent and statistically significant: whether one assesses civic engagement by means of membership in civic associations or by means of voluntary activity, Canadians rank lower than Americans.

Previous research has found that the more individuals participate in their communities, the more they trust others, but, in addition, the more that they trust others, the more they participate in their communities—though the effect of participation on trust is stronger than the effect of trust on participation (Brehm and Rahn 1997). If participation does lead to trust, then one might expect

Americans, given their higher levels of civic engagement, to be more trusting than Canadians—assuming, of course, that such differential patterns of civic engagement have persisted meaningfully over time. But the data reveal Canadians to be more socially trusting than Americans. However, it may well be that social trust and civic engagement are not as closely linked as some have suggested. For example, some analysts have shown that participation tends to beget more participation (Houghland and Christenson 1983). In addition, several recent surveys have suggested that civic volunteering is not strongly related to social trust and, therefore, that social trust needs to be considered separately from civic engagement (for example, Guterbock and Fries 1997; Pew Research Center 1997).

However, since organizational membership and involvement are both tied to political participation, it is likely that those factors that affect variation in political participation will be associated with variation in these measures of civic engagement. Thus the lower levels of civic engagement in Canada may be a function of differential levels of other factors (such as education and race) that have been found to be associated with levels of political participation as well.

Consequently, the relationships between several sociodemographic variables (specifically, gender, race, age, and education) and an index tapping answers to the two social trust questions among Canadians and Americans are examined in Table 5. These same sociodemographic variables are also examined in terms of their relationship with an index tapping membership in social organizations and voluntary activity within them, that is, the index of civic engagement. Finally, Table 5 examines the relationship between two variables tapping religious characteristics of the respondent (specifically, religious tradition and church attendance) and the index of social trust as well as the index of civic engagement.

The values of eta reported in Table 5 reflect variation in the sociodemographic categories rather than variation cross-nationally. The value of eta for cross-national differences on the index of social trust is .06, while the corresponding value of eta for cross-national differences related to the index of social engagement is .10 (data not shown). Thus, if one wishes, for example, to assess whether differences in some particular sociodemographic variable outweigh cultural differences between the two countries, then the value of eta for that variable as presented in Table 5 needs to exceed .06 for the social trust index and .10 for the social engagement index.

With regard to social trust, the data reveal that differences between males and females are virtually nonexistent within each country—though men and women in Canada tend to be somewhat more trusting than their counterparts within the United States. However, with regard to organizational membership and voluntary activity, significant differences emerge between males and females, with females much more likely to report membership and

TABLE 5

**SOCIAL TRUST AND CIVIC ENGAGEMENT, BY SOCIAL AND
RELIGIOUS CHARACTERISTICS, CONTROLLING FOR COUNTRY**

	Index of Social Trust			Index of Civic Engagement		
	Canada	United States	Eta	Canada	United States	Eta
Gender						
Male	3.47	3.28		2.83	3.56	
Female	3.41	3.27	.01	3.23	4.35	.07
Race						
White	3.46	3.42		3.04	4.10	
Nonwhite	3.20	2.87	.14	3.03	3.61	.01
Age						
Under 35	3.41	3.13		2.14	2.96	
35-54	3.52	3.33		3.64	4.84	
55 and over	3.37	3.38	.05	3.35	4.06	.16
Education						
High school or less	3.24	2.95		2.01	2.01	
Postsecondary						
vocational or technical	3.41	3.22		3.02	4.27	
Some college	3.53	3.40		3.26	4.38	
College graduate	3.64	3.53		3.64	5.25	
Postgraduate	3.80	3.67	.17	5.36	6.33	.29
Church attendance						
Rarely	3.39	3.15		1.67	2.00	
Occasionally	3.44	3.28		2.50	2.85	
Periodically	3.59	3.34		4.47	4.13	
Regularly	3.41	3.39		4.41	4.60	
Frequently	3.39	3.18	.05	5.65	6.33	.32
Religious tradition						
Evangelical Protestant	3.40	3.18		4.40	3.94	
Mainline Protestant	3.65	3.57		4.13	4.85	
Black Protestant	2.84	2.71		1.96	5.00	
Roman Catholic	3.36	3.50		2.65	3.65	
Other	3.42	3.18	.14	2.37	3.31	.16

voluntary activity than males in both settings. But, while such gender differences persist within both cultural contexts, such differences are not nearly as great as the national differences.

Likewise, the data in Table 5 reveal that whites are more trusting and more socially engaged (particularly in the United States) than are nonwhites. However, differences between whites and nonwhites are greater and more significant with regard to expressions of social trust than with regard to reported social engagement. In fact, while nonwhites are less trusting than whites in both the United States and Canada, Table 5 reveals that much of the differential levels of social trust across the two countries is due simply to the much lower level of social trust reported by nonwhites in the United States compared to nonwhites in Canada—as the mean score on the social trust index is virtually identical for white Canadians and white Americans. On the other hand, with regard to patterns of civic engagement, national differences persist in both racial categories. Regardless of whether respondents are white or not, respondents from the United States were much more socially engaged than those from Canada. Thus both region and race are associated with differential levels of social capital (as measured by social trust and social engagement).

Generally speaking, age appears to be monotonically related to expressions of social trust, with those who are older more likely to express higher levels of social trust. However, the exception to this pattern is evident among those Canadians in the oldest age category, who were the least trusting of all Canadians in terms of age. Cross-national differences also continue to persist within age categories, as Canadians in a particular age group tend to be more trusting than their American counterparts in the same age category— except among those 54 years or older, as the means scores on social trust among those in the oldest age category are virtually identical across the two countries. On the other hand, social organizational membership and voluntary activity are curvilinearly related to age, as those younger than 35 and those 55 or older are less likely to be socially engaged than those who are 35 to 54 years of age. National differences are not as strongly related as age is to social organizational membership and voluntary activity. Nevertheless,

national differences in social engagement persist in all three age categories.

Education is both monotonically and strongly correlated with social trust and social engagement. Education is positively correlated with social trust, as those with higher levels of education tend to report higher levels of interpersonal trust. Yet national differences also continue to persist with regard to the relationship between education and social trust, as Americans are less trusting of others than their counterparts with similar levels of education residing in Canada. Education is likewise strongly related to levels of civic engagement, as those with higher levels of education are much more likely to report increased levels of organizational membership and involvement. However, the impact of country on this relationship between education and social engagement is less consistent; it is only among those who report more than a high school level of education that it becomes apparent that Americans are much more engaged than their educational counterparts in Canada.

Church attendance, on the other hand, is curvilinearly related to expressions of social trust: those who attend church least frequently and those that attend most frequently are more likely to express lower levels of social trust. Whether this lower level of reported interpersonal trust among frequent church goers is a reflection of personal experience or theological understanding cannot be ascertained from the data, but it is clear that, regardless of region, levels of interpersonal trust generally increase among respondents as their level of church attendance increases—until church attendance reaches its zenith. However, overall, the range of differences in levels of interpersonal trust across differing levels of church attendance did not vary widely, though cross-national differences persisted consistently within all five categories of church attendance. On the other hand, church attendance is much more strongly related to social engagement; higher levels of reported church attendance are monotonically and strongly related to higher levels of organizational membership and activity. Once again, national differences continue to persist with regard to the relationship between church attendance and civic engagement; generally speaking, across almost all levels of reported church attendance, Canadians are less likely to report social organizational membership and activity than their religious counterparts in the United States.

Finally, Table 5 presents the relationship between religious tradition and social trust and civic engagement within Canada and the United States. The United States is home to large numbers of those who belong to churches tied to the evangelical Protestant and black Protestant traditions. The data reveal that religious tradition is moderately related to both social trust and civic engagement, though somewhat more strongly so in terms of civic engagement than social trust. Black Protestants, as a whole, were more likely to express lower levels of social trust than were those associated with other religious traditions; this was true within both Canada and the United States. Evangelical Protestants were also relatively untrusting socially, with Canadian evangelicals somewhat more trusting than their counterparts in America. Mainline Protestants, regardless of country, were the most likely to report higher levels of social trust, and reported levels of social trust differed little across the two countries. Roman Catholics in Canada tended to mirror evangelical Protestants in terms of their level of social trust, while Roman Catholics in the United States tended to be more trusting on the whole and generally mirrored mainline Protestants in terms of their level of social trust.

On the other hand, despite their relatively high levels of reported social trust, Roman Catholics tended to be relatively unengaged socially in the United States, ranking ahead only of those who fall into the "other" category in terms of religious tradition. Likewise, despite their ranking lowest in terms of reported levels of interpersonal trust, those affiliated with the black Protestant religious tradition in the United States ranked the highest in terms of social organizational affiliation and involvement. Cross-national differences, moreover, were not always consistent. While civic engagement tends to be lower in Canada than in the United States, regardless of religious tradition, such a pattern does not hold true for evangelical Protestants. Evangelical Protestants in Canada are more civically engaged than evangelical Protestants in the United States.

Multivariate analysis

Not surprisingly, a variety of sociodemographic factors have been found to be related to social trust and civic engagement. The questions remaining, then, for the purposes of this study are (1) whether the relationships between the religious variables and civic engagement analyzed in Table 5 are simply a function of sociodemographic variation across such religious categories, and (2) whether national residence has an independent effect upon variation in measures tapping civic engagement. Consequently, in order to assess the relative effects of these religious variables as well as country of residence itself, a multiple classification analysis was run. For the purposes of this analysis, the index tapping civic engagement (that is, the additive index tapping affiliation with social organizations and voluntary activity within such organizations) serves as the dependent variable. The additive index tapping social trust was used as an independent variable, positing that increased social trust leads to increased levels of civic engagement; the variables of education, church attendance, religious tradition, and national residence were also used as independent variables. Three sociodemographic variables, namely, age, race, and gender, were introduced as covariates or control variables in the analysis. The results of this analysis are presented in Table 6.

Multiple classification analysis is based upon the extent to which the mean values of the dependent variable within different categories of the independent variables deviate from the grand mean, once controls for the various covariate variables and other independent variables have been introduced. Several important points emerge from this multiple classification analysis. First, education continues to be strongly related to levels of civic engagement, with increases in education being associated with higher levels of such engagement. Even after controls have been introduced, the respondents' level of education and level of civic engagement continue to be monotonically related, with the resultant beta for education ranking relatively high at a value of .27.

Second, it is clear that the two religious variables (church attendance and religious tradition) have an independent impact on civic engagement even after controls have been introduced for education, level of social trust, race, age, gender, and national residence. Not surprisingly, church attendance has a stronger impact on such engagement (beta = .31) than does the particular religious tradition with which the respondent is associated (beta = .11)—as the mean scores for civic engagement not only monotonically increase with increases in church attendance, but the adjusted mean score jumps considerably as one moves from those who attend church "regularly" to those who attend church "frequently" (from 1.07 more than the grand mean to 2.69 more than the grand mean). More surprising, perhaps, is the fact that the impact of church attendance (beta =

TABLE 6
CIVIC ENGAGEMENT: A MULTIPLE CLASSIFICATION ANALYSIS

Grand mean = 3.52	N	Unadjusted Deviation from Grand Mean	Eta	Adjusted for Independent Variables and Covariates	Beta
Education					
High school or less	2119	−1.50		−1.40	
Postsecondary vocational or technical	1109	−.04		.11	
Some college	976	.49		.27	
College graduate	1031	.93		.88	
Postgraduate	751	2.53	.29	2.36	.27
Church attendance					
Rarely	1477	−1.73		−1.70	
Occasionally	1573	−.85		−.82	
Periodically	1103	.77		.61	
Regularly	1038	1.02		1.07	
Frequently	751	2.65	.32	2.69	.31
Religious tradition					
Evangelical Protestant	1038	.58		−.22	
Mainline Protestant	1185	.97		.72	
Black Protestant	304	1.15		.74	
Roman Catholic	1582	−.49		−.63	
Other	1833	−.72	.16	.08	.11
Social trust index					
Low	758	−1.00		−.76	
2	827	−.47		−.13	
3	1339	−.64		−.56	
4	1556	.47		.38	
High	1462	.86	.15	.57	.11
Country					
Canada	2965	−.47		−.06	
United States	2976	.47	.10	.06	.01

Multiple R = .456
R squared = .208

.31) exceeds the impact of education (beta = .27) in terms of civic engagement. One important point should also be noted with regard to religious tradition. Specifically, it is clear that, once controls have been introduced for the other variables included in the analysis, the level of social engagement among black Protestants far exceeds the average level of such engagement (the grand mean) and mirrors the level exhibited by mainline Protestants. This pattern is consistent with the findings of previous research that religious involvement, particularly among those who lack the resource of money, imparts civic skills and engenders civic involvement (Verba, Schlozman, and Bardy 1995, chap. 11). On the other hand, it is also clear that, once one controls for the various sociodemographic variables (as well as variation in church attendance across religious traditions), the expected level of civic engagement declines among evangelical Protestants and Roman Catholics.

Third, the data in Table 6 reveal that increased levels of social trust are positively associated with increased levels of civic engagement. While these two variables are likely to be reciprocally related, it is also true that, once one has controlled for both various sociodemographic variables and several religious variables, the independent impact of social trust on civic engagement continues to be evident and continues to be relatively strong. The beta value for the index of social trust (.11) is the same as that for religious tradition.

Finally, it is also clear that national residence no longer has much of an independent impact on civic engagement once controls for the other variables have been introduced, as the beta value for place of residence diminishes to .01.[4] However, even after the impact of church attendance, religious tradition, education, and social trust have also been addressed, the mean score for Canadians on the civic engagement variable still resides below the grand mean, suggesting a residue of cultural difference.

CONCLUSION

This article has sought to provide an examination of the level of social trust and civic engagement evident in the United States and Canada and how religious variables may affect their distribution cross-nationally. Several conclusions can be drawn from the analysis presented here.

First, in terms of social trust, Canadians appear to be slightly more trusting than Americans, but Canadians trail Americans in terms of membership and activity within social organizations. Canadians were less likely than Americans to report being members of social organizations and less likely to report volunteering within those organizations of which they were a part.

Second, a variety of different sociodemographic and religious variables were found to be associated with different levels of social trust and civic engagement. Education, in particular, was strongly related to both expressions of social trust and reports of civic engagement. Gender differences were only moderately evident only in terms of civic engagement, while racial differences were only evident, though strongly so, in terms of social trust. Age differences were moderately associated with differential levels of social trust and more strongly associated with civic engagement. Similarly, both church attendance and religious tradition helped to shape social trust and civic engagement. Church attendance was strongly related to social engagement, though curvilinearly related to social trust; religious tradition was moderately related to both social trust and civic engagement.

Third, even when analyzing the relationship of the various sociodemographic and religious variables to social trust and civic engagement, national differences generally persisted. For example, in Table 5, the mean scores of Canadians with regard to social trust exceeded those of Americans in 20 of the 22 comparisons made, while the mean score of Americans with regard to civic engagement exceeded those of Canadians in 19 of the 22 comparisons made.

Fourth, even when controls were introduced for education, age, race, gender, region, and social trust, it is clear that both church attendance and religious tradition have an independent impact upon respondents' reported levels of civic engagement. Consequently, social analysts who choose to focus on civil society and associational activity need to take religion seriously and incorporate religious variables within their analyses.

Finally, perhaps the most important finding reported here is that the relationship between social trust and civic engagement appears to vary by religious tradition. The guiding assumption of most analyses of social capital is that social trust and social engagement are closely intertwined. However, while black Protestants express relatively low levels of social trust, they nevertheless exhibit relatively high levels of social engagement, once proper controls have been introduced. Just how it is that such low levels of social trust get transformed into relatively high levels of social engagement is not clear. But these findings suggest that future analyses that focus on the interrelationship between social trust and civic engagement will need to pay closer attention to how that interrelationship may be affected by membership in a particular religious tradition.

Notes

1. Religious tradition is a concept used to designate a grouping of religious communities that share a distinctive worldview (Kellstedt et al. 1996). It is typically measured by denominational affiliation, and scholars typically recognize six major traditions in the United States: evangelical Protestant, mainline Protestant, black Protestant, Roman Catholic, Jewish, and the nonreligious or secular population. In the analysis here, however, all respondents who do not belong to any of the four specified Christian traditions are classified as "other."

2. "Regularly" is used here to denote "weekly," while "frequently" is used to denote "more than once a week."

3. It may be that Americans are more religious in terms of their beliefs, or it may be that the connection between religion and culture is stronger in the United States than Canada, so as to encourage Americans to provide a more religious answer. See Reimer 1995.

4. The resultant multiple R for this eight-variable model used to account for variation in the index tapping civic engagement is .46. Accordingly, the model accounts for approximately 21 percent of the variation in the dependent variable (multiple R squared).

References

Brehm, John and Wendy Rahn. 1997. Individual-Level Evidence for the Causes and Consequences of Social Capital. *American Journal of Political Science* 41(3):999-1023.

Coleman, James. 1988. Social Capital in the Creation of Human Capital. *American Journal of Sociology* 94 (supp.):95-120.

———. 1990. *Foundations of Social Theory*. Cambridge, MA: Belknap.

Greeley, Andrew. 1997. Coleman Revisited: Religious Structures as a Source of Social Capital. *American Behavioral Scientist* 40(5):587-94.

Guterbock, Thomas and John C. Fries. 1997. *Maintaining America's Social Fabric: The AARP Survey of Civic In-*

volvement. Washington, DC: American Association of Retired Persons.

Houghland, J. G. and J. A. Christenson. 1983. Religion and Politics: The Relationship of Religious Participation to Political Efficacy and Involvement. *Sociology and Social Research* 67:405-20.

Kellstedt, Lyman, John Green, James Guth, and Corwin Smidt. 1996. Grasping the Essentials: The Social Embodiment of Religion and Political Behavior. In *Religion and the Culture Wars: Dispatches from the Front*, ed. John Green, James Guth, Lyman Kellstedt, and Corwin Smidt. Lanham, MD: Rowman & Littlefield.

Lipset, Seymour Martin. 1990. *Continental Divide*. London: Routledge.

Peterson, Steve. 1992. Church Participation and Political Participation: The Spillover Effect. *American Politics Quarterly* 20:123-39.

Pew Research Center for the People and the Press. 1997. *Trust and Citizen Engagement in Metropolitan Philadelphia: A Case Study*. Washington, DC: Pew Research Center for the People and the Press.

Putnam, Robert. 1993. *Making Democracy Work: Civic Traditions in Modern Italy*. Princeton, NJ: Princeton University Press.

———. 1995. Tuning in, Tuning out? The Strange Disappearance of Social Capital in America. *PS: Political Science & Politics* 28(4):664-83.

Reimer, Samuel. 1995. A Look at Cultural Effects on Religiosity: A Comparison Between the United States and Canada. *Journal for the Scientific Study of Religion* 34(4):445-57.

Tocqueville, Alexis de. 1969. *Democracy in America*. Ed. J. P. Mayer. Trans. George Lawrence. Garden City, NY: Doubleday, Anchor Books.

Verba, Sidney, Kay Schlozman, and Henry Brady. 1995. *Voice and Equality: Civic Volunteerism in American Politics*. Cambridge, MA: Harvard University Press.

Wuthnow, Robert. 1991. *Acts of Compassion*. Princeton, NJ: Princeton University Press.

ANNALS, *AAPSS*, **565**, September 1999

Death and Civil Society

By LORENA MELTON YOUNG OTERO

ABSTRACT: By comparing death and burial rituals in neighboring communities in western Mexico, much can be learned about civil society. Four communities are examined, two traditional and two in the process of change as they struggle with the influx of a sizable number of U.S. retirees as well as the growing number of Protestant church denominations that are appearing in the area.

Lorena Melton Young Otero graduated with an M.A. in political science from California State University–Sonoma and is in a doctoral program in sociology at the Instituto de Ciencias Sociales y Humanidades of the Benemerita Universidad Autónoma de Puebla, in the state of Puebla in Mexico. Her fieldwork in the doctoral program was done in the Lake Chapala area of western Mexico; its main focus was on U.S. retirees who migrate to Mexico after retirement.

THERE is an ongoing discussion of democratization in civil society and the question of how it is measured. On the one hand, open elections are pointed to, while, on the other, the strength of the economy is used. Yet there are signs that this is not the whole story and might even camouflage the actual situation within civil society, and Mexico is a case in point. Even though strides have been made along the road toward democracy, problems still appear to be surfacing. The most obvious, of course, is the Chiapas rebellion, which burst into headlines at the end of 1994 and continues to this day. It illustrates that, within civil society as it exists in Mexico, only some of its citizens are benefiting from political or economic changes. If the North American Free Trade Agreement has made a difference in the health of the national economy and if the more open and honest elections that are now being held are used as the yardstick to measure the democratization process, then it would seem that Mexico should be headed in the right direction, regardless of Chiapas.

Others, however, have suggested that democracy is dependent on more than what is apparent on the surface, that civil society actually rests on a broader base. This, then, suggests that a turn to what is happening at other levels within Mexican civil society might be more revealing of the true state of affairs. Because ritual and the culture of politics have been shown to have threads throughout the whole of society (De Los Reyes and Rich 1997; Rich and De Los Reyes 1996), investigations into rituals carried out at the base of civil society, the community, should reveal more about society in general than any number of top-down studies would. To this end, the following investigation into death and burial rituals is presented in detail.

One of the most important rituals in the lifetime of an individual is one where the main protagonist has only a silent part—the act of being buried, or sent in some manner to a final resting place, by others after death. Burial rituals thus have a social as well as a religious significance. These rituals, however, are not always the same and can vary widely. When studying differences in death and burial rituals, any variations between groups should be more readily apparent and understood when two contrasting social groups come into contact. Such is the case in western Mexico, where a number of U.S. citizens have chosen to relocate in the Lake Chapala area after retirement (for the sake of expediency, all retirees will be labeled as being from the United States, although there are an increasing number of Canadians and a few Europeans also in the area).

The following discussion will focus on four communities within 40 miles of each other. Two share a U.S. retiree population of 4000 to 6000 persons, while the other two have relatively few retirees. Differences in burial rituals both within and between the four communities will be described, and the possible social significance of the differences will be discussed.

RITUALS

In any discussion of rituals, it must be understood that there are quotidian rituals and rituals of great significance. Everyday life is replete with rituals—acts that constitute a type of ceremony that surrounds and forms a part of how the mundane may be performed. How clothes are laid out, how a table is set, or the order in which groceries are purchased and then stored upon arriving home are all rituals of a sort. They are done to be esthetically pleasing, to make a task easier, or to emphasize one pattern or process over another; in other words, there is something personal in how and why such an act is performed. Other rituals, however, demark important ceremonial activities that are socially significant in civil society and may be religious, can involve a number of people, and deal with transitional events. Such is the case with burial rites, which are a part of a significant, and the ultimate, life transition.

For a number of years, sociologists, anthropologists, historians, and philosophers have been discussing the role of ritual in civil societies (see Giddens 1972, 232-38). Most agree that ritual is not empty, that, if it exists, it performs some function within the social group and for the individuals composing the group. Among other functions, Durkheim felt that religious rituals "reaffirm the social solidarity of the group" and also that rituals can "counter the individuals' experiences of loss or inadequacy—such as the inevitability of death" (Hall and Neitz 1993,

51). Therefore, burial rituals encountered in the four communities in western Mexico should reflect not only the religious inclination of the members of the local communities but also the form and manner of social reaffirmation inherent in the specific rituals practiced.[1]

THE FOUR COMMUNITIES

The four communities of Ixtlahuacan de los Membrillos, Chapala, Ajijic, and San Luis Soyatlan are located within 40 miles of each other on the shores of Lake Chapala in the state of Jalisco in western Mexico. According to the Instituto Nacional de Estadística, Geografía e Informática (INEGI), there are approximately 40,252 residents in the area, of whom 5000-6000 are people from the United States who have settled there after retirement (INEGI 1997a, 71; Ayuntamiento de Chapala 1997).

Ixtlahuacan de los Membrillos is a farming village of about 3000 people, of whom only 20 or so are U.S. retirees. It is about 10 miles from the outskirts of Chapala, the largest town in the area, and is separated from Chapala by a natural barrier of low mountains. Situated in its own valley, Ixtlahuacan can be seen from the highway that runs between Guadalajara and Chapala, but is off the highway. Without a car, it is necessary to either walk out to the highway to flag down a bus or to wait for the second-class bus that arrives intermittently every 30 to 45 minutes during the day in the center of town. Additionally, the town is not really oriented toward tourism, having few restaurants (and none on the main square) and no art or craft products. The community, although close to Chapala, remains more or less separated or isolated from it and from the hustle and bustle that marks the larger town.

San Luis Soyatlan is about 25 miles from Ajijic on the highway that goes around the lake. Although it is located on a through highway, its bus service is more oriented toward the second route into Guadalajara, more than an hour or so away. It, too, is relatively isolated, because it takes about two hours to traverse the bus and change-of-bus routes necessary to get to either Ajijic or Chapala. The majority of its 5000 inhabitants are dedicated to agriculture, although it does have some small restaurants for the through-highway traffic. It has a resident population of only about 15 U.S. retirees.

Chapala and Ajijic are the two largest towns in the area. Chapala is a vacation resort destination, with attendant hotels, restaurants, and other service providers. It is also the seat of government for the entire area, including police and security forces. In Chapala, there are 17,998 inhabitants, including 2500-3000 resident U.S. retirees (INEGI 1997b, 030-6). Ajijic, on the other hand, is the arts and crafts center of the area. It has 11,000 inhabitants, including another 2500-3000 U.S. residents, some of whom own boutiques, galleries, restaurants, and so forth.

It is said that, during the winter months, the foreign population in the area comprising Chapala and Ajijic doubles with the arrival of the so-called snow birds (those who come during the winter months and stay for three to six months only). The retiree presence at that time increases to between 10,000 and 12,000 persons (Ayuntamiento de Chapala 1997).

In the four communities, there is one Catholic church in Ixtlahuacan, and another in San Luis Soyatlan. In Chapala and Ajijic, there are several Catholic churches as well as churches for Episcopalians, Baptists, Presbyterians, Mormons, Seventh Day Adventists, and Jehovah's Witnesses; two nondenominational churches; and the controversial cult church of The Light of the World. There is one cemetery each in Ixtlahuacan, San Luis, Chapala, Ajijic, and the small community of San Antonio Tlayacapan (located between Chapala and Ajijic). Chapala has the largest cemetery in the area. It is divided into three parts: one for the local Mexican residents, and a separate parcel of land on either side of the Mexican section, which two parcels are dedicated for foreign—mostly U.S., plus a few Canadian—burials only.

DEATH AND BURIAL:
SAN LUIS SOYATLAN
AND IXTLAHUACAN
DE LOS MEMBRILLOS

The vast majority of persons die at home in Ixtlahuacan and San Luis. A clinic or a hospital is reached only with some difficulty from either town, and, in addition, both are relatively poor towns. This situation matches the practice in many parts of Mexico, where most patients receive treatment at a small local clinic or hospital, and, if they are gravely ill and can afford it, they might be sent on to a bigger hospital, in this case to Guadalajara. Otherwise, they are sent home to either recover or die. In many cases, patients prefer to die at home, and doctors acquiesce in this decision.

At the moment of death, several things happen simultaneously. Immediate and extended family, *compadres* (ritual family, such as god-parents), friends, neighbors from the *barrio* (the demarked area of a neighborhood), and other community members are summoned. Some wash the body, dress it, wrap it in a sheet, and bind the jaws (embalming is not normally a part of burial practice in Mexico). Someone else goes to the church to begin the death toll on the church bell(s), which informs everyone in the *barrio* that someone has died. The doctor is called to verify death and fill out the death certificate. One copy of the certificate is delivered to the local governmental authorities, who will issue a burial permit and collect the appropriate fees for the cemetery plot, or for the burial if the family already owns a plot. The other copy is for the local *panteonero* (person in charge of the cemetery and digging the grave). Unless the government authorities issue the permit and the *panteonero* receives it, appropriately signed and stamped, the burial will not be allowed to take place.

At the same time, a family member goes to the local funeral parlor to buy either a coffin of wood (plain, or carved and varnished) or the more ornate metal coffin lined with satin. The funeral parlor also loans out chairs, a large cross, and flower urns, to be used at the home of the deceased during the nights of prayer that will follow, all included in the cost of the coffin. Meanwhile, back at the house, those present have begun reciting the Rosary, which will be repeated hourly all night long. If death occurs during the day, the same ritual is carried out, with burial the following day. Everyone will take turns staying with the family and the body, and the body will not be left alone until burial. During this night (or day and night) of vigil, called the *velorio*, liquor often appears, most likely having been purchased by a compadre. It is served to the men, with soda pop or coffee and Mexican sweet bread served to the men, women, and any children present.

If death occurs at night, the following morning arrangements are made both for burial in the local cemetery and for a mass in the local church called Misa con Cuerpo Presente (Mass with the Corpse Present). After this mass, neighbors and friends will come forward to console the bereaved family members and will quietly press whatever money they can afford into the palms of the bereaved while admonishing, "Conform to God's will." The coffin, draped in black, will then be carried on the shoulders of male family members or *compadres* and friends (or driven in a hearse or, occasionally, in the back of a pickup truck) through town to the cemetery, with everyone else following on foot. Occasionally, a local musical group will be hired to play while accompanying the mourners on their journey through town to the cemetery.

At the cemetery, a cross of ashes will be made where the coffin will rest, after which the coffin is lowered into the grave. The grave is then filled in, the earth tamped down, flowers are placed on the grave, and cigarettes are handed out to the mourners. Even those who never smoke will light up and blow the smoke around. This is said to "keep away bad air." No one will leave until these ritual acts are completed.

That evening, which begins the nine nights of the Novenario, family, compadres, friends, and barrio neighbors will again gather for the saying of the Rosary, after which coffee and Mexican sweet bread will be served. During these nine nights of prayer, new compadres will be found who agree to provide the cross (grave marker) that will be placed at the grave in the cemetery. On the last night of the Novenario, the cross presented by the new compadres will be placed flat on an improvised altar in front of where the Rosary will be said, and each hour it will be raised a little higher, until, around 11:00 p.m. or midnight, it will be straight up. This ritual is called the Levantada de la Cruz (Raising of the Cross), and it prepares the cross for its placement at the grave on the following day. After the placement of the cross in the cemetery, everyone who participated in the nine nights of prayer is invited to a midday meal prepared by

the bereaved and which also honors the new compadres, called Compadres de la Cruz (Compadres of the Cross).

These nine days and nights of very open expression of grief and consolation in the company of family, friends, neighbors, and compadres, where the Rosary is said over and over for the soul of the departed, are very intense. Emotions are wrung dry. At the end of this period, the bereaved are expected to return to normal, become functioning community members once again, and put sadness behind them (at least publicly).

In both Ixtlahuacan and San Luis, family members will return to the cemetery for an all-night vigil beginning midday on 1 November and lasting through the night to midday 2 November. This is the Day of the Dead Ceremony. The family brings flowers, candles, and food; they clean and decorate the graves; and they may bring radios, cigarettes, and liquor (which they offer the dead by pouring a bit on the ground by the grave). They will also set up special and elaborate house altars in their homes, called ofrendas, to honor the dead. Ofrendas are erected in many communities in the states of Guerrero, Michoacán, Puebla, and Oaxaca, but they are not erected in either Chapala or Ajijic, with two exceptions. In Ajijic, the foreign art colony erects ofrendas on the sidewalks in front of their studios or galleries, and, in both Chapala and Ajijic, the local schools may erect an ofrenda in either a classroom or the entrance to the school.

BURIAL FOR A CHILD UNDER 5: SAN LUIS SOYATLAN AND IXTLAHUACAN DE LOS MEMBRILLOS

When a child under the age of 5 dies, it is another story. Before becoming 5 years old, the child is considered to be innocent, and upon death the child becomes an *angelito* (little angel). Public grief and mourning are thus considered inappropriate. An all-night celebration for children is arranged, to be attended by as many children as possible, plus families, *compadres*, and other *barrio* members. There will be *tortas* (a type of sandwich), drinks, candy, games, music, and laughter. The object is to keep the children awake, happy, and excited all night with the continual games, to accompany the new angel, who will be resting on a prominently placed table and surrounded by flowers. Pictures will be taken of the new angel with the parents, and with any other family, friends, or children who wish such a memento.

Of course, the same preparation of the body takes place as happens for an adult, but the child will be dressed in white, if a girl, and in Sunday best, if a boy. Similar arrangements must also be made regarding the death certificate, burial permits, purchase of a coffin, mass in the church before the actual burial, and so on.

For the procession to the cemetery for burial, the child's body will be carried on a table surrounded and covered by flowers, with fireworks shot off at intervals while the church bell(s) ring a joyous one-bell toll, rather than the two-bell toll used to signify death for adults. It is at the cemetery where the body is transferred to the coffin. However, in cases where the family elects to place the child's body in the coffin for the procession through town to the cemetery, the coffin will be draped in white.

The nine-day Novenario will take place in the home of the deceased child, with coffee, soft drinks, sweet bread, and candy served daily. It will be held from 4 p.m. to about 8 p.m., rather than at night as is done for an adult death. The same Rosary will be said hourly, but joyously. The raising of the cross will also take place on the ninth afternoon, with the Compadres of the Cross being especially honored because the deceased is now an angel.

DEATH AND BURIAL IN CHAPALA AND AJIJIC

Because both Chapala and Ajijic have sizable numbers of U.S. retirees (2500-3000 each) and because the area Protestant churches are also located in or between these two communities, burial rituals must first be discussed in light of religious affinity and then in light of nationality.

Catholic

For the majority of Catholics in Chapala and Ajijic, much has changed. Unlike for their neighbors 15 miles down the road in either direction, death and burial rituals have not remained the same. The body is prepared, the doctor is called, the permit process remains the same, and family, friends, *compadres*, and neighbors come for the first-night *velorio*. However, after the mass and the procession to the cemetery the next day, any subsequent saying of the Rosary, usually for three days in most cases, is most often done at the church and only occasionally now in the home of the deceased.

After death in Chapala and Ajijic, there are few or no Novenario gatherings at the home of the deceased for nine nights, and the cross is bought by family members so there are no Compadres of the Cross. Consequently, there is no communal bread and coffee each night, and no midday meal for everyone at the end of the nine-day public mourning period. There may be a dinner, but it will be for family members and a few close friends only. There are also few or no all-night celebrations for the death of a child under 5 years old. Another change is the election of cremation instead of burial, cremation being permitted by the church now. In this case, the funeral parlor makes the arrangement for cremation, and the ashes will be taken to a mass for blessing, after which the ashes may be kept in an urn at home, buried, or set in the burial plot in the cemetery.

Even though much modified, the rituals that still exist take place in the company of family and friends, so that the bereaved are not left totally alone in their grief. However, the shortening of the number of days and nights in which the bereaved are surrounded by caring individuals means that they are certainly not supported to the extent that people in the communities of Ixtlahuacan de los Membrillos and San Luis Soyatlan are.

Hand in hand with this change, in Chapala and Ajijic there are no all-night cemetery vigils on 1-2 November, and few people do more than clean the graves, place flowers, and pray the Rosary at graveside. There is also little more than a perfunctory change to the house altar made for the dead, and certainly nothing elaborate such as an *ofrenda* (with the exceptions mentioned previously in regard to foreign artists in Ajijic erecting altars in front of their businesses as well as a few local schools erecting a general *ofrenda* in the school entrance).

It must be mentioned that most change in ritual comes slowly. Remnants would exist today that reflect a more elaborate and generalized practice in times past. Older men and women who have spent their lives in Chapala and Ajijic remember that, in their youth, there were still some burial rituals like those that exist today in Ixtlahuacan and San Luis but that the customs were beginning to disappear even then.

Protestant

Protestants, whether Mexican or from the United States, most frequently will have the body sent to a local funeral parlor in either Chapala or Ajijic, and they may or may not keep an all-night vigil there accompanied by family, friends, and other church members. They will also have to go through the same permit procedures as mentioned earlier, for the doctor, government, and cemetery. Someone will go and stay with the bereaved that night, after prayers at the funeral parlor, if it is not an all-night vigil, or stay with the family if they have decided to have the vigil at their home with the body present.

There will be a church service the next day for the deceased, there can be a funeral procession with family, friends, and church members, and there can be either burial or cremation. After these initial rituals, the family members return home, usually alone. Some people may drop by for short visits or to bring food during the first few days, but the bereaved will be minimally supported, as they are expected to deal with their grief privately.

U.S. RETIREES AS A SEPARATE CASE

At this point, nationality must be discussed. Not all retirees are church members, and some are only social association members and attend church infrequently or not at all. The vast majority are Protestants; only a few are Catholics. There is the question of what people do, or should do, if a foreigner drops dead on the street. To address this situation, in 1974 the American Society of Guadalajara started a registration program for all retirees living in Mexico. This program is now run by the Memorial Society of Guadalajara, and the Chapala Society in Ajijic and the American Legion in Chapala assist by enrolling members from their own associations.

Retirees complete a form that gives all the necessary data for death certificates and burial or cremation permits in Mexico. This form also asks who should be notified, preferences for church services or not, which church or none, which hymns or scriptures they want or not, where they should be buried or sent after death, whether they want cremation and, if so, what should happen to the ashes afterward, whether they want a plaque in the local cemetery or not, and whether they want a small memorial service (in addition to, or instead of, a church service) or not. The form lists costs, and there is a prepayment plan with a safe set-aside bank account in which to deposit the required sum of money under the retiree's name until needed. After signing and being witnessed, the form becomes legally binding.

On the one hand, this appears to be an intelligent solution to what has created problems in the past. Indeed, a local newspaper reported that 150 U.S. citizens die each year in just the states of Jalisco, Colima, and Nayarit (*Colony Reporter*, 17-23 May 1997). This does not include those who might have died elsewhere in Mexico. On the other hand, it is an excellent example of preprogrammed do-it-yourself death and burial ritual. Even the act of filling out the form becomes a modern addition to the ritual of burial. At the time of death, once the deceased has been identified as a foreigner, the U.S. Consulate Offices will be notified, and they, in turn, notify the Memorial Society, which takes over from there. The paperwork will be completed, and the wishes carried out to the letter.

Problems of a different sort can occur, however, when the retiree has married a Mexican woman. In at least one case (and it was said that there were several others) when the retiree died walking home from a morning of sports activities, his body was taken to a funeral parlor in Guadalajara, his last wishes were carried out as he had requested, and he was cremated. The wife, who was Catholic, then combined the death and burial rituals of both Protestantism and Catholicism. She did not know where the body had been taken, so no one could pass the night with the deceased. Instead, an all-night *velorio* was held at her home, with family and friends saying the Rosary; no Novenario was held; and when she finally got the urn with the ashes, she took them to the local church, had a mass said and the ashes blessed, and took them home to remain with the family.

CEMETERIES AND CEMETERY PLOTS

As a final note, it should be mentioned that it is one thing to die, it is another to get buried. In the five communities of Ixtlahuacan, San Luis, San Antonio, Chapala, and Ajijic, as in many other parts of Mexico, having a cemetery plot and owning a cemetery plot are two different things. The civil side of burial rituals consists of more than obtaining a permit for burial; it also consists of obtaining the plot in which to bury the dead. In the cemeteries in all five of the communities under discussion, the deceased can own a plot for seven years. Even though the ownership is called "in perpetuity," it still means only seven years, depending on the amount paid in fees. Seven years is long enough, it is said, for the body to be buried and then become a skeleton, after which time it is disinterred

by cemetery workers and reburied in the *fosa comun* (common grave) if additional fees are not paid.

The plot is then available for others to purchase for use in the same manner for the next seven years. In a sense, the plot is rented, not owned. However, there is another type of ownership, also called "in perpetuity," in which the plot is actually purchased and a title to the plot is given to the family in the same manner in which they would hold a title to any other piece of land. With this type of ownership, the body will not be disinterred after seven years.

Those who own a plot in true perpetuity then have other choices: to line the plot with cement shelves (the plot can accommodate shelves enough to hold up to five caskets) or to leave the plot as is but retain the right to bury up to five caskets one on top of the other. Large families often buy two plots side by side, and they then have room for ten family members. Cement crypts can be constructed on top of the ground for yet more bodies on the plot space. To the same plot space, above or around these crypts, the family may add cement or stone small benches, miniature churches, crosses, angels, flower urns, large arches or conch shells to shelter the figure of Christ or the Madonna, plus headstones with the engraved names of most or all of those buried beneath. This above-ground cemetery furniture can be quite impressive and rise quite high. The furniture pieces are not added all at once; it might actually take a number of years, when money is available, to complete the task. In addition, families may also squeeze in flower plants, bushes, and even small trees.

Mexican cemeteries are therefore noted for their elaborate and profuse use of above-ground decoration. To the contrary, however, the cemetery in Ajijic has only minimal above-ground decoration beyond headstones. But plot owners have created a new innovation, the installation of waist-high wrought-iron fences to enclose individual plots and which proclaim that the plot is owned in perpetuity by land title.

The most unusual cemetery in the communities under consideration is that in Chapala. It is actually divided into three sections, one large center section for townspeople and a section on either side of the center portion, which are reserved for foreigners (mainly U.S. citizens). The difference between the center section and the two side sections is amazing! The center, or Mexican, section, is resplendent with above-ground crypts and all the stone and cement cemetery furniture previously mentioned. In stark contrast, the "American Cemetery" (as the two side sections are called by local townspeople) is bare except for a lawn and flush-to-the-ground bronze plaques, which give a name and the date of death. Also, in these sections, each grave plot contains only one body.

The Daughters of the American Revolution, a social-civic organization, which has a chapter in Guadalajara, has recently completed an investigation and registration of all foreign burials in the Chapala cemetery (Daughters of the American Revolution 1997). They found 305 burials of U.S. citizens in the American Cemetery: 103 females, 202 males. Of the 305, 72 were veterans. The earliest date found for interment of U.S. citizens was 1956; where or whether earlier burials occurred has not been ascertained. (This ongoing project will next focus on the cemetery in Ajijic.)

Considering the number of deaths that occur in the area (*Colony Reporter*, 17-23 May 1997), it is apparent that a shift in burial ritual choice is taking place among retirees. With the number of older retirees in the area increasing each year, there should be a commensurate increase in the number of local burials, and this does not seem to be the case. It appears that many more U.S. retirees are now electing to be cremated, with the ashes sent home, or requesting that their bodies be sent home intact. Another option is that, when the retiree becomes fairly feeble or disabled, he or she returns to the United States for the final months or years of care.

One final option, according to some who claim to be in the know, is that an increasing number of retirees who elect cremation ask their friends to dispose of their ashes around flower beds at the local Protestant churches, in the city parks, on the grounds of the local association gardens, or in the lake. All these arrangements are said to be forbidden by Mexican law, but they are occurring anyway. With this sort of disposal, there would be a cremation record but no record of just what happened to the deceased after cremation and no burial record. This, too, is a self-selected burial ritual.

DISCUSSION

What are the basic components of death and burial ritual in civil society in Ixtlahuacan de los Membrillos and San Luis Soyatlan as opposed to Chapala and Ajijic? Ritual in Ixtlahuacan and San Luis requires more people, prayers, crosses, a church service, and communal sharing of food. Family, friends, *compadres*, *barrio* neighbors, and other community members come to begin the prayers, prepare the body, stay for an all-night vigil immediately after death, and pray, grieve, and console the bereaved in their home, at the church, at the cemetery, and afterward for nine days with nightly saying of the Rosary. The communal food is shared in two ways: with the sweet bread and coffee each night and with the final communal dinner at the end of the nine days. Additionally, new *compadres* are gained through the ritual of the raising of the cross that is later placed at the grave site.

In Chapala and Ajijic, Catholics will come for the all-night vigil, will help prepare the body, will attend mass the next day, and will participate in the funeral procession, but there will only be three nights of Rosary said in lieu of the nine-night Novenario still practiced in Ixtlahuacan and San Luis. In addition, there is no traditional coffee and sweet bread, no communal dinner (only one involving family members and, possibly, a few close friends), and no

Compadres of the Cross. In other words, the ritual acts focus more on family involvement and much less on community involvement in death and burial.

For the Protestants in the area, death and burial rituals are even more reduced. Although church members, family, and possibly other community members may or may not attend an all-night vigil, in many cases the vigil will take place in a funeral parlor rather than at home. After the church service and the burial, there may be occasional short visits by family and friends, with food brought to the bereaved home; however, grieving is expected to be done privately.

For retirees, the services are similar to those of most Protestant denominations but may be even further reduced to a short memorial service at one of the associations to which the deceased belonged. Cremation or burial would comply with whatever wishes the deceased had previously indicated on the Memorial Society of Guadalajara's registration form (called the "post-life" form by the Chapala Society in Ajijic).

All of the death and burial rituals that have been discussed contain items, objects, and services of religious and social significance: the cross; Jesus Christ or the Virgin or both; a church service for the deceased; flowers; food exchanges of some type; and cremation or burial. What changes between the four communities of Ixtlahuacan de los Membrillos, San Luis Soyatlan, Chapala, and Ajijic is the degree or amount of involvement by others in the death and burial process. There is also a shift from public and shared grieving to more private and individual grieving.

It is evident that the change from an agriculturally oriented community to one of product and service provision to outsiders has changed the social focus in local society. Notwithstanding the influence of the wide variety of Protestant churches in the area, and the influx of a large number of U.S. retirees, each of which has an orientation of individualism in expression in religious and social spheres (Bellah et al. 1985, 222), even the Catholic church in both Chapala and Ajijic has experienced a shift in the social-religious rituals surrounding death. It is no longer the totality of the community that offers sustenance and solace in times of need to any one member, but a much smaller number of people on whom individual community members must now rely in Chapala and Ajijic.

In speaking of Mexico and Mexicans, Condon (1990) tells us that "every person is part of a larger family grouping . . . [and] cannot be regarded as a completely isolated individual" (88). Each person is part of an extended family, and interlacing ties with *compadres* lead to the larger social group, the community. Through the communal sharing of death, burial, and grieving, burial and death rituals reaffirm group unity, and, at the end of public grieving, family members are expected to take up their roles again, as valued members within a community of members.

On the other hand, in Chapala and Ajijic, there is evidence of a shift in death and burial ritual from a family-community group focus to an individual focus, with the ultimate expression of this lying in the much-reduced self-selected burial rites of many U.S. retirees. A study on individualism and religious and social-civic practices stated that "individualism lies at the very core of American culture. . . . Anything that would violate our right to think for ourselves, judge for ourselves, make our own decisions, live our lives as we see fit, is [seen as] not only morally wrong, it is sacrilegious" (Bellah et al. 1985, 142). Each person is encouraged to be the sole authority for his or her actions, be it work or play, public or private. Protestantism reinforces, and is reinforced by, this belief in self-responsibility, wherein each person is ultimately responsible for himself or herself before God. In this case, death and burial rites reaffirm the individualism of society's members, and the bereaved are expected to overcome their grief and resume their life as individuals, taking care of themselves as before.

The death and burial rituals seen in Ixtlahuacan de los Membrillos and San Luis Soyatlan still reflect an orientation toward community and community members as a part of the whole. The rituals in Chapala and Ajijic, including those of U.S. retirees residing permanently in the area, show an increasing focus on individualism, with an orientation toward the self and away from the community as a whole. The change in death and burial rituals is thus the reflection of the shift from a community focus to an individual orientation; the care of the individual is shifting from the community to the self.

This investigation into death and burial rituals has demonstrated that a shift is occurring at the community level that does not bode well for the development of any broad-based democratic processes. The shift in the amount of involvement by others in the death and burial process, coupled with a shift from public and shared grieving to more private and individual grieving expressions, reflects an erosion of one of the real strengths that Mexican civil society has: its family-community orientation. If that is taken away, on what do the seeds of true democracy and equal access to opportunity fall?

Note

1. All the following information on death and burial rituals comes from interviews in Otero 1997.

References

Ayuntamiento de Chapala. Secretario de administración. 1997. Interview by author. May.

Bellah, Robert, Richard Madsen, William Sullivan, Ann Swidler, and Steven Tipton. 1985. *Habits of the Heart.* Berkeley: University of California Press.

Condon, John. 1990. So Near the United States. In *Culture Bound: Bridging the Cultural Gap in Language Teaching,* ed. J. Valdes. New York: Cambridge University Press.

Daughters of the American Revolution. 1997. U.S. Burials in the Chapala, Jalisco Cemetery. Ajijic, Jalisco, Mexico. Mimeographed.

De Los Reyes, Guillermo and Paul Rich. 1997. Myth-Making and Political Culture: Creating Mystiques of Power. Paper presented at the Second Congress of the Americas, 27 Feb., Universidad de las Américas–Puebla, Mexico.

Giddens, Anthony, ed. 1972. *Emile Durkheim: Selected Writings.* New York: Cambridge University Press.

Hall, John and Mary Jo Neitz. 1993. *Culture: Sociological Perspectives.* Englewood Cliffs, NJ: Prentice Hall.

Instituto Nacional de Estadística, Geografía e Informática (INEGI). 1997a. *Jalisco: Perfil sociodemografico.* Aguascalientes, Ags.: INEGI.

———. 1997b. *Monografías, municipales: Chapala.* Guadalajara, Jalisco: INEGI.

Otero, Lorena. 1997. Field notes, Sept.-Nov. Instituto de Ciencias Sociales y Humanidades, Universidad Autónoma de Puebla, Mexico.

Rich, Paul and Guillermo De Los Reyes. 1996. Mexican Caricature and the Politics of Popular Culture. *Journal of Popular Culture* 30(1):133-44.

ANNALS, *AAPSS*, **565**, September 1999

Ritual and Community Networks Among Laborer Groups in Mexico

By OLGA LAZCANO and GUSTAVO BARRIENTOS

ABSTRACT: As a symbolic act of cultural reproduction and re-elaboration of networks of community cohesion, so crucial to civic society at times of discontinuity of the social sense, ritual provides a temporary but necessary reorientation of the daily lives of industrial workers of Nahua origin in the Puebla-Tlaxcala region. This community phenomenon contrasts with the purpose of ritual connected to the workplace, where reaffirmation of identity as a worker is accentuated, subsuming ethnic identity and enhancing cohesion within the labor group and the factory. It is in this dual context that ritual becomes an intermediary in a sincretic process of both community and worker cohesion and ethnic and worker identity. What is important, then, is to distinguish between the two types of ritual, analyzed within the inter- and extra-workplace sphere of interaction, and the different symbols found in each. The purpose of this article is to present such an analysis using the voice of blue-collar workers.

Olga Lazcano is associate professor in the Anthropology Department at the Universidad de las Américas–Puebla, Mexico. Her research interest focuses on labor groups in Mexico. She is currently conducting research on community networks and labor groups in Huejotzingo, Puebla.

Gustavo Barrientos is research professor in the Anthropology Department of the Universidad de las Américas–Puebla, Mexico. He has published a number of articles related to urban issues and anthropology. His current research interest concerns anthropology applied to industry and urban problems.

RITUALS OF COMMUNITY COHESION IN THE REDEFINITION OF SOCIAL SENSE

We have an important example of the processes of community network redefinition in the foundry workers of Teziutlán, Puebla, Mexico, a mountainous area 300 miles north of Puebla City. Many of the foundry workers are bilingual speakers of Spanish and Nahua. They have formed traditional dance groups that participate in regional religious celebrations such as the feast days of patron saints and the Virgin Mary, the raising of the cross, Corpus Christi, and Holy Week. The members of each group—the *quetzalines*, *tocotines*, *santiaguitos*, and *negritos*—make sure that the steps and routines of their particular dance are handed down from generation to generation, as they were taught by their fathers and grandfathers, who in turn were taught by their ancestors. Skilled performers who know the significance of their particular dance believe that they are privileged to conserve this tradition and knowledge in their community.

There is a connection with the factory in the need to work double shifts in order to be able to go to the hills to obtain the traditional elements that the different parts of the dance costume must include. For example, the headdress of a *quetzaline* includes a framework of slender sticks taken from the trunk of the *tarro* tree that might require several days to obtain. Another important element is the so-called *cera puerca*, a resin that is used as glue and that can take from several hours to a whole day hiking rough canyons to find. The *quetzalines* argue that "it's not important how long it takes to find the materials Mother Nature provides; these are the ones our fathers taught us [to use] and the ones that tradition requires us to use."

The feathers are taken from a white hen, of a type called *ranchera*, after it has been purified by cutting off its head, hanging it by the feet to bleed, and plunging it into hot water. The rest of the costume elements, such as paper and woven components, are purchased in the market.

Constructing the headdress takes about a month, and each dancer must make his own in order to be able to carry the fullest significance of the tradition and the protection of the ancestors on his head, the part of the body that guides the rest. The dancers all compete to see who can produce the most attractive headdress.

The other important part of the costume is the cape, which is made of royal blue satin and features a nineteenth-century national coat of arms surrounded by a border of beads and spangles sewn by the participant's wife. The dancers say that with the coat of arms they reaffirm that they are "Mexican Indians" and that the wife sews the border as an act of sharing family honor and respect for the community. They note that the coat of arms is an old one because the tradition is as well.

A recent costume innovation is replacement of the traditional sandal with *charro* (Mexican cowboy)–type boots. The dancers argue,

Now we're not just *campesinos* [poor peasants]; we're workers too. We need to show our progress, and we do it by using shoes or especially boots, which we combine with red satin pants, but now made by a tailor because they look more presentable.

The complete costume costs perhaps $200, which is about two months' salary, and requires another month's effort to put together. In order to get the money for the costume, which tradition requires be redone each year, the dancers take out a loan from the union, which charges interest at 60 percent. They repay the loan from the small proceeds from the sale of corn in the local market, work done by the wife.

An individual participates in an average of 14 festivals a year and, in order to do so, works double shifts or asks for leave without pay. To avoid problems at work, the extra shifts worked are usually the ones from 3:00 p.m. to 7:00 a.m. the day before the festival. So, after working continuously for 16 hours at high-risk job sites such as the crucible of a foundry, they head for the sacristy of the church in Acateno, where the other dancers and family members are waiting to help them don their costumes. The community or *barrio* (quarter, where social relations are strong) that has invited the group will have sent transportation, frequently a truck with stock racks, to take them to the festival site, where their first task will be to assemble the quetzal star, a wooden wheel where the quetzal ceremony will be performed.

The dancing starts at about 9:30 a.m. and does not stop until 2:00 p.m., when the *quetzalines* mount the quetzal star. Stabilizing themselves by pressing their legs against the wooden frame, they use body motions to make the star spin like a wheel of fortune, leaving them alternately upright and upside down. After the quetzal ceremony, all go to mass and, upon leaving, continue to dance. From the beginning, the participants have been drinking *aguardiente*, a strong, clear alcoholic beverage. The rule for drinking is to avoid falling down drunk like the *tocotines* since the next day they will have to be at work. Further, severe intoxication detracts from the prestige and status of the group.

The dance ends at about 8:00 p.m., when the dancers are served a meal. If it is a sponsored event, they are taken to the home of the sponsor. If it is a church festival, they are served in the atrium of the church. After the meal, they remove their costumes in a private ceremony held in the sacristy of the church or in a separate room in the home of the sponsor. In street clothes, they can continue the camaraderie for as long as they might care to, frequently into the early hours of the morning. The next day they need to be at the factory to work their regular shift. They return to dangerous job sites with reflexes slowed by fatigue, which on unfortunate occasions has resulted in job accidents. Don Gerardo comments, "We know it's dangerous, but for us the primary thing in life must be to preserve tradition. In the end, God will protect us since we went to worship him, and, if nothing happens to us in the quetzal star, nothing will happen in the factory."

Another interesting ritual, called Carnaval, takes place in Huejotzingo, a small town with a Nahuatl-speaking population (Nutini and Isaac 1974). Huejotzingo is located 20 kilometers east of Puebla City. The ritual takes place on Shrove Tuesday, with lesser festivities during the two days before. In order to participate in this festival, individuals work double shifts, exchange shifts that they will have to pay back (often two days for one) on their days off, and, in extreme cases, take job suspensions.

Carnaval in Huejotzingo is an example of symbolic interaction within a region where different social groups share or dispute the meanings of symbols. In this case, to share meanings implies common symbols, what Bordieu (1988) calls "habitus" and defines as "a system of shared social dispositions and cognitive structures which generates perceptions, appreciations and actions" (279). In other words, it is the relationship between the reality of things and the conception that people have of those things.

For Bordieu (1990), only a case analysis could demonstrate the decisive break with the vision of the social world that results from the act of substituting the relationship between the individual and the society for the relationship constructed between two modes of existence of the social, the "habitus," or the history made by the individual, and the "field of action," the history of the festival Carnaval. Thus we note the difference between the history of the individual in relation to the significance of his or her participation as a distinct entity and the collective history of the participants in the interaction and negotiation of meanings within a common space that leads them to participate in a regional traditional festival. In this sense, the negotiation of meanings is effected in relation to each of the symbols that characterize participation in Carnaval: status, inclusion in a social group, competition, entertainment, disorder, integration, and victory over the rich and powerful, among others.

Preparations for Carnaval begin six months before. The first step is to select which battalion to be part of by talking to the general who organizes each group. Each of Huejotzingo's four *barrios* might organize its own battalions of *zuavos, turcos, zapadores, franceses, zacapoaxtlas, indios*, and *negros*, the last being a recently incorporated group, while the others have been a tradition since the middle of the last century. If accepted, each individual must begin to put together the costume (or to repair or rent one) and save up for the sign-up and music fees. Participation in a specific battalion depends in part on the three-part process Berger (1989, 75) has described as "internalization," "objectivization," and "externalization." The pleasure gained from participation is internalized through sharing a regional culture. In the process of objectivization, one realizes that Carnaval is a festival relevant to his or her daily life. Through the process of externalization, the significance that the festival has for the participants is acted out. In this way, the participant indicates with which battalion he or she identifies, and the joy found in being part of that battalion, its costume, and the significance given each group. Despite such feelings, choosing a battalion depends as well on the participant's economic situation at that time, given that the cost of the costume depends on the battalion.

The general of a battalion is selected by a group of friends or is perhaps self-appointed. He organizes and obtains the *ranchos*, or food and refreshments, for his battalion and contracts for the music that will accompany them. This individual acquires the position of boss when he manages to form a battalion and, for that reason, has power as a personal attribute (Wolf 1990). That is, the participants respect and obey him because for them he is the person who knows how to manage and control. The general, for his part, understands these to be his central obligations, which free him even to strike those participants who do not obey orders meant to control, such as those against excessive drinking or firing muskets toward the crowd, or orders meant to protect women participants.

Don Jorge, general of the *turcos* (Turks), and an employee at Crisol, a textile factory, spoke to us about his participation:

My father's the one who taught me the joy of Carnaval since I was eight years old. I remember back then he was usually broke and we were 11 in all, 6 sisters and 5 brothers, and he was a worker in a sweater factory where he worked like a dog and they paid him next to nothing. Back then all of us boys in the family went as devils because that was the cheapest costume. My mother and sisters were in charge of making us the outfits. At 14, when I started as an apprentice where my father worked and began to earn my few pennies I went as an "Indio Serrano" [mountain Indian] which is the least special Battalion but you have to start somewhere. One of my sisters made me the costume.

I ended up in a bad financial situation. My father got sick and my brothers and I had to leave the family early. That's how at the age of 18 I started going as an "Arriero" [courier] like the ones who transported the money that, according to tradition, "Agustín Lorenzo" used to steal to give to the poor. I was able to go in whatever clothes I had, only needing a horse to be in that group. That was real nice. You could shine with the ladies since you have to be real clever to be able to handle a horse at full gallop and with those guns thundering, since that scares the horses. When I finally got a stable job at Crisol and began to earn well and steady I stopped going as an Arriero. At 24 I decided to form my Battalion of Turcos because it was a Battalion that had disappeared and I wanted to retrieve a tradition that was being lost and now I have 16 years organizing it.

As a result of my going out as a General, well dressed and done up, my wife fell in love with me. She used to come from Zacatepec accompanying her brothers who went out in Carnaval and there she saw me because I've never liked going out in a mask, mostly because of the cost of the costume and besides, that way they know who you are. That's how we met in the parade and then right away we got married and now we have 16 years together, the same as I've been General. An uncle who has worked a long time in a clothing factory designs the costumes for me and my sister sews them.

Being a General is my greatest pride in life, for that reason I spend good money on the costumes, even though my sister charges me very little and my uncle charges what is fair. I like to wear a different costume for each of the 3 days of Carnaval. The more a person shines the greater his distinction among the people. The costume consists of a turban, sword, jacket, shirt, cartridge belt, cape, and horse. That's how with the three costumes I've spent approximately 120 dollars.

I have 5 children, 3 girls and 2 boys, and for me it's very satisfying that they go out for Carnaval. My 15, 14, and 13 year old daughters go as belly dancers and are standard bearers for my Battalion. They look so pretty in their costumes that they make my Battalion shine even more. My six year old son has his little outfit and goes out even though it can be tough because the little guy still gets tired, but it makes my wife and me very proud to see him in Carnaval.

My wife, my sisters, and my mother are in charge of preparing the food, which nearly always consists of rice and mole [a chili-based sauce], for my Battalion. Some 500 people attend who all need drinks as well. These days the food is purchased with the fees from the participants since it was getting very expensive when I purchased it myself, and the times make it more difficult each year, especially now that my oldest daughter is in prep school.

I lose a week's work in which I don't earn any money because they give me the time off but without pay. Sometimes I'm lucky and they pay me but I have to work extra hours including my days off and frequently one day extra. But like I said, the pride, the satisfaction, and the joy of participating is part of my life. Because of that I don't care at all—and before being

a factory worker, I'm from Huejo. (Lazcano 1995, 17)

For Levi (1981), Novelo (1984), and Satriani (1985), the different cultural expressions of the subaltern classes are re-elaborated by the dominant culture and, at the same time, constitute forms of resistance that conserve their intimate or particular culture, depending on the social group involved. One must discuss, therefore, not civil society but civil societies. In this sense, Carnaval is a form of cultural resistance. Participation in Carnaval, as with other actions in the daily life of the workers, constitutes a kind of subversive act, although the intention is not to challenge the rules of the workplace but rather to unite oneself with community networks. It would be unimaginable in any other part of the year that a secretary might dare to say to her boss, "I'm very sorry but I won't be at work because I have to go to the festival." Let us not forget that Batkin (cited in Reynoso 1991, 25) has characterized carnival festivals as myth and ritual in which the celebration of fertility and abundance converge and the values of the established order are inverted with a cosmic sense of the destruction and regeneration of times past. Batkin observes that this vision of popular culture constitutes a marked contrast with the conservative culture of the dominant classes.

Huejotzingo is a market city that serves as a center for the different communities in its hinterland. These neighboring cities, such as Cholula, San Miguel Tianguizolco, and San Luis Coyotzingo, among others, celebrate Octavos de Carnaval on the Sundays during Lent by reenacting nearly to the letter what occurs in Huejotzingo, although on a much smaller scale and with evident reduction in splendor and expense. The Octavos de Carnaval are conceived as very local festivities wherein intimate peasant culture is shared (Lomnitz-Adler 1992). Because the Octavo participants are worker-peasants, the Carnaval participants who live in Huejotzingo say that the Octavos de Carnaval are "very common" festivities "since they're Indian." Curiously, of his symbolic identification with a battalion, Don Ignacio, a worker at Politex, a factory that manufactures thread for textiles, tells us,

Despite the fact that I'm from Huejotzingo I like to go with the Battalion of the Indios [Indians] because it's the one I identify with our ancestors, it's a feeling that you're participating with the weaker and the poorer. But I don't like to participate in the Octavos de Carnaval because I believe that these days they're not first rate.

The worker-peasants, for their part, are anxious to participate in the main carnival at Huejotzingo and send their local group leader, or *general de comunidad*, to talk to the general of the specific battalion they would like to join.

The use of muzzle-loaders is as fundamental as are the mask and the diverse elements of the different costumes. There exists a commercial infrastructure where these various elements are sold at different qualities and prices according to the budget of the participant. For some, it is very important to point out that they use muskets or costumes that they themselves or someone in their household has made. It is important to note that frequently the *gasne* (cape) is made by the young man's girlfriend as a way to contribute to his fine presentation and as a way to recognize him amid the festivities.

Referring to the costume, Don Fidel, who works at a thread factory, says,

The costume shows the personality one is trying to project. If the costume is lavish and well cared for, you notice right away and say, "This is worthwhile, look at that outfit." But for that you have to go to great lengths to have the best. In that way everything shines, the individual as much as Carnaval.

The price of a musket varies between $30 and $1000; a mask, between $1 and $30; and a cape, between $20 and $400, depending on the style. There exist as well maintenance workshops where muskets are repaired and painted and where costumes are put in order. If one decides to use the same costume, repairs can be made by a maintenance workshop or by the participant himself.

As noted before, the Carnaval festivities in Huejotzingo begin two days before Shrove Tuesday. Sunday at 11:00 a.m. all gather at the *villita* (chapel) where, after prayers, the groups take their parade positions and fire the first volleys to announce Carnaval. From there they leave at 11:30 for the main square, where they march around the plaza, never ceasing to fire off their muskets. At

1:00 p.m. they reenact *el rapto de la dama* (the kidnapping of the heiress) by Agustín Lorenzo, a figure of local myth. At 3:30 p.m. *la boda india* (the Indian wedding) of Agustín Lorenzo and his lady takes place. Later, the hut of the lovers is set aflame, they flee, and the battles between the battalions begin. There are frequently many accidents as a result of incautious use of muskets and abuse of alcoholic beverages. When the battles are over, the festival ends. The same itinerary is repeated on Monday.

On Shrove Tuesday, each battalion assembles at 6:00 a.m. and goes to every house that has offered them *rancho*, which consists of big baskets of bread, cases of beer, bottles of liquor, pots full of tamales, cases of soft drinks, and so on. All of the things that are gathered together in the *rancho* are taken to the general's house, where breakfast is taken. At approximately 9:00 many of the battalions go to the cemetery to pay respects to a member who has recently passed away. At 11:00 all head for the *villita* and at 11:30 the circling of the main plaza begins anew. At 1:00 *el rapto de la dama* is enacted and at 3:30, *la boda india*. Then the couple's hut is torched, they flee, and the battles ensue.

At the dinner hour, some battalions are invited to eat at the home of a distinguished individual. Those battalions without an invitation gather at the home of the general; each of the members has contributed in order to prepare *barbacoa* (a popular meat dish) or *mole* (turkey cooked in chili sauce). Participants from the communities eat in the main square or near Huejotzingo's sixteenth-century convent, in family groups.

We believe that participation in the festival, the idea of Carnaval as a space and time of equality that ends with the lifting of the mask, and the use of the costume as a symbol of temporary status are regional symbolic features shared by all of the participants in the festival, independently of gender or social position.

Negotiating with employers the times and ways to be able to participate and the use of one's salary as an element that permits showier participation during Carnaval are traits characteristic of workers. An intriguing phenomenon is that these workers do not organize in order to participate together nor in relation to an identity with the workplace. This is in contrast to the festivities that are organized within the factory, where a strong identity with the factory is reinforced. We can thus speak of celebrations whose intent is to renew an identity with one's community of origin and celebrations that renew an identity with the workplace.

RITUALS OF REAFFIRMATION
AND IDENTIFICATION
WITH THE WORKPLACE

The processions from factories to parish churches that take place during the festivities of the Virgin of Carmen are an interesting example of rituals that strengthen worker identity. For the processions in which the employees of the clothing factories of Teziutlán, Puebla, participate, preparations begin three months in advance. Each of approximately 25 factories organizes contributions from its employees to prepare for the celebrations.

The Virgin is represented by a young girl, who rides in the procession on an elaborately decorated sedan chair. The majority of the factories select their girl, either by contest or by vote, from the daughters of their workers. Selection is an honor for the parent whose daughter is chosen. In some plants, the girl selected is a daughter of the owners. The outfit worn by the representative is designed and sewn by the best seamstresses, with the costs paid by the contributions from all the workers. Each of the factories competes to see who has presented the best throne for their Virgin and who is dressed the best.

The processions are organized so that each hour a contingent leaves from its workplace for the church, where the Virgin will be carried to the altar. There a worker representative delivers an expression of thankfulness to the patroness of Carmen and a mass is offered. The elaborateness and solemnity of the mass that follows each procession depend on the money gathered by the workers to pay for the mass. Thus there might be a mass with a red carpet extending to the door, with lighted lamps, and with one, two, or even three priests. A mass in the morning costs less than a mass in the afternoon. The floral arrangements vary in both size and quality and are changed each hour as a new mass begins. The companies with a larger number of workers and relatively better salaries are the ones that try to have a

more ostentatious mass, the most richly decorated throne, and the most carefully dressed Virgin. Each vies for the noon mass, which is the most expensive. Thus the timing of the processions depends on the amount of money raised by the workers at each factory to pay for the ritual.

During the day of the processions, then, a work interruption occurs each hour starting at 8:00 a.m. and progressing from factory to factory. Each procession begins when the workers gather in formation at the factory gates. There the owners or their representatives present the company's banner to inaugurate the procession. Everybody returns about an hour and a half later, the owners retrieve the banner presented earlier, and the workers return to their job sites.

An even more interesting case of cohesion and group identity involves the workers from the La Estrella clothing factory in Tlaxcala. There, despite the bankruptcy and closure of the plant, workers continue to celebrate the Virgin of Pilar, the patroness of the factory, even though many of them are in very difficult financial situations. When the factory was running, they would have a big annual festival and carry the Virgin's image in procession to the Church of Santa Ana to celebrate mass. The company would pay some of the costs while the union required a fee from each employee in order to make the celebration "showier and better."

With the closure of the factory, the workers continued with the procession, even in the most uncertain of times. A commission was formed and charged with organizing the procession and mass. Fees were collected, and the commission would go to the home of Don Tomás, the ex-leader of the union, to borrow the image. This continued until five years ago, when Don Tomás became ill with cancer and decided not to lend the image any more. He told the commission, "I need her, more than any of you because I'm very ill, and . . . she gets angry because we remove her and mistreat her and don't take care of her and she doesn't like it."

For this reason, the ex-workers organized an effort to have the money the following year to send for a replica of the image even though they were convinced it was not the same. As Don Paco, one of the participants, affirmed to us:

The other Virgin is the good one, the original, the one the owners brought directly from Spain, and the one that for all that time took care of us from the door of the factory. There's nothing more to that bastard Tomás, he took the best in the liquidations and still takes away our protection.

This is a group of former factory workers who, now in their sixties, are without economic security. The procession and the mass have become the only basis of identity and belonging for them, as individuals who have seen themselves lose their importance in other community and family networks.

The importance of ritual as reaffirmation of identities and maintenance of community is crucial in the daily lives of those workers of Nahua origin in the Puebla-Tlaxcala region who faced, historically, impacts from the creation of industrial corridors in traditionally agricultural areas. In response to the process of economic globalization, and within a fuller process of culture in transition, they have retaken traditional ceremonies as the link to their ethnic identity. This can clearly be seen with the *quetzalines* and the festival of Carnaval. On the other hand, in this process of change, worker identities have forcefully penetrated as well and have syncretized with traditional festivals, as in the case of the Virgin of Carmen. An extreme case of worker identity reproduction and the continuance of a rite of protection is that of the ex-workers from the La Estrella factory in Tlaxcala, where, even though the factory gates are closed, they continue to celebrate the feast of their patroness, the Virgin of Pilar.

Ritual is converted into a veneration of the sacred as a symbol of economic security, of protection at work, of family integration, of reaffirmation of nationalism, with a reemphasis on the national, on things religious, and on livelihood, taking place in the spaces of community and the factory. In rural Mexico, without ritual there is no civil society.

References

Berger, Peter. 1989. *La construcción social de la realidad*. Buenos Aires: Amorrortu Editores.

Bordieu, Pierre. 1988. *Homo Academicus*. Stanford, CA: Stanford University Press.

————. 1990. *Sociología y cultura*. Mexico City: Grijalbo.

Lazcano, Olga. 1995. Ser obrero en Huejotzingo. Master's thesis, Universidad de las Américas–Puebla.

Levi, Giovana. 1981. Vida cotidiana de un barrio obrero: La aportación de la historia oral. *Cuicuilco* 11:65-73.

Lomnitz-Adler, Claudio. 1992. *Exits from the Labyrinth: Culture and Ideology in the Mexican National Space*. Berkeley: University of California Press.

Novelo, Victoria. 1984. La cultura obrera: Una contrapropuesta cultural. *Nueva antropología* 6:45-55.

Nutini, Hugo and Barry L. Isaac. 1974. *Los pueblos de habla náhuatl de la región de Puebla y Tlaxcala*. Mexico City: Instituto Nacional Indigenista.

Reynoso, Carlos. 1991. *El surgimiento de la antropología postmoderna*. Mexico City: Gedisa Editorial.

Satriani, Luigi Lombardi. 1985. *Apropiación y destrucción de las culturas populares*. Mexico City: Editorial Nueva Imgen.

Wolf, Eric. 1990. Facing Power: Old Insights, New Questions. *American Anthropologist* 92:586-96.

ANNALS, *AAPSS*, **565**, September 1999

Civil Society and Volunteerism: Lodges in Mining Communities

By GUILLERMO DE LOS REYES and ANTONIO LARA

ABSTRACT: This article discusses the contributions of secret ritual-istic societies to the social construction of mining communities and to nineteenth-century life in the United States in general. The role of se-cret societies in nineteenth-century American life has not been fully assessed. What attention they have received often overlooks their ef-fect on associational life and volunteerism, including those in the mining community. This article points out the influence that Free-masonry had upon much of American organizational life in the nine-teenth century. The study of Masonic institutions thus may well be important to understanding American mining culture.

Guillermo De Los Reyes is a Ph.D. candidate at the University of Pennsylvania. His current research interests are the study of political and popular culture in Mexico and the influence of civil society in the democratization of Mexico.

Antonio Lara is a graduate student at the Universidad de las Américas–Puebla. He is currently doing research on voluntary associations and democracy and the role of the Catholic Church in Mexican politics.

THE contributions of secret ritualistic societies to the social construction of mining communities and to nineteenth-century life in the United States in general have not been fully assessed. What attention they have received often overlooks their effect on associational life and volunteerism, including those in the mining community. That the societies were a significant influence seems clear. Mary Murphy (1997) writes about Butte, Montana:

On most nights, a large proportion of Butte's population could be found congregated in one of the city's many labor or fraternal halls . . . nearly every organized fraternal group in the country had a chapter in Butte. By the advent of World War I, the Masons, Elks, Odd Fellows, Good Templars, Knights of Columbus, Ancient Order of Hibernians, Sons of St. George, and Scandinavian Brotherhood, among others, had built impressive halls. (8)

FRATERNAL LIFE
IN NINETEENTH-
CENTURY AMERICA

The extent of fraternal life among miners is perhaps not surprising considering the early reputation that America had acquired for its enthusiasm about voluntary societies. "In no country of the world," wrote Alexis de Tocqueville (1990), "has the principle of association been more successfully used or applied to a greater multitude of objects than in America. . . . There is no end which the human will despairs of attaining through the combined power of individuals united into a society" (191-92).

However, there are surprisingly few nonpolemical books and even fewer dissertations when it comes to the fraternal aspects of this subject. Mary Ann Clawson, in her pioneering study *Constructing Brotherhood* (1989), writes about this scholarly neglect:

To the great majority of historians who have even noticed it, the presence of fraternal association has been as uninteresting as it was insignificant . . . scholars have tended to strip away the epiphenomenal fraternal "trappings" so as to concentrate on the religious, economic, or political "core," which is then seen as the only meaningful part of the institution. This lack of awareness is most pronounced in the study of nineteenth-century American society, where a Masonic type of fraternalism served as the organizational model for trade unions, agricultural societies, nativist organizations, and political movements of every conceivable ideological stripe, as well as for literally hundreds of social organizations. (5)

If we accept her view, and we do, that Freemasonry was an influence on much of American organizational life in the nineteenth century, then the study of Masonic institutions may well be important to understanding American mining culture. There is considerable evidence that this is the case. Such was the importance of Freemasonry in early mining communities that "Masonic" was the name applied to at least a few significant California mining areas (Billeb 1968, 92-199).

Despite its strange rituals and peculiar customs, Masonry was the earliest social organization in many mining communities. For example, Mary Murphy (1997) writes,

The first voluntary association organized in Montana seems to have been the Masons' Grand Lodge of Montana, established in Virginia City in January 1866. Freemasonry was the forefather of the many fraternal lodges that multiplied in the late nineteenth and early twentieth centuries until millions of Masons, Shriners, Odd Fellows, Pythians, Woodmen, Elks, Moose, and Eagles walked America's streets. Butte, Montana's fastest growing city, proved fertile ground for the cultivation of fraternal life. By 1900 there were lodges representing more than two dozen fraternal orders in the city. The Odd Fellows alone had eighteen branches, and the Masons closely trailed with fifteen. (138)

Freemasonry was certainly the lodge of choice in most mining towns. In California, for example, Masonry accompanied the gold rush, and the growth of Masonic lodges among the miners was nothing less than extraordinary. Since Freemasonry was not a working-class phenomenon, this is historiographically noteworthy, as it bears out the thesis of Sean Wilentz (1990) that, "in smaller single-industry cities and mining towns, divisions between workers and the independent middle classes tended to be less sharp than in larger cities" (124).

Investigation may show that Masonry was a part of Californian life even before the growth of mining. California was part of the Spanish Empire and then part of the New Mexican Republic. Since Freemasonry as an organized movement possibly arrived in Mexico with Spanish soldiers and officials in the period 1810-15, and since individual Freemasons were persecuted by the Inquisition in eighteenth-century Mexico, it is possible that there were Mexican Masons in California sometime before the 1840s. There were American Masons there in the 1830s and early 1840s while an independent Mexico held the territory.[1]

FREEMASONRY IN MINING COMMUNITIES

Freemasonry is not an American or Mexican movement in its origins. It has antecedents long before American or Mexican national independence, though not nearly as ancient as dedicated Freemasons sometimes claim. It found its way to the Western Hemisphere at least by the early 1700s. Its rituals are highly dramatic, subjecting candidates for membership to harrowing experiences, which include a mock assassination in the third, or Master Mason, degree. Evidence abounds that the focus of these rituals was to cement ties of friendship and fellowship between the members, and that sense of community was much prized in the rough-and-tumble of early mining.

Writing about California, John Walton Caughey (1975) remarks, "Masonry, the Odd Fellows, and other fraternal orders came early to the diggings. After all the men of mines were, most of them, Americans and ready joiners" (191). He adds that the mining industry supported at least one rival secret ritualistic society that was for miners almost exclusively, E Clampus Vitus.

This fraternity was active at least as early as 1857, although its zealots claimed it originated in the Garden of Eden and included Solomon as one of its members (as the Masons claimed also). With officers bearing titles such as "Clampatriarch" and "Royal Grand Musician," the members of E Clampus Vitus gave the Masons a good deal of competition, and Caughey comments, "Some would say, as a matter of fact, that the convivial, raucous, fun-loving Clampers best embody the spirit of gold rush society" (192).

In any event, a Freemason, James W. Marshall (1812-85), discovered gold in California in January 1848. Marshall's life encapsulates the vagabond experiences of many California gold rush participants. Born in New Jersey, he emigrated in 1839 to Kansas and in 1844 to California. He providently went to work for John A. Sutter (1803-80) in the lumber business at Coloma, California. It was while examining a millrace on 18 January 1848 that he found a gold nugget. This was actually two weeks before the official end of the war between the United States and Mexico, which formally ended with the signing of the Treaty of Guadalupe on 2 February 1848.

Marshall not only took the first three steps, or degrees, of Masonry—the Entered Apprentice, Fellowcraft, and Master Mason degrees—but also became a Royal Arch Mason, which involved four more of the degrees, or initiatory pageants (Denslow 1959, 3:139). Sutter, who employed Marshall, was also, allegedly, a Mason. He was born in Germany of Swiss parents and

served in the French Army in its campaign against Spain in 1823-24. He emigrated to America and settled in St. Louis in 1834. Taking up fur trading, he traveled to Oregon, Hawaii, and Alaska. In 1839, he came to California, first to San Francisco and then to Sacramento, where he settled and became a Mexican citizen. He did poorly as a gold prospector and was the victim of claim-jumpers, with the result that his own financial gain was negligible. Sutter was elected to receive Masonic degrees in Corinthian Lodge of Maryville, California, in 1853, but there is a controversy over whether or how he received them (Denslow 1959, 4:210).

The gold rush brought thousands of people like Marshall and Sutter to California. They were forced to live in hardship and danger. Masonic lodges offered fellowship and friendship in this hostile environment, so it is no wonder they were created so early. A similar phenomenon was noted among miners during Canada's Klondike Gold Rush of 1896-99, when organizations such as the Yukon Order of Pioneers played an important social role (Klondike 1987, 29).

The California grand lodge chartered all the original lodges in Nevada. The first Nevada lodge was founded in Carson City in 1862. Between 1862 and 1864, 10 more were organized. The Grand Lodge of Nevada was formed in 1865, and its headquarters, library, and museum are in Reno (Henderson 1984, 293-94).

Not only did these lodges strain to conduct Masonic rituals according to the time-honored tradition, but also they were very careful to have the permission to operate from Masonic organizations elsewhere. To appreciate the amazing fidelity to custom of the mining lodges in California during the gold rush as far as Masonry was concerned, it is well to keep in mind that Masonic lodges derive their legitimacy from grand lodges, which usually are sovereign for a particular geographic unit such as an American state. Mindful of this, the miners brought their Masonic permissions and licenses with them in the same baggage as their shovels and pans.

The Grand Lodge of Missouri issued a charter for a Masonic lodge in California on 10 May 1848. This document is often, in error, called the Lassen Charter because it was carried to California in a party led by Peter Lassen (1800-1859). Lassen was born in Copenhagen, Denmark, and arrived in America in 1830. He worked as a blacksmith in Missouri, and it was there that he became a Mason. In 1839, he went west to Oregon. In 1840, he went by ship to California, where he wandered around for several years. In 1844, he, like Sutter, became a Mexican citizen. In 1847, he was back in Missouri, organizing the wagon train that carried the charter (Denslow 1959, 3:58-59).[2]

The lodge was organized on 30 October 1849, with a Presbyterian minister, the Reverend Saschel Woods (d. 1854), as the presiding master. Lassen was also an officer. Woods was a member of the wagon party that Lassen had headed, and it was Woods who actually was entrusted with the charter. He had been made a Mason in Missouri in 1842, where he fought in the Mormon War (Stansel 1975, 12; Denslow 1959, 4:348).[3] Apparently the lodge met in Lassen's trading post at Benton City (now Vina), California. The lodge, named "Western Star Lodge," still exists, although, soon after its establishment, it moved to Shasta, California, where it meets to this day (Stansel 1975, 14).

Parenthetically, California Masonry continued to have a colorful history in the post–gold rush era. Hawaii continued to be under the jurisdiction of the Grand Lodge of California for many years and, after the American conquest of the Philippines during the Spanish-American War, the grand lodge began chartering lodges there. In fact, during World War II, California chartered a lodge in China. Meanwhile, the Grand Lodge of the Philippines chartered lodges in California (see Haffner 1988)!

Masonic lodges were formed early in other mining locales. The Russell party exploring Colorado had established a camp at Cherry Creek for only 10 days before a Masonic meeting was held, on 3 November 1858. One of the participants wrote,

We agreed to meeting every Saturday night and as our object in locating in Colorado was to get gold (we were supposed to be out prospecting during the week) we decided that any ideas concerning the country we were in, which might come to us, news of any mines we might discover, or any information which might be beneficial to the brethren, Masonically or financially, would, at the next meeting, be given to the Masons, there assembled. (Clark 1936, 56-57)

FREEMASONRY
AND CIVIL SOCIETY

The history of Freemasonry and similar widespread fraternal organizations as part of the mining story goes far to illustrate Leon Fink's assertion about mining history: "The new literature [on Freemasonry], while acknowledging diversity in economic development and political situation, has, in fact, discovered remarkable parallels in labor movements, worker culture, and popular aspirations otherwise separated by geographical distance, national identity, and political autonomy" (Fink 1963, 5). For the early miners, there were often no churches to attend, no organized amusements other than saloons and brothels, and even no cemeteries if they died. The Masonic lodge therefore

became almost all things to its members, a lodge, a religious center, a social rendezvous, a league for self-protection, and a sieve with which to sift the wheat from the chaff among the American adventurers, miners, trappers, and traders who began to come in from the East in a continuing stream . . . a lighthouse of friendship, charity, and social life. (Haywood 1963, 206)

The influence this was to have on the development of the mining unions and on the politics of those towns and states where miners were important remains a mystery, which, considering the notorious secretiveness of the Masons, is perhaps appropriate.

Notes

1. For a discussion of the situation in California during the brief period of its inclusion in the Mexican Republic, see Forbes 1973 and Francis 1976. Further information will be found in Weber 1976.

2. There seems to be a pattern in which the early settlers did not benefit from their adventures. For example, Lassen lost his ranch and was killed by an Indian in 1859.

3. The sword that Woods used in the Mormon War is now the property of the Masonic lodge in Carrollton, Missouri.

References

Billeb, Emil W. 1968. *Mining Camp Days*. Las Vegas: Nevada.

Caughey, John Walton. 1975. *The California Gold Rush*. Berkeley: University of California Press.

Clark, George B. 1936. *Our Masonic Heritage: A Glimpse of the Historical Background of Freemasonry*. Denver: Grand Lodge A.F. and A.M. of Colorado.

Clawson, Mary Ann. 1989. *Constructing Brotherhood: Class, Gender and Fraternalism*. Princeton, NJ: Princeton University Press.

Denslow, William R. 1959. *10,000 Famous Freemasons*. Richmond, VA: Macoy.

Fink, Leon. 1963. Looking Backward: Reflections on Workers' Culture and Certain Conceptual Dilemmas Within Labor History. In *The Masonic Essays of H. R. Haywood*, ed. Harry Leroy Haywood. Vol. 20. Fulton: Transactions of the Missouri Lodge of Research.

Forbes, Alexander. 1973. *California: A History of Upper and Lower California*. New York: Arno Press.

Francis, Jessie Davies. 1976. *An Economic and Social History of Mexican California, 1822-1846*. Vol. 1. New York: Arno Press.

Haffner, Christopher. 1988. *The Craft in the East*. Hong Kong: District Grand Lodge of Hong Kong and the Far East.

Haywood, Harry Leroy, ed. 1963. *The Masonic Essays of H. R. Haywood*.

Vol. 20. Fulton: Transactions of the Missouri Lodge of Research.

Henderson, K. W. 1984. *Masonic World Guide*. London: Lewis Masonic.

Klondike, Pierre Berton. 1987. *The Last Great Gold Rush, 1896-1899*. Toronto: McClelland & Steward.

Murphy, Mary. 1997. *Mining Cultures: Men, Women, and Leisure in Butte, 1914-41*. Chicago: University of Illinois Press.

Stansel, Edwin N., comp. 1975. *A History of Grand Lodge of Free and Accepted Masons, State of California, 1850-1975*. San Francisco: Grand Lodge of Free and Accepted Masons of the State of California.

Tocqueville, Alexis de. 1990. *Democracy in America*. Vol. 1. Henry Reeve text rev. Francis Bowen and Phillips Bradley. New York: Random House.

Weber, David J., ed. 1976. *Northern Mexico on the Eve of the United States Invasion: Rare Imprints Concerning California*. New York: Arno Press.

Wilentz, Sean. 1990. Rise of the Working Class. In *Perspectives on American Labor History: The Problems of Synthesis*. Dekalb: Northern Illinois University Press.

Book Department

INTERNATIONAL RELATIONS AND POLITICS

DUMMETT, MICHAEL. 1997. *Principles of Electoral Reform*. Pp. xi, 193. New York: Oxford University Press. $65.00. Paperbound, $23.95.

Michael Dummett, a professor emeritus of logic at Oxford, has been interested in the properties of voting systems for a number of years. This book follows his *Voting Procedures* (1984) but is less technical and more policy oriented. Although there is some discussion of countries other than the United Kingdom, it is obviously addressed to the debate about electoral systems for the United Kingdom. For decades this was a private argument for Liberals (who would benefit from any reform) and ignored by supporters of the other parties (who would suffer). But the Blair Labour government, which won 64 percent of the seats on 43 percent of the vote in its 1997 victory, appointed the centrist politician Lord (Roy) Jenkins to head a commission on electoral systems for the United Kingdom. Jenkins had to recommend, by fall 1998, an electoral system to be put head-to-head in a referendum against the plurality ("first-past-the-post") system.

Dummett's pedagogical problem is that most people who think they know about electoral reform do not even know that social choice theory underpins the subject. Dummett aptly says, "The intransitivity of majority preference is the source of all the unwelcome facts about voting, and of all the difficulty of the subject." He introduces the concepts of Condorcet criterion, Borda and Copeland scores. And he stresses that the question "Who is the right person to represent this constituency [district]?" is a quite different question from "What should the balance of parties in the legislature be?" The German electoral system allows these questions to be separated.

Dummett attacks the Irish single transferable vote (STV) system but concedes that STV secures as many seats for each concentrated minority as it has quotas. He then proposes a modification of the Borda rule for multimember districts that achieves the same end. As Dummett knows, however, the Borda rule is severely manipulable ("My scheme is only intended for honest men," said Borda when French academicians manipulated his scheme as soon as it was introduced for their elections).

Although almost nobody favors multimember districts for U.S. elections, American and European debates about proportional representation are not as remote as they seem. Americans discovered the problems and solutions for proportional representation a century before Europeans—in the context of apportionment of seats in Congress to the states. Alexander Hamilton's apportionment system is exactly the largest-remainder proportional representation system; Thomas Jefferson's is exactly Victor d'Hondt's. Dummett deserves to be widely read in the United States as well as Europe.

IAIN McLEAN

Nuffield College
Oxford
England

FOOT, ROSEMARY. 1995. *The Practice of Power: U.S. Relations with China Since 1949*. Pp. viii, 291. New York: Oxford University Press. $35.00.

Rosemary Foot has written a useful survey of U.S.-China relations from 1949 to 1980. Foot demonstrates convincingly that this relationship has been very important to both countries. The United States consistently saw a Communist China as a major competitor in the post–World War II world. China represented both a competing model of development and a challenge to various U.S. world-order goals. The Chinese frequently saw the United States as the major obstacle to their own development and, at the same time, as a determiner of China's status in the world. The accommodations between the two powers, evident by the 1970s, channeled the relationship in more constructive directions without eliminating the remaining underlying tensions.

Foot employs a topical approach in her analysis. She begins with the U.S. effort to isolate China through a trade embargo and opposition to Chinese membership in the United Nations. After examining American public opinion about China, Foot considers the American view of Chinese military capabilities and the role of the Sino-Soviet relationship in American policy toward China. Two themes are prominent in this analysis. First, the U.S. attempt to isolate China always faced serious opposition. America's allies

were never convinced of the efficacy of the effort and often sought to ignore or revise the U.S. attempts to isolate China. Indeed, by the late 1960s, American public opinion started to encourage American policy to undertake more contact with China. Second, American policy toward China was often more subtle and realistic than the public comments of U.S. officials tended to indicate. This was particularly true in the 10-15 years before the 1971-72 Nixon opening to China.

I have two reservations about the book. First, Foot's attempt to connect the events she describes to general ideas about power in international relations is not very successful. Second, I wish that more attention had been paid to the Taiwan issue in U.S.-Chinese relations. This issue has been and remains the really dangerous point of dispute in the relationship. It deserves more attention than it received in this volume. These reservations, however, should not cause the book to be neglected. It remains a sophisticated and careful survey of a most important relationship in international affairs.

JAMES FETZER

State University of New York
Bronx

GRANT, RUTH W. 1997. *Hypocrisy and Integrity: Machiavelli, Rousseau, and the Ethics of Politics*. Pp. xii, 201. Chicago: University of Chicago Press. Paperbound, $22.50.

In this unusually interesting and well-written volume, one of the best historians of political thought within the discipline of political science presents an original analysis of certain assumptions shared by Machiavelli and Rousseau that distinguish them from the later liberal tradition (Hobbes, Locke, and Smith) in ways not anticipated by previous interpreters. Ruth Grant shows how these earlier theorists focused on the notion of dependency. Political relationships arise because people not only have competing interests but also have endless needs for each other. Flattery, lying, and manipulation arise as means of influencing others and are unavoidable at some levels. The ethical man must rise above such dependence, but the reality is that few can accomplish this. Morality and ethics emerge inescapably at the center of politics.

Beyond the universal focus on self-interest, men are subject to political passions such as vanity, pride, and ambition, which continually undermine the cool calculations of interests that liberal theorists assume to predict law, order, and peace. Reason is perverted into rationalization, and men are hypocrites. But hypocrisy, being unavoidable, is to be judged by its results.

Grant's original analysis results from systematic examination of the underlying assumptions that the earlier writers shared and the different paths they followed in their political theories. (The detailed and complex findings cannot be recapitulated here.) Machiavelli, it turns out, recommended the pursuit of power as a means to independence and recognized the necessity of using hypocrisy to achieve this, given the corruptness of many people and the private interests that divide us. While Rousseau's assumptions of a natural unity and goodness of the self enabled him to postulate an ideal of a unified political community, the real-life needs and moral weaknesses of men lead almost all of them into dependence—either on their superiors or on their inferiors. Either way, they are corrupted, and moral integrity is compromised. Only a few moral purists can escape through rigorous adherence to a combination of an altruistic attention to the common good and the needs of others and an ascetic inattention to one's own interests.

This analysis leads Grant to identify a weakness in the liberal theory that informs democratic theorists. Because it "does not take sufficient account of the distinctive character of political relations, of political passions, and of moral discourse," it underestimates the place of hypocrisy in politics. While liberal theorists will argue back that Hobbes and Locke paid more attention to these issues than she recognizes, she has made an important point that can shift the focus of an old debate between political theorists to new and possibly more fertile ground.

NOEL B. REYNOLDS
Brigham Young University
Provo
Utah

HARLE, VILHO. 1998. *Ideas of Social Order in the Ancient World*. Pp. xvii, 252. Westport, CT: Greenwood Press. $25.00.

This volume is an important contribution to the interdisciplinary literature on social order. The author, a professor of international relations at the University of Lapland in Finland, offers a comparative analysis of ideas of social order from the leading religious traditions, political theories, and literary sources of antiquity. Harle draws material from Chinese political philosophy, Indian epic and statecraft literature, Zoroastrianism, Judaism, Greek and Roman political thought, and early Christianity. Although concededly handicapped by an inability to read the texts in their original ancient languages (and perhaps also an unwillingness to draw more from classical historiography or philology), Harle succeeds admirably in the technical treatment of his subject.

Harle's primary thesis is that there were two strands of ideology for the establishment and maintenance of social order in antiquity: one emphasizing moral principles, the other exalting political power. Although the distinction between principle-oriented and power-oriented patterns of social order is hardly novel, it receives full vindication in Harle's study. Indeed, the book is roughly divided between the treatment of these two patterns. When Harle considers moral principles as the basis of social order, he gives attention to Indian notions of dharma and caste, Zoroastrian principles of *asha* and social contract, and Jewish paradigms of Torah and national identity. When Harle discusses power-oriented principles of social order, the methodology shifts somewhat. The treatment becomes less focused on explicating particular idea traditions, and, instead, a superb cross-cultural analysis is made of power approaches to social order (not all of which are coercive). Of particular interest to scholars of ancient international relations (or, like me, of ancient international law) will be those chapters in which Harle considers how the ancient mind was able to solve the dilemma of balancing particularism and exclusion with peace and coexistence in a world of different ethnic, religious, and linguistic groupings.

The culmination of Harle's work is a useful typology and concordance of ancient ideas of social order. Although I am somewhat dubious of the "scoring" system used to characterize the affinity of different ancient ideologies for particular principles of social order, this is nevertheless a useful contribution to the literature. Nor am I sure the book overcomes (despite Harle's claims) all vestiges of Eurocentrism, to the extent that is even necessary or desirable. This book will be a useful addition to the work of peace and

international studies as well as political and international theory.

DAVID J. BEDERMAN
Emory University
Atlanta
Georgia

THOMPSON, NORMA. 1996. *Herodotus and the Origins of the Political Community: Arion's Leap.* Pp. xiv, 193. New Haven, CT: Yale University Press. No price.

Norma Thompson claims that Aristotle, founder of the Western rationalistic tradition, "defined himself against Herodotus." In this self-defining activity, Aristotle introduced the "idea of a theory" that allowed him to unjustly denigrate the creative or myth-making propensities of the poet and especially the storytelling propensities of the historian. Thompson, in her thought-provoking book, seeks to defend Herodotus, a "poetic historian" who seems "both pre-Socratic and strikingly post-modern," or perhaps Heideggerian, to be more exact, against the charges of Aristotle. Her defense, which brings to light the primary thesis of her book, takes the form of an explanation of why Herodotus includes both "serious" or factual and "ridiculous" or mythical stories in his *History*. According to Thompson, Herodotus does this because he believes that all such stories, including, for instance, his own story of the battle of Marathon (1.103-1.124), whether they be factual or mythical, serve to found the various political communities to which such stories belong, define that community's "culture," and guide that community or culture into the future. Thus Herodotus is not in contradiction with Aristotle's famous tenet that humans are political animals but only with Aristotle's teaching of the place of the "rational" in that political world.

Thompson also claims that the telling of such "fighting stories" can reveal to the reader or listener the "national character" or "culture" of a people that the historian, such as Herodotus, wishes to convey. Thompson gives a most insightful example of this Herodotean method in her discussion of the Persian debate about the future of their regime at the end of Book III and of the Greek debate about the future of Athenian democracy in Book V. These debates, as told by Herodotus, ultimately reveal the Greeks (as well as Herodotus), despite Persian pretensions to be such, as the real "truthtellers" because they place a much higher value on free discourse or speech in general, which reflects the Greeks' creative or artistic, if slightly irrational, stance toward both the human and divine realms. Thompson, as she defends Herodotus against Aristotle, also defends him against three contemporary commentators and critics, Martin Bernal, Francois Hartog, and Edward Said, none of whom, she writes, "has done justice to the historiographical teaching in *The History*."

Thompson, in her secondary, and perhaps questionable, thesis, suggests that Herodotus does not believe in an unchanging or universal human nature, and, even if there were such an objective or universal human nature, human beings would not have access to it because all thought, including their own, is bound by cultural subjectivity: for Herodotus, "acts and words enter the realm of [myth] instantaneously, and . . . it is not possible to prevent any act or any words from doing so." This does not mean that Herodotus "retire[s] in relativistic despair; cultures make out better and worse in his portrayal." For instance, in Thompson's analysis of Herodotus's famous custom-is-king passage (3.38), which "reveals him thinking like a Greek," she claims that he portrays the "intellectual" Greeks

as superior to the "traditional" Indians and the "cynical" Persians. However, it is hard to understand how Herodotus could make what Thompson calls these "impartial" judgments or rankings of the customs or conventions of various peoples if he does not do so from a standard that exists externally to the conventional. Thompson resists the notion that Herodotus could have a simply human perspective, because she believes that any perspective outside of culture is subhuman, which she makes clear in her analysis of the story of Arion (1.23-1.24), the hero of her title and afterword. Thompson does not consider that Herodotus may have two standards of what is natural for man, a higher and a lower, revealed, for instance, in his discussion of Cambyses's "Sacred Sickness" (3.35). Perhaps, for Herodotus, man's lower nature is located in his body (3.99), a life in accordance with which may indeed exist animal-like beneath convention or culture (3.101, 4.106), but perhaps man's higher nature is located in his mind or soul, the life in accordance with which, for Herodotus, may exist beyond convention or culture. For Thompson's Herodotus, however, convention or culture does not point beyond itself. Perhaps this is the reason why Thompson never systematically deals with the question of justice in *The History*, which seems odd for someone interested in Herodotus's view of the founding of and interaction between different political communities. Neither does Thompson deal with the relationship between eros and justice, or injustice, powerfully raised by Herodotus in the opening of his *History* (1.1-1.5), as well as in the story of Gyges (1.8-1.12), the story of Hermotimus (8.104-8.106), and the story of Xerxes's love and Masistes's death (9.108-9.113).

ANN WARD

Fordham University
Bronx
New York

AFRICA, ASIA, AND
LATIN AMERICA

MOORE, ROBIN D. 1997. *Nationalizing Blackness:* Afrocubanismo *and Artistic Revolution in Havana, 1920-1940.* Pp. xii, 320. Pittsburgh, PA: University of Pittsburgh Press. $45.00. Paperbound, $19.95.

Nationalizing Blackness, Robin D. Moore's social history of Cuban popular culture, focuses on race relations and racial discourse in the construction of Cuban "national" culture.

Each of Moore's early chapters explores a fascinating and underresearched corner of Cuban popular culture. Chapter 2, "Minstrelsy in Havana," is the first comprehensive English-language treatment of the Cuban blackface theater, Teatro Vernáculo, with its triangle of *negrito, mulata,* and *gallego* (white Spaniard) archetypes. Moore argues that although it reflected and perpetuated racial oppression, it also opened up a needed discourse on black, working-class culture. Chapter 3 explores the history of the black processional groups called *comparsas,* originally associated with the Día de Reyes (Kings' Day) but later permitted to join in Havana's Carnival. Like the *sones* of chapter 4 or the *rumbas* of chapter 6, *comparsas* were reviled by whites and middle-class blacks of the early twentieth century but achieved a gradual acceptance, at least in their stylized versions. Moore perceptively traces this shift in reception to the growing Cuban resentment of American imperialism, to the modernist fascination with "primitivist" arts, and to the need to construct an inclusive sense of national identity.

The chapter on *rumba* journeys far from Havana to demonstrate how foreign markets, fads, and expectations (in Paris and New York, for example) shaped Cuban music. Two additional chapters

sketch the trajectory of the *afrocubanismo* movement and its artistic circle known as the Minoristas, situating various developments in music, theater, dance, literature, and visual arts in the political and intellectual ferment of the time.

Nationalizing Blackness provides a timely challenge to conventional wisdom on Afrocuban culture. Most Cuban scholars and writers present Cuba as a bastion of racial tolerance and claim Afrocuban culture for the whole nation. In contrast, Moore chronicles a history of virulently racist discourse over African influences in Cuban culture and of Afrocuban cultural marginalization. Moore also reveals the ideological contradictions and ambivalence that characterized the early exponents of *afrocubanismo*, who are typically lauded as champions of racial tolerance. Because he views Cuban popular forms as the product of mediations, negotiations, and translations, Moore questions whether scholars have overemphasized distinctions between "pure" and "adulterated" Afrocuban expressions.

In short, Moore's fascinating and well-written study is intellectually daring in its argument, thorough in its social-historical research, and deserving of a wide audience in the social sciences.

GAGE AVERILL
New York University
New York City

SEYMOUR, JAMES D. and RICHARD ANDERSON. 1998. *New Ghosts, Old Ghosts: Prisons and Labor Reform Camps in China.* Pp. xvii, 313. Armonk, NY: M. E. Sharpe. $39.95.

China has the largest population of any country in the world (1.2 billion), and, with a long tradition of harsh discipline, it should not be surprising that China has a large prison population.

While Seymour and Anderson suggest that China's prison population may be hovering close to 2.0 million, in terms of imprisonment rates, Chinese incarceration rates are close to the world average. The United States, with some 1.7 million prisoners, ranks at the top with over 600 prisoners per 100,000. However, the descriptions of Chinese prisons offered by Seymour and Anderson conjure up the image of a Russian gulag from the Stalinist times.

Seymour and Anderson examine the prison system in three provinces in northwest China: Xinjiang, Qinghai, and Gansu. Most readers will not be familiar with these provinces, and that is a problem with this book. Just how representative these three remote provinces are of the rest of China is not adequately addressed. China publishes scant information on its correctional system, and Seymour and Anderson obtained information via secret documents, interviews with former prisoners, and published documents from three provinces. A second difficulty with the book is the liberal use of Chinese terms that many readers will find troubling. For example, the word "cadre" is difficult to translate into operational English. Similarly, the use of Chinese terms like *bingtuan, laogai,* and *jiuye* can befuddle the reader. Lastly, parts of the book read like an agricultural economics report as we examine grain and cotton production, industrial output, and livestock holdings.

The real merits of this work appear in the second half of it. Seymour and Anderson describe the management of the prison, pointing out the corruption and low competency of prison guards, the power of the "top cell boss" who runs the cell or cell block, and the pervasive subculture of resistance that becomes a code of honor among prisoners. Food is scarce, health care almost nonexistent, and working conditions brutal. For example, uranium mining, coal mining, and asbestos mining are done by prisoners. While all Chinese prisons are essentially factories, the authors argue that prison output does not make a significant contribution to the gross domestic product. Prison-made products are not competitive with the outside economy, and many countries refuse to import them.

Seymour and Anderson paint a different picture of prison outcome in China from the official Chinese depiction. Anyone who has visited China hears repeatedly that recidivism is 4.6 percent. While no one knows the accurate recidivism rate, the authors are highly dubious of this success rate. Second, the official line is that, once prisoners complete their sentence, they are reintegrated into the community and the label of ex-offender does not exist. The authors point out the fallacy of this assertion. Some ex-prisoners are not permitted to leave the locale of the prison; others are unable to find work; still others are not accepted into any residential community.

In their conclusion, Seymour and Anderson suggest that individual rights need to be protected at the trial stage in China. The authors do not seem to recognize that common law procedures that are the bedrock of the American legal system are simply not part of the Chinese legal system. The authors do suggest that prison conditions have changed since the oppressive penal system of the 1950s, but the conditions are still less humane than those found in Western prisons. Overall, this book makes an important contribution to understanding Chinese social control practices and the dismal record of inhumane treatment of prisoners throughout the world.

DEAN G. ROJEK

University of Georgia
Athens

UNITED STATES

FILENE, PETER G. 1998. *In the Arms of Others: A Cultural History of the Right-to-Die in America.* Pp. 282. Chicago: Ivan R. Dee. No price.

In a moment of self-discovery, University of North Carolina historian Peter G. Filene found he wanted to write about Karen Ann Quinlan, which he does in his book in vibrant and piercing detail. But Filene does much more than dramatize the misfortunes and tremendous pressures faced by families in deciding what to do for their hopelessly ill loved ones and getting physicians and medical institutions to comply. He also links the right to die to parallel social changes that have been important in basing end-of-life decision making on personal rights and autonomy. The march of medical technology permits physicians—driven by the mandate to heal—to prolong life, and the accompanying ambiguity about the definition of death creates a crisis in individual cases of treatment that did not exist a few decades ago. New right-to-die issues, especially artificially administered food and hydration and assisted suicide and advocacy for AIDS sufferers, further complicate our choices. The modern civil rights movement and women's political drives for equality, individual rights, and personal empowerment, along with the prominence of courts as case-by-case decision makers, also are heavily responsible for emphasizing personal control and autonomy. Much of this territory has been covered well by others, but Filene unfolds the story through especially expressive, arresting, and nontechnical clarity that captures the reader in both the drama and the social context of the continuing dilemma over what to do in hopeless medical cases.

Besides leading the reader to care deeply for people trapped in the ambiguity and subjectivity of modern death and dying, Filene emphasizes that so long as we base the right to die on individual self-determination and rights, everyone is vulnerable when individuals no longer are able to assert those rights or have left no advance written instructions about their wishes for end-of-life care. Instead, the right to die needs to be based on "relatedness" in which death and dying are managed by individuals with their families, friends, and supportive institutions such as hospice. His final chapter examines the disparate cultures of Bali and the Netherlands in order to make us aware that how we in the United States cope with death and dying is not the only way. He urges Americans to remove death and dying from impersonal medical institutions and specialist-strangers, with their medical machinery at the ready, to a compassionate setting in which family and friends and hospice, coupled with realism, reassurance, and access to effective pain relief—"in the arms of others"—make dying less fearful, painful, prolonged, and lonely.

HENRY R. GLICK

Florida State University
Tallahassee

PALMER, NIALL A. 1997. *The New Hampshire Primary and the American Electoral Process.* Pp. xx, 195. Westport, CT: Praeger. $55.00.

Every four years, like an electoral Brigadoon, Iowa and New Hampshire take center stage in American politics. Presidential candidates and reporters flock to the two states, and, for weeks and even months in advance of these two contests, little else matters in politics than what the voters in these states think. Within days of the conclusion of these contests, however, Iowa and New Hampshire disappear from national consciousness for another four years. The verdicts rendered by their voters, however, continue to reverberate throughout the rest of the campaign.

Yet, despite all of the attention lavished on these two states by candidates and reporters and despite the apparent importance of the results of their elections, little scholarly attention has been devoted to them. This omission is corrected in part by Palmer's volume on the New Hampshire primary. There is no grand theory behind this study, no rigorous testing of hypotheses. Instead, Palmer provides a solid review of what political scientists and journalists have learned about the New Hampshire primary and its place in the nomination process. The result is a satisfying work that pulls together information from a variety of sources and greatly informs and expands a reader's understanding of the event and its importance.

The account of the history of the Granite State's primary, for example, is very useful because it helps remind people what really happened in each contest. (I think it is important to point out, as Palmer does, why President Johnson's performance in the 1968 contest was deemed a failure, even though he finished first with almost 50 percent of the votes as a write-in candidate!) Palmer goes on to challenge conventional wisdom in several other instances, most notably in regard to the exaggerated influence of the Manchester *Union Leader* and, perhaps, the underestimated power of WMUR-TV, the state's only major commercial television station. The idea that New Hampshire is unrepresentative of the rest of the nation and therefore an inappropriate choice to lead off the primary season is tackled head on, with Palmer offering persuasive arguments in favor of retaining the state's current role.

In sum, this is not a volume that will alter the way we think about New Hampshire and its role in the presidential nomination process. It is, however, a thoughtful and well-grounded work that any student of presidential elections will find informative.

PEVERILL SQUIRE
University of Iowa
Iowa City

TRUBOWITZ, PETER. 1998. *Defining the National Interest: Conflict and Change in American Foreign Policy.* Pp. xvi, 353. Chicago: University of Chicago Press. $55.00. Paperbound, $18.95.

"One nation, under God, indivisible": whatever the position may be of the Almighty, Peter Trubowitz intends in this provocative book to demonstrate that the remainder of this phrase is clearly inaccurate. His argument is that the United States is best understood not as one nation but as three mutually suspicious regions. What is defined as the national interest is the material interest of the currently dominant alliance of any two regions against the third. Trubowitz finds evidence for all three possible combinations: the Northeast and the West's making common cause against the South in the 1890s through the 1920s, the Northeast and the South's dominating the West from the 1930s into the 1970s, and the West and the South's allying against the Northeast beginning in the 1980s.

This, then, is geopolitics as that term is used here: the intraregional politics in these three sections, based on their differing material interests, the outcome of which drives the weak American state in its policies toward the outside world. The economic forces dominant in the regions that succeed in forming a coalition employ the machinery of government to sustain their prosperity at the expense of neglecting or even exploiting the region left without a partner when the music stops each generation in this three-sided dance.

Reminding us of the domestic forces that shape foreign policy is a useful corrective to the overly deterministic reliance on international structure as a way of explaining the actions of states. Yet in this picture of American politics, the outside world seems almost to disappear, and with it any way of assessing the wisdom of policies for dealing with that world. Trubowitz does not ignore international events, but the lens of uneven regional economic development through which they are filtered is so thick that they seem very faint indeed.

Ideas on the purposes of the United States in the world and the proper uses of governmental power at home also play a highly subsidiary role here. Their subordination is particularly clear in the handful of pages devoted to what might be thought to form one of the central parts of the story of twentieth-century American foreign policy: the Cold War.

Trubowitz has written a thoroughly researched and well-organized study. Like most revisionist works, it runs the risk of carrying its argument too far, but it is an argument worth hearing.

DAVID CLINTON

Tulane University
New Orleans
Louisiana

SOCIOLOGY

FISHMAN, TALYA. 1997. *Shaking the Pillars of Exile: "Voice of a Fool," an Early Modern Jewish Critique of Rabbinic Culture.* Pp. xviii, 362. Stanford, CA: Stanford University Press. $49.50.

The riddle of the composition of the elusive treatise *Voice of a Fool (Kol Sakhal)* has engaged scholars of the Jewish past since the middle of the nineteenth century. *Kol Sakhal* attacks rabbinic culture and especially its reliance on and interpretation of the Oral Law, but it dismisses the Christian notion that the Bible is to be interpreted differently at different times. A number of *Kol Sakhal's* criticisms owe much to the Karaites, yet other passages condemn the harshness of Karaite law. At times, *Kol Sakhal's* assessment of the Oral Law reads like the writing of a heretic, while its author steadfastly maintains the Divine origin and perfection of the Torah.

In *Shaking the Pillars of Exile*, Talya Fishman convincingly argues that *Kol Sakhal*, which was alleged by the Venetian rabbi Judah Aryeh (Leone) Modena to have been composed in Spain in the year 1500 and given to him in manuscript form by an acquaintance in 1622, was actually written by Modena himself. Although Fishman is not the first to make this claim, most recent treatments of *Kol Sakhal* have held that Modena was not its author. Indeed, some modern scholars maintain that this attribution borders on slander, given Modena's public defense of rabbinic Judaism on other occasions.

At the heart of Fishman's argument is the intriguing assertion, supported by a number of examples, that critical scrutiny of rabbinic texts and practices, and even suggestions for reform and change, often came from within the ranks of otherwise traditional Jewish thinkers. *Kol Sakhal* is an extreme example or perhaps an overextension of what Fishman calls "tolerated dissent."

In the first half of the book, Fishman advances her claim regarding Modena's authorship by noting the existence of a parallel attack on the papacy by the Venetian friar Paolo Sarpi, by examining the categories of law and approaches to codification that Modena adopted from medieval Jewish writers ranging from Maimonides to the Karaites, and by outlining the differences between the skepticism of Modena and the heretical beliefs of Uriel da Costa and others. Fishman concludes her analysis with some illuminating remarks about Modena's pseudepigraphic attribution of *Kol Sakhal* to one Amitai bar Yedaiah ibn Raz.

In three appendices, Fishman provides additional data regarding the place and date of composition, notes significant similarities between *Kol Sakhal* and Modena's acknowledged writings, and discusses the manuscripts of *Kol Sakhal*. (Interestingly, this discussion points to a correlation between *Kol Sakhal* and *Besamim Rosh*, a purported collection of responses by Rabbi Asher ben Yehiel, published by the forger Saul Berlin.) The second half of *Shaking the Pillars of Exile* consists of an annotated English translation of *Kol Sakhal*. In her informative notes, Fishman seeks to identify the sources of the rabbinic beliefs and practices that Modena critiques, a particularly important endeavor with regard to the third part of *Kol Sakhal*, which is structured as a revisionist code of law.

I came across only one assertion that is not ironclad. One of the three main passages that Fishman adduces from *Kol Sakhal* to demonstrate her contention that it was composed after 1500 is a critique of the rabbinic ceremony of blessing or sanctifying the new moon, which contains, among other elements, the recitation of the phrase "David King of Israel lives and endures." The earliest written source that includes these words as part of the ceremony, according to Fishman, is the *Mappah* (Rabbi Moses Isserles's glosses to the *Shulḥan 'Arukh*), published in 1569-71. The thirteenth-century *Commentary to the Torah* by Rabbi Baḥya ban Asher (which Isserles notes as his source for this phrase in both his glosses to *Shulḥan 'Arukh* and in his *Darkhei Mosheh* to Rabbi Jacob ben Asher's *Arba 'ah Turim*) ought not be considered, according to

Fishman, as an earlier written source for this passage in part because Rabbi Baḥya "associates the chanting of this phrase with the renewal of the moon (*ḥiddush levanah*) rather than with the sanctification of the new moon (*kiddush levanah*)," as Isserles does. In fact, however, rabbinic sources ranging from the Palestinian Talmud to the liturgical collection of Rabbi Amram Gaon to Maimonides' *Mishneh Torah* and Rabbi Moses of Coucy's *Sefer Miṣvot Gadol* use a form of *ḥiddush levanah* in referring to the blessing made over the new moon. (See the sources listed in Yaakov Gartner, *Gilgulei Minhag be-'Olam ha-Halakhah* [Jerusalem: Hemed Press, 1995], 192-93.)

Moreover, the passage "David King of Israel lives and endures" does appear as part of the blessing of the new moon in the kabbalistic prayer commentary composed by Meir ibn Gabbai (b. 1480). (See *Tola 'at Ya 'aqov* [1560; reprint, Jerusalem: Shvilei Orhot Hayyim, 1996], 101 [*sod birkat ha-levanah*].) This work was first published in Constantinople in 1560, but it was written in 1507 and could easily have been known to the generation of the Spanish exile. The presence of this passage in ibn Gabbai's work, in the commentary of Rabbenu Baḥya, and in Menaḥem Recanati's kabbalistic Torah commentary from the early fourteenth century (a reference noted by Fishman but dismissed as a talmudic citation rather than as an indication of any formal ritual) suggests that it was a part of the ceremony for the sanctification of the new moon in kabbalistic circles at least, well before its inclusion by Isserles.

At the same time, Fishman's contention (163-65) that the practices referred to (and critiqued) by *Kol Sakhal* are rooted in Ashkenaz (or Italy) rather than in Spain (which conflicts with the claim of Spanish origin made on *Kol Sakhal*'s title page) is succinctly demonstrated and beyond question. Indeed, it is possible to locate additional examples of Ashkenazic customs and practices, and venerable ones at that, to which *Kol Sakhal* refers. (Regarding the custom not to begin things on Monday or Wednesday [*Shaking the Pillars*, 271, n.561], see *Sefer Roqeah*, sec. 215 [p. 106], and ms. Parma 541, fol. 264v [end]; on refraining from meat and wine from the seventeenth of the Hebrew month of Tammuz onward [*Shaking the Pillars*, 290, n.22], see *Sefer Rabiah* 3:659-60, and ms. Bodleian 781, fol. 72v [cited in Avraham Grossman, *Hakhmei Ashkenaz ha-Rishonim* (Jerusalem: Mosad Bialik, 1981), 288]. On the obligation to give priestly gifts in the Di-

aspora [*Shaking the Pillars*, 265, n.465], see Grossman, 194-95. [For the view of Rabbi Meir of Rothenburg, cf. the *Commentary of Rosh to Hullin*, chap. 11, sec. 1, and *Qisur Pisqei ha-Rosh*, ad loc.].)

Written in a lucid and engaging style, and with palpable erudition, *Shaking the Pillars of Exile* sheds new light not only on *Kol Sakhal* and Leone Modena but also on a wide range of issues within the rubrics of Jewish intellectual history and the history of religion. Generalist and specialist alike will come away with many new insights and ideas.

EPHRAIM KANARFOGEL

Yeshiva University
New York City

OTHER BOOKS

ALLISON, SARAH E. and KATHERINE E. McLAUGHLIN-RENPENNING. 1998. *Nursing Administration in the 21st Century: A Self-Care Theory Approach.* Pp. xxi, 298. Thousand Oaks, CA: Sage. $48.00. Paperbound, $22.50.

ANTAKI, CHARLES and SUE WIDDICOMBE, eds. 1998. *Identities in Talk.* Pp. ix, 224. Thousand Oaks, CA: Sage. $74.00. Paperbound, $26.95.

AVRUCH, KEVIN. 1998. *Culture and Conflict Resolution.* Pp. xv, 153. Washington, DC: United States Institute of Peace. $29.95. Paperbound, $14.95.

BAKER, DAVID and DAVID SEAWRIGHT, eds. 1998. *Britain for and Against Europe: British Politics and the Question of European Integration.* Pp. xiv, 252. New York: Oxford University Press. $65.00.

BAUMANN, FRED E. 1998. *Fraternity and Politics: Choosing One's Brothers.* Pp. ix, 150. Westport, CT: Praeger. $55.00.

BEARDEN, WILLIAM O. and RICHARD G. NETEMEYER. 1998. *Handbook of Marketing Scales: Multi-Item Measures for Marketing and Consumer Behavior Research.* 2d ed. Pp. xiv, 535. Thousand Oaks, CA: Sage. $75.00.

BELDEN, JOSEPH N. and ROBERT J. WIENER, eds. 1998. *Housing in Rural America: Building Affordable and Inclusive Communities.* Pp. xi, 218. Thousand Oaks, CA: Sage. $55.00. Paperbound, $22.95.

BELL, MICHAEL MAYERFELD and MICHAEL GARDINER, eds. 1998. *Bakhtin and the Human Sciences.* Pp. x, 235. Thousand Oaks, CA: Sage. $74.00. Paperbound, $25.00.

BENNAHUM, DAVID S. 1998. *Extra Life: Coming of Age in Cyberspace.* Pp. 238. New York: Basic Books. $23.00.

BERMAN, WILLIAM C. 1998. *America's Right Turn: From Nixon to Clinton.* 2d ed. Pp. xii, 221. Baltimore: Johns Hopkins University Press. $38.95. Paperbound, $14.95.

BHALLA, A. S., ed. 1998. *Globalization, Growth and Marginalization.* Pp. xvii, 224. New York: St. Martin's Press. $65.00. Paperbound, $30.00.

BILLINGTON, JAMES H. 1999. *Fire in the Minds of Men: Origins of the Revolutionary Faith.* Pp. xiv, 677. New Brunswick, NJ: Transaction. Paperbound, $29.95.

BOCKER, ANITA, KEES GROENENDIJK, TETTY HAVINGA, and PAUL MINDERHOUD, eds. 1998. *Regulation of Migration: International Experiences.* Pp. 279. Amsterdam, Netherlands: Het Spinhuis. Paperbound, no price.

BOEMEKE, MANFRED F., GERALD D. FELDMAN, and ELISABETH GLASER, eds. 1998. *The Treaty of Versailles: A Reassessment after 75 Years.* Pp. xii, 674. New York: Cambridge University Press. $85.00.

BOGGS, GRACE LEE. 1998. *Living for Change: An Autobiography.* Pp. xvi, 301. Minneapolis: University of Minnesota Press. Paperbound, no price.

BRADFORD, NEIL. 1998. *Commissioning Ideas: Canadian National Policy Innovation in Comparative Perspective.* Pp. viii, 226. New York: Oxford University Press. Paperbound, $29.95.

BURK, JAMES, ed. 1998. *The Adaptive Military: Armed Forces in a Turbulent World.* 2d ed. Pp. ix, 227. New Brunswick, NJ: Transaction. Paperbound, $24.95.

CAMPBELL, DAVID. 1998. *Writing Security: United States Foreign Policy and the Politics of Identity.* Pp. xiii, 289. Minneapolis: University of Minnesota Press. Paperbound, no price.

CARDEN, MAREN LOCKWOOD. 1998. *Oneida: Utopian Community to Mod-*

ern Corporation. Pp. xxx, 228. Syracuse, NY: Syracuse University Press. Paperbound, $16.95.

CHAPA, JUAN BAUTISTA. 1997. *Texas and Northeastern Mexico, 1630-1690.* Pp. xii, 235. Austin: University of Texas Press. No price.

CHARLES, NICKIE and HELEN HINTJENS, eds. 1998. *Gender, Ethnicity and Political Ideologies.* Pp. xi, 195. New York: Routledge. $75.00. Paperbound, $24.99.

CLASTRES, PIERRE. 1998. *Chronicle of the Guayaki Indians.* Pp. 349. Cambridge: MIT Press. $25.50.

COLUMBUS, FRANK, ed. 1998. *Central and Eastern Europe in Transition.* Vol. 1. Pp. vii, 245. Commack, NY: Nova Science. $59.00.

———. 1998. *Central and Eastern Europe in Transition.* Vol. 2. Pp. vii, 220. Commack, NY: Nova Science. $59.00.

CUBITT, SEAN. 1998. *Digital Aesthetics.* Pp. xiii, 172. Thousand Oaks, CA: Sage. $66.00. Paperbound, $22.95.

DEAN, HARTLEY with MARGARET MELROSE. 1999. *Poverty, Riches and Social Citizenship.* Pp. xiv, 211. New York: St. Martin's Press. No price.

ELIASSEN, KJELL A., ed. 1998. *Foreign and Security Policy in the European Union.* Pp. x, 246. Thousand Oaks, CA: Sage. $78.95. Paperbound, $28.50.

FERREE, MYRA MARX, JUDITH LORBER, and BETH B. HESS. 1998. *Revisioning Gender.* Pp. xxxvi, 500. Thousand Oaks, CA: Sage. $73.50. Paperbound, $35.95.

FRIEDMAN, MEYER and GERALD W. FRIEDLAND. 1998. *Medicine's Ten Greatest Discoveries.* Pp. xiii, 263. New Haven, CT: Yale University Press. $30.00.

GALLIGAN, YVONNE, EILIS WARD, and RICK WILFORD, eds. 1998. *Contesting Politics: Women in Ireland, North and South.* Pp. xvii, 278. Boul-

der, CO: Westview Press. $65.00. Paperbound, $25.00.

GOLDSTENE, PAUL N. 1998. *The Collapse of Liberal Empire.* 2d ed. Pp. xxi, 138. Novato, CA: Chandler & Sharp. $24.95. Paperbound, $12.95.

GUIGNI, MARCO G., DOUG McADAM, and CHARLES TILLY, eds. 1998. *From Contention to Democracy.* Pp. xxvi, 285. Lanham, MD: Rowman & Littlefield. $60.00. Paperbound, $25.95.

GUNNELL, JOHN G. 1998. *The Orders of Discourse: Philosophy, Social Science, and Politics.* Pp. xv, 252. Lanham, MD: Rowman & Littlefield. $68.00. Paperbound, $24.95.

HALPERN, LASZLO and CHARLES WYPLOSZ, eds. 1998. *Hungary: Towards a Market Economy.* Pp. xx, 390. New York: Cambridge University Press. $74.95.

HAMBURG, G. M., ed. 1999. *Liberty, Equality, and the Market: Essays by B. N. Chicherin.* Pp. xxxv, 457. New Haven, CT: Yale University Press. $45.00.

HAMLET, JANICE D., ed. 1998. *Afrocentric Visions: Studies in Culture and Communication.* Pp. xiv, 266. Thousand Oaks, CA: Sage. $52.00. Paperbound, $23.95.

HARE, PAUL. 1998. *Angola's Last Best Chance for Peace: An Insider's Account of the Peace Process.* Pp. xix, 182. Washington, DC: United States Institute of Peace. Paperbound, $14.95.

HARRE, ROM, JENS BROCKMEIER, and PETER MUHLHAUSLER. 1998. *Greenspeak: A Study of Environmental Discourse.* Pp. xi, 204. Thousand Oaks, CA: Sage. $65.00. Paperbound, $28.95.

HERRICK, WILLIAM. 1998. *Jumping the Line: The Adventures and Misadventures of an American Radical.* Pp. xxiii, 283. Madison: University of Wisconsin Press. $21.95.

HETHERINGTON, KEVIN. 1998. *Expressions of Identity: Space, Performance, Politics.* Pp. vii, 181. Thousand Oaks, CA: Sage. $66.00. Paperbound, $22.95.

HOOVER, STEWART M. 1998. *Religion in the News: Faith and Journalism in American Public Discourse.* Pp. xi, 234. Thousand Oaks, CA: Sage. Paperbound, $22.95.

HUFF, ROBERT M. and MICHAEL V. KLINE. 1998. *Promoting Health in Multicultural Populations: A Handbook for Practitioners.* Pp. xvii, 554. Thousand Oaks, CA: Sage. $75.00. Paperbound, $36.95.

JACOBS, HARVEY M., ed. 1998. *Who Owns America? Social Conflict over Property Rights.* Pp. xvii, 268. Madison: University of Wisconsin Press. $50.00. Paperbound, $19.95.

JONES, STEVEN G., ed. 1998. *Cybersociety 2.0: Revisiting Computer-Mediated Communication and Community.* Pp. xvii, 238. Thousand Oaks, CA: Sage. Paperbound, $25.50.

KAUFFMAN, BILL. 1998. *With Good Intentions? Reflections on the Myth of Progress in America.* Pp. xii, 124. Westport, CT: Praeger. $35.00.

KEATING, W. DENNIS, MICHAEL B. TEITZ, and ANDREJS SKABURSKIS. 1998. *Rent Control: Regulation and the Rental Housing Market.* Pp. xiii, 246. New Brunswick, NJ: Center for Urban Policy Research. Paperbound, $14.95.

KELLY, JAMES. 1998. *Henry Flood: Patriots and Politics in Eighteenth-Century Ireland.* Pp. 486. Notre Dame, IN: University of Notre Dame Press. $42.00.

KORT, MICHAEL. 1999. *The Columbia Guide to the Cold War.* Pp. xiv, 366. New York: Columbia University Press. $40.00.

LAHAN, NICHOLAS. 1998. *The Reagan Presidency and the Politics of Race: In Pursuit of Colorblind Justice and Limited Government.* Pp. xv, 240. Westport, CT: Praeger. $59.95.

LEE, KENNETH K. 1998. *Huddled Masses, Muddled Laws: Why Contemporary Immigration Policy Fails to Reflect Public Opinion.* Pp. xii, 168. Westport, CT: Praeger. $35.00.

LEE, LOYD E., ed. 1998. *World War II in Asia and the Pacific and the War's Aftermath, with General Themes: A Handbook of Literature and Research.* Pp. xv, 507. Westport, CT: Greenwood Press. $95.00.

LEIGH, ANNE. 1998. *Referral and Termination Issues for Counsellors.* Pp. ix, 150. Thousand Oaks, CA: Sage. $45.00. Paperbound, $19.95.

MAAGA, MARY McCORMICK. 1998. *Hearing the Voices of Jonestown.* Pp. xx, 187. Syracuse, NY: Syracuse University Press. $29.95.

MAGEN, ZIPORA. 1998. *Exploring Adolescent Happiness: Commitment, Purpose, and Fulfillment.* Pp. xix, 228. Thousand Oaks, CA: Sage. $46.50. Paperbound, $21.95.

MAZRUI, ALI A. and ALAMIN M. MAZRUI. 1998. *The Power of Babel: Language and Governance in the African Experience.* Pp. xii, 228. Chicago: University of Chicago Press. $40.00. Paperbound, $19.00.

MENY, YVES and ANDREW KNAPP. 1998. *Government and Politics in Western Europe: Britain, France, Italy, Germany.* 3d ed. Pp. xvi, 490. New York: Oxford University Press. $75.00. Paperbound, $24.95.

METCALF, LINDA. 1998. *Solution Focused Group Therapy: Ideas for Groups in Private Practice, Schools, Agencies, and Treatment Programs.* Pp. xiv, 242. New York: Free Press. $27.95.

MILES, STEVEN. 1998. *Consumerism: As a Way of Life.* Pp. viii, 174. Thousand Oaks, CA: Sage. Paperbound, $22.95.

MILLER, TIMOTHY. 1998. *The Quest for Utopia in Twentieth-Century*

America. Vol. 1, *1900-1960*. Pp. xxv, 254. Syracuse, NY: Syracuse University Press. $34.95.

MINAHAN, JAMES. 1998. *Miniature Empires: A Historical Dictionary of the Newly Independent States*. Pp. xvi, 340. Westport, CT: Greenwood Press. $75.00.

MULDOON, JAMES P., JR., JOANN FAGOT AVIEL, RICHARD REITANO, and EARL SULLIVAN, eds. 1998. *Multilateral Diplomacy and the United Nations Today*. Pp. xii, 260. Boulder, CO: Westview Press. $55.00. Paperbound, $22.00.

MURRAY, GEOFFREY. 1998. *China: The Next Superpower*. Pp. x, 260. New York: St. Martin's Press. $39.95.

NAJITA, TETSUO, ed. 1998. *Tokugawa Political Writings*. Pp. lxxiii, 156. New York: Cambridge University Press. $59.95. Paperbound, $18.95.

NORDHAUS, WILLIAM D., ed. 1998. *Economics and Policy Issues in Climate Change*. Pp. ix, 324. Washington, DC: Resources for the Future. $45.00.

PARK, SE HARK and WALTER C. LABYS. 1998. *Industrial Development and Environmental Degradation*. Pp. xiii, 187. Northampton, MA: Edward Elgar. $75.00.

PETERSEN, ALAN. 1998. *Unmasking the Masculine: "Men" and "Identity" in a Sceptical Age*. Pp. vi, 149. Thousand Oaks, CA: Sage. Paperbound, $22.95.

PISZKIEWICZ, DENNIS. 1998. *Wernher Von Braun: The Man Who Sold the Moon*. Pp. x, 240. Westport, CT: Praeger. $27.95.

PREEG, ERNEST H. 1998. *From Here to Free Trade: Essays in Post-Uruguay Round Trade Strategy*. Pp. xi, 154. Chicago: University of Chicago Press. $38.00. Paperbound, $18.00.

RANDALL, VICKY and GEORGINA WAYLEN, eds. 1998. *Gender, Politics and the State*. Pp. x, 214. New York: Routledge. Paperbound, no price.

ROSS, ROBERT S. 1998. *After the Cold War: Domestic Factors and United States–China Relations*. Pp. xiv, 194. Armonk, NY: M. E. Sharpe. $59.95. Paperbound, $22.95.

SAFFIAN, SARAH. 1998. *Ithaka: A Daughter's Memoir of Being Found*. Pp. xi, 308. New York: Basic Books. $23.00.

SEATON, JEAN, ed. 1998. *Politics and the Media: Harlots and Prerogatives at the Turn of the Millennium*. Pp. 135. Cambridge, MA: Basil Blackwell. Paperbound, $24.95.

SHANDLEY, ROBERT R., ed. 1998. *Unwilling Germans? The Goldhagen Debate*. Pp. x, 295. Minneapolis: University of Minnesota Press. Paperbound, no price.

STAM, HENDERIKUS J., ed. 1998. *The Body and Psychology*. Pp. ix, 240. Thousand Oaks, CA: Sage. $66.00. Paperbound, $24.95.

STEEPLES, DOUGLAS and DAVID O. WHITTEN. 1998. *Democracy in Desperation: The Depression of 1893*. Pp. 261. Westport, CT: Greenwood Press. $59.95.

TAROCK, ADAM. 1998. *The Superpowers' Involvement in the Iran-Iraq War*. Pp. xiv, 251. Commack, NY: Nova Science. $49.00.

UNDERHILL, LINDA. 1999. *The Unequal Hours: Moments of Being in the Natural World*. Pp. xi, 145. Athens: University of Georgia Press. No price.

VAN MAANEN, JOHN. 1998. *Qualitative Studies of Organization*. Pp. xxxii, 360. Thousand Oaks, CA: Sage. $65.00. Paperbound, $29.95.

VARADY, DAVID P., WOLFGANG F. E. PREISER, and FRANCIS P. RUSSELL, eds. 1998. *New Directions in Urban Public Housing*. Pp. xviii, 286. New Brunswick, NJ: CUPR Press. Paperbound, $19.95.

WRIGHT, STEPHEN, ed. 1998. *African Foreign Policies*. Pp. xi, 260. Boulder, CO: Westview Press. $65.00. Paperbound, $26.00.

INDEX

Affordable

Money in the bank. It may seem like just a dream. A little price-shopping can help make it a reality. Insurance coverage offered through your AAPSS membership features competitive group rates negotiated especially for members like you.

Take advantage of one of your best membership benefits. Affordable coverage. Reliable providers. Portable benefits. **Call 800 424-9883, or in Washington, DC 202 457-6820,** to speak to a customer service representative. Because quality insurance coverage doesn't have to empty your wallet.

· GROUP INSURANCE FOR AAPSS MEMBERS
Cancer Expense • Catastrophe Major Medical
Dental Plan • High Limit Accident • Medicare
Supplement • Member Assistance • Term Life

PRESIDENTIAL STUDIES QUARTERLY

Official Publication of the Center for the Study of the Presidency

Editor: Gary L. Wamsley, *Virginia Polytechnic Institute*

COMPREHENSIVE EXAMINATION

Continually viewed by businesspersons, scholars, and professionals as an indispensable resource for understanding the complex office of the President, **Presidential Studies Quarterly** provides articles and book reviews not only on the presidency, but also its relations with Congress, the Courts, the States, and on public policy issues facing the Nation in both the domestic and international arenas.

SINGLE THEME FOCUS

The journal publishes research on one particular topic per issue, ensuring that you receive the most complete investigation of the current issues being discussed.

Recent Issue Topics:

Volume XXVIX, Number 1 / Winter 1999
THE HUMAN PRESIDENCY

Volume XXVII, Number 4 / Fall 1998
THE CLINTON PRESIDENCY IN CRISIS

Volume XXVII, Number 3 / Summer 1998
**GOING GLOBAL:
THE PRESIDENCY IN THE INTERNATIONAL ARENA**

Volume XXVIII, Number 2 / Spring 1998
**THE BUCK STOPS HERE:
DECISION MAKING IN THE OVAL OFFICE**

Volume XXVIII, Number 1 / Winter 1998
WHEELING AND DEALING IN THE WHITE HOUSE

Quarterly: March, June, September, December
Yearly rate: $84
896 pages /
ISSN: 0360-4918

Presidential Studies Quarterly is abstracted and/or indexed in *ABC POL SCI, ABS POL SCI Advance Bibliography of Contents, Academy Abstracts, America: History and Life Historical Abstracts, Communication Abstracts, Human Resources Abstracts, International Political Science Abstracts, Political Science Abstracts, Public Affairs Information Service Bulletin, Sage Family Studies Abstracts, Sage Public Administration Abstracts, Sage Urban Studies Abstracts,* and in *United States Political Science Documents*.